Water Safety

Instructor's Manual

Printed in the United States of America

StayWell
780 Township Line Rd.
Yardley, PA 19067

ISBN 978-1-58480-445-1

11 12 13 / 9 8 7 6 5 4 3

Acknowledgments

The American Red Cross Swimming and Water Safety program and supporting materials were developed through the dedication of both employees and volunteers. Their commitment to excellence made this possible.

The following Red Cross national headquarters and USA Swimming staff contributed to the development, design and review of this program and supporting materials. The Swimming and Water Safety project team included:

Jean Erdtmann
Senior Director
Program Development and Sales Support

Pat Bonifer
Director
Research and Product Development

Jennifer Deibert
Project Manager
Program Development and Sales Support

Mike Espino
Project Manager
Research and Product Development

Florence E. Fanelli
Manager
Program Development and Sales Support

Connie Harvey
Technical Manager
Program Development and Sales Support

John E. Hendrickson
Project Manager
Program Development and Sales Support

Greta Petrilla
Manager
Communication and Marketing

Greg Stockton
Project Manager
Program Development and Sales Support

Bobby Broome
Senior Associate
Program Development and Sales Support

Martha Chapin
Senior Associate
Program Management and Field Support

Lindsey Darrah
Senior Associate
Product Management and Business Planning

Kelly Fischbein
Senior Associate
Evaluation

Allanea Foreman
Senior Associate
Research and Product Development

Tom Heneghan
Senior Associate
Product Management and Business Planning

Don Lauritzen
Senior Associate
Operations and Program Management

Lindsay Oaksmith, CHES
Senior Associate
Program Development and Sales Support

John Thompson
Senior Associate
Operations and Program Management

Erich Ericson
Associate
Program Development and Sales Support

Denise González
Associate
Operations and Program Management

Betty J. Butler
Administrative Assistant
Operations and Program Management

Guidance and support was provided by the following individuals:

Scott Conner
Senior Vice President
Preparedness and Health and Safety Services

Don Vardell
National Chair
Preparedness and Health and Safety Services

The StayWell team for this edition included:

Nancy Monahan
Senior Vice President

Paula Batt
Executive Director
Sales and Business Development

Reed Klanderud
Executive Director
Marketing and New Development

Ellen Beal
Editorial Director

Mary Ellen Curry
Director of Publication Production

Bryan Elrod
Senior Developmental Editor

Shannon Bates
Senior Production Manager

Kate Plourde
Marketing Manager

The following members of the American Red Cross Advisory Council on First Aid, Aquatics, Safety and Preparedness (ACFASP) also provided guidance and review:

Stephen J. Langendorfer, PhD
Associate Professor, Kinesiology
School of Human Movement, Sport and Leisure Studies
Bowling Green State University
Bowling Green, Ohio

Linda Quan, MD
Professor
Department of Pediatrics
University of Washington School of Medicine
Attending, Emergency Services
Seattle Children's Hospital
Seattle, Washington

The Sounding Board for this edition included:

Patricia L. Bennett
Aquatics Coordinator
District 196 Community Education
Rosemount, Apple Valley and Eagan, Minnesota

Catherine L. Bradshaw, CTRS
Senior Recreation Supervisor II, Aquatic Fitness Instructor
Department of Recreation, Parks and Open Space
Therapeutic Recreation Center
Norfolk, Virginia

Susan T. Dempf, PhD
Associate Professor
The School of Education
The Sage Colleges
Troy, New York

John A. Kaufmann
Supervisor, Training Specialist
United States Navy
Pensacola, Florida

Kathy L. Ray
Safety Outreach Specialist
American Red Cross St. Louis Area Chapter
St. Louis, Missouri

Dave Thomas
Sport Development Consultant
USA Swimming
Colorado Springs, Colorado

Wendy Westberg
Health and Safety Service Manager
American Red Cross Lower Bucks Chapter
Levittown, Pennsylvania

The following individuals provided external guidance and review:

Janet Gabriel
Liaison-Safety, Coach Development and Sports Science
USA Diving
Fort Lauderdale, Florida

Russell Mark
Biomechanics Manager
USA Swimming
Colorado Springs, Colorado

Laura Mase
Coach (former Education Director)
USA Synchro
New Canaan, Connecticut

Stefanie Sinno, PhD
Assistant Professor of Psychology
Muhlenberg College
Allentown, Pennsylvania

John A. Waterhouse
Henderson, Nevada

Leah H. Wright-Ansorge
Special Education Teacher
Minneapolis, Minnesota

Special Acknowledgments

The American Red Cross would like to thank the following individuals who provided talent and locations for much of the photography in this manual and the other products supporting this program:

Nancy Cataldo
Director of Service Center Operations
The American Red Cross of Central South Carolina
Sumter, South Carolina

Jay Fitzgerald
Head Swim Coach
Pine Crest Aquatic Center-Woodson Pool
Fort Lauderdale, Florida

Janet Gabriel
Dive Coach
Pine Crest Aquatic Center-Woodson Pool
Fort Lauderdale, Florida

Tim Godwin
Aquatics Supervisor
20th Force Support Squadron
Shaw Air Force Base, South Carolina

Peter Karl
Assistant General Manager, Aquatics
Army Navy Country Club
Arlington, Virginia

Peggy Kubala
Aquatics Director
City of Sumter
Sumter, South Carolina

Mike McGoun
Director of Aquatic Services
City of Coral Springs
Coral Springs, Florida

Briane Schonfeldt
Aquatics Supervisor
City of Irvine
Irvine, California

Jean Skinner
Fairfax County Park Authority
Fairfax, Virginia

Photo Locations

Army Navy Country Club
Arlington, Virginia

Audrey Moore Recreation Center
Fairfax County Park Authority
Annandale, Virginia

City of Sumter Aquatics Center
Parks and Recreation
Sumter, South Carolina

Coral Springs Aquatic Complex
City of Coral Springs
Parks and Recreation
Coral Springs, Florida

Mullins Park Pool
City of Coral Springs
Parks and Recreation
Coral Springs, Florida

Pine Crest Aquatic Center-Woodson Pool
Pine Crest School
Fort Lauderdale, Florida

Spring Hill Recreation Center
Fairfax County Park Authority
McLean, Virginia

University of Maryland
College Park, Maryland

William Woollett Jr. Aquatic Center
City of Irvine
Community Services
Irvine, California

Woodlands Pool
20th Force Support Squadron
Shaw Air Force Base, South Carolina

Special thanks go to the following individuals for their assistance:

Bill Smith Design
Interior Designer

Simon Bruty
Photographer

John Healy
Production Assistant

Water Safety Instructor's Manual
Table of Contents

Part A

Administration

CHAPTER

1

Introduction

The purpose of the American Red Cross Swimming and Water Safety program is to teach people how to be safe in, on or around water and to teach individuals of different ages and abilities how to swim. Programming for people with special needs, such as those with disabilities, and different skill levels is a key component. In a logical progression, the program covers the knowledge and skills needed for aquatic skill development. As participants develop these skills, they will become safer and better swimmers.

Before you teach any of these courses or presentations, you should be familiar with the *American Red Cross Swimming and Water Safety* manual, the *Water Safety Instructor's CD-ROM,* this instructor's manual and the following additional materials and resources:

- Instructors intending to teach water safety courses and presentations must use the leader's guides provided on Instructor's Corner (*www.instructorscorner.org*).
- Instructors who wish to teach Longfellow's WHALE Tales must use the *Longfellow's WHALE Tales K–6 Educational Packet.* An optional *Longfellow's WHALE Tales DVD* also is available.
- Instructors intending to teach the Safety Training for Swim Coaches course must also use the *American Red Cross Safety Training for Swim Coaches Supplement* and *American Red Cross Safety Training for Swim Coaches Instructor's Manual.*

Program Materials

Swimming and Water Safety program materials are available from your local Red Cross chapter. Contact your chapter to purchase any materials necessary when teaching your class. Materials also can be purchased on Instructor's Corner (*www.instructorscorner.org*) or *www.shopstaywell.com.*

Water Safety Instructor's Manual and CD-ROM

This manual and CD-ROM are resources for those authorized by the Red Cross as Water Safety instructors to teach the following Red Cross Swimming and Water Safety courses and presentations:

- Parent and Child Aquatics
- Preschool Aquatics
- Learn-to-Swim
- Basic Water Rescue
- Personal Water Safety
- Water Safety Presentations
  - Water Safety Today
  - General Water Safety
  - Home Pool Safety
  - Parent Orientation to Swim Lessons
  - Sun Safety
  - Rip Current Safety

This instructor's manual is the primary resource that explains and describes the Red Cross Swimming and Water Safety program. The manual will direct you to the appropriate resource, the accompanying CD-ROM and to Instructor's Corner (*www.instructorscorner.org*) for course materials. This manual suggests teaching concepts, strategies, best practice steps and progressions, along with tips to ensure participant's success. It includes detailed information for instructors to plan, prepare and teach the Red Cross Swimming and Water Safety program. The instructor's manual has six parts:

- **Part A: Administration.** Introduces the Swimming and Water Safety program, describes course organization and course completion procedures and discusses class safety and instructor responsibilities.
- **Part B: Learning Theory.** Builds on information learned in the Fundamentals of Instructor Training course regarding the teaching and learning process, including the principles of motor learning. It contains some strategies and suggestions to use when teaching your courses.
- **Part C: Course Planning and Management.** Explains how to prepare block plans and lesson plans, as well as how to organize courses. It explains how to integrate water safety knowledge and skills into classes and presents concepts for planning how to teach different ages and abilities. It also explains the importance of communication with parents, including effective use of the Learn-to-Swim booklets in working with children. Additionally, this section discusses issues that affect young learners and their parents.
- **Part D: The Courses.** Details each of the levels of Parent and Child Aquatics, Preschool Aquatics and Learn-to-Swim. For each level, it explains learning objectives, defines readiness for the level, provides an outline of skills and details skill steps and progressions.
- **Part E: Teaching Water Safety.** Describes the Water Safety courses and presentations

available in the Swimming and Water Safety program. It directs you to the appropriate resources for specific lesson plans and participant materials. It also identifies target audiences and provides suggestions for offering the courses and presentations in the community.

The accompanying CD-ROM is a valuable resource for instructors as well as a great resource for program coordinators. For instructors, it contains information and resources to help them plan and prepare to teach. The CD-ROM includes–

- Sample block plans and lesson plans for each level.
- Teaching activities, games and drills.
- Sample forms, such as skill checklists.
- Newsletters for each level.
- Certificates of achievement for each level.

For program coordinators, the CD-ROM provides tools to assist in managing a swimming and water safety program and a team of instructors, including–

- Sample instructor evaluation forms.
- Sample job description.
- Sample records and reports, such as performance reports and registration forms.
- Instructor recruitment information.
- Information about managing and promoting Red Cross Swimming and Water Safety programs.

Swimming and Water Safety

The basic resource for instructors is the *American Red Cross Swimming and Water Safety* manual. The manual, combined with the *American Red Cross Swimming and Diving Skills DVD*, is also a resource for participants in Learn-to-Swim Levels 5 and 6 and adults who are interested in learning to swim, refining their strokes or learning more about aquatics. *Swimming and Water Safety* is required for participants in the Safety Training for Swim Coaches course. The manual describes and illustrates the skills in the Swimming and Water Safety program.

Swimming and Water Safety provides information regarding the components of aquatic safety as well as skill analysis for basic aquatic skills, strokes, diving and competitive swimming. This manual also presents more information for instructors teaching swimmers with disabilities or who want to incorporate more fitness activities into their teaching.

Water Safety Handbook

The *American Red Cross Water Safety Handbook* is used to support the water safety presentations on Instructor's Corner (*www.instructorscorner.org*). It is designed to increase safety wherever and whenever water sports are enjoyed. It includes easy-to-remember safety tips for pools, spas, waterparks, lakes, rivers, oceans and more. The handbook is ideal for parents, the general public, youth in grades 4–12 or youth organizations, and people who participate in activities in and around the water, such as camp staff and campers.

Raffy Learns to Swim and Waddles in the Deep

Two booklets are integral to Red Cross Preschool Aquatics and Learn-to-Swim lessons–*Raffy Learns to Swim* and *Waddles in the Deep*. These booklets provide a written communication mechanism between instructors and parents and participants, and they reinforce the content learned during the lessons.

Raffy Learns to Swim contains–

- A story line that supports and reinforces what participants are learning.
- Achievement cards that indicate a participant's progress toward passing Red Cross Preschool Aquatics Levels 1 and 2 and Learn-to-Swim Level 1. The instructor completes the appropriate achievement card at the end of each session.
- Activities to help parents practice with their child.
- General water safety tips to help parents keep their family safe whenever they are in, on or around water.
- A chart that provides an overview of Red Cross Preschool Aquatics and Learn-to-Swim.

Waddles in the Deep contains–

- A story line that supports and reinforces what participants are learning.

- Achievement cards that indicate the participant's progress toward passing Red Cross Preschool Aquatics Level 3 and Learn-to-Swim Levels 2 and 3. The instructor completes the appropriate achievement card at the end of each session.
- Activities to help parents practice with their child.
- Tips for safe diving to help keep parents and their family safe from injuries to the head, neck and back.
- A chart that provides an overview of Red Cross Preschool Aquatics and Learn-to-Swim.

Longfellow's WHALE Tales K–6 Educational Packet and Longfellow's WHALE Tales DVD

Longfellow's WHALE Tales targets children ages 5–12 and teaches safe behavior in, on and around the water. The materials in the *Longfellow's WHALE Tales K–6 Educational Packet* are designed to give children an awareness of being safe around the water and to help promote healthful aquatic recreation.

Longfellow's WHALE Tales is designed to be flexible to meet the needs of the participants. Leaders can pick or choose activities from 11 safety topics when developing a presentation. There is no set format and no minimum or maximum time requirements for presenting the information. An optional DVD is available.

Safety Training for Swim Coaches Supplement and Safety Training for Coaches Instructor's Manual

Safety Training for Swim Coaches, developed in collaboration with USA Swimming, is designed to provide participants training in aquatic safety that focuses on basic knowledge and skills to prevent and respond appropriately to many of the emergencies that can occur in a competitive swimming environment.

The Safety Training for Swim Coaches course has several delivery options that fit individuals' needs and provide flexibility in making it easy to attain and maintain this important certification. Participant materials include *Swimming and Water Safety* and the *Safety Training for Swim Coaches Supplement.* The supplement is available in electronic format from your local Red Cross chapter and on the Health and Safety Services section of the Red Cross Web site at *www.redcross.org.* Instructors use the *Safety Training for Swim Coaches Instructor's Manual* to teach the course, which is also available in an electronic format from your local Red Cross chapter.

DVDs

The DVDs, which are required for the Water Safety Instructor course, may also be used as teaching aids for the Swimming and Water Safety program. The following three DVDs are part of the *Swimming and Water Safety Program DVD Set*:

- *American Red Cross Swimming and Diving Skills*
- *American Red Cross Teaching Swimming and Water Safety*
- *American Red Cross Longfellow's WHALE Tales*

Instructor's Corner

Instructor's Corner is a Web site (*www.instructorscorner.org*) dedicated to Red Cross instructors. It contains additional information designed to help you as an instructor, including frequently asked questions, instructor updates, program updates and course-related forms. In addition, lesson plans for the following water safety courses and presentations also are on Instructor's Corner:

- Basic Water Rescue
- Personal Water Safety
- Water Safety Presentations
  - Water Safety Today
  - General Water Safety
  - Home Pool Safety
  - Parent Orientation to Swim Lessons
  - Sun Safety
  - Rip Current Safety

Additional Instructor Resources

Depending on the courses you teach, you may find it useful to consult the following materials:

- *American Red Cross Fundamentals of Instructor Training Participant's Manual*
- *American Red Cross Lifeguarding*
- *American Red Cross Lifeguarding Instructor's Manual with CD-ROM*

- *American Red Cross Lifeguarding DVD*
- *American Red Cross Lifeguard Management*
- *American Red Cross Basic Water Rescue*
- *American Red Cross Small Craft Safety*

Course Participants

The Red Cross has developed age guidelines for the Swimming and Water Safety courses. The recommended ages are only general guidelines. For children, take into consideration readiness, experience and maturity level when determining the course level in which participants should enroll.

- Parent and Child Aquatics is intended for infants and toddlers from 6 months to about 3 years of age.
- Preschool Aquatics is intended for children about 4 and 5 years of age.
- Learn-to-Swim is intended for children from about 6 years of age through older adults. Learn-to-Swim courses can be customized for different ages and abilities. Generally, classes should have participants of similar ages and abilities so you can conduct appropriate activities. Participants should also have the knowledge, skills and readiness appropriate for each level. For more information on these topics, see the individual Level Notes sections.
- For most water safety courses and presentations, there are no age prerequisites to participate. However, courses and presentations should have participants of similar ages and abilities so you can conduct appropriate activities. Also, some courses and presentations are more suited to older audiences. For more information on these topics, see the individual Course or Presentation Notes section.

Working with the Local Red Cross Chapter

If you wish to teach any part of the Swimming and Water Safety program, you should start planning well before the first class begins. Meet with your local Red Cross chapter. The chapter will assist you with–

- Your authorization to teach.
- The *Instructor Agreement* and, if applicable, the *Authorized Provider Agreement*
- Local policies and procedures, in addition to national guidelines.

The chapter may want to know the dates, times and locations of the course(s). Contact your local Red Cross chapter for any other information you need before your first lesson and any time thereafter if you have questions. The instructor's CD-ROM and Instructor's Corner (*www.instructorscorner.org*) are valuable resources to help you plan and teach any courses or presentations in the Swimming and Water Safety program.

Staffing

Water Safety Instructors

Your responsibilities as a Red Cross Water Safety instructor include–

- Ensuring that all participants have the physical ability to perform the skills and know to consult you if they have concerns about their physical ability to do so.
- Ensuring the classroom, pool and all practice areas are free of hazards.
- Administering and scoring the final written exam(s).
- Being familiar with and knowing how to use course materials and training equipment effectively.
- Planning, coordinating and managing training with your local Red Cross chapter, including advising the local Red Cross chapter in advance of any classes you are scheduled to teach.
- Informing participants about knowledge and skill evaluation procedures and course completion requirements.
- Creating a non-threatening environment that is conducive to achieving the learning objectives.
- Preparing participants to meet the course objectives.
- Adapting your teaching approach to match the experience and abilities of the participants, identifying participants who are having difficulty and developing effective strategies to help them meet course objectives.
- Supervising participants while they are practicing course skills and providing timely, positive and corrective feedback as they learn.

- Evaluating participants as they perform skills, focusing on critical performance steps as described in the skill sheets and/or outlines.
- Conducting courses in a manner consistent with course design.
- Issuing course completion certificates.
- Submitting completed course records and reports to the Red Cross representative within 10 working days from course completion.
- Being familiar with and informing participants of other Red Cross courses and programs.
- Being prepared to answer participants' questions or knowing where to find the answers.
- Providing a positive example by being neat in appearance and not practicing unhealthy behaviors, such as smoking, while conducting Red Cross courses.
- Identifying potential instructor and instructor aide candidates and referring them to the appropriate Red Cross representatives.
- Abiding by the obligations in the *Instructor Agreement and Code of Conduct* and, if applicable, the *Authorized Provider Agreement.*
- Representing the Red Cross in a positive manner.
- Promoting volunteer opportunities available through the Red Cross.

The Red Cross also recommends the following minimum instructor-to-participant ratios:

- Parent and Child Aquatics: 1 instructor for every 10 parent and child pairs
- Preschool Aquatics levels 1 through 3 and Learn-to-Swim levels 1 through 3: at least 1 instructor for every 6 participants
- Learn-to-Swim levels 4 through 6 and Basic Water Rescue: at least 1 instructor for every 10 participants

Close supervision is necessary to make practice effective and the class safe. To increase safety and instructional quality, consider having fewer participants per instructor.

Co-Instructors and Instructor Aides

Using co-instructors is an effective way to increase the amount of individual attention each participant receives. Co-instructors should be certified and authorized Water Safety instructors. Inexperienced Water Safety instructors and seasoned instructors can be paired to provide additional instructional attention for participants while at the same time helping the new instructor gain experience and confidence.

Water Safety instructor aides can assist Water Safety instructors with clerical, supervisory and maintenance responsibilities. Instructor aides must work under the direct supervision of a Water Safety instructor who is actively teaching the course. Effective use of aides allows the instructor to focus more time on the instructional aspects of the classes. Water Safety instructor aides should be able to–

- Demonstrate the skills being taught.
- Assist participants under the direction of the Water Safety instructor.
- Recognize unsafe conditions and behaviors and respond either by addressing or reporting situations to the instructor or swimming and water safety program coordinator.

It is important when using additional staff, such as co-instructors and instructor aides, to define their roles and responsibilities clearly. This helps eliminate confusion and lapses in supervision. Remember, you are ultimately responsible for your participants' safety.

To find candidates for Water Safety instructor aides, consider individuals who exhibit a strong sense of maturity and responsibility. Water Safety instructor aides must have successfully completed the level or demonstrated the knowledge and skills for the level for which they are serving as an aide. Water Safety instructors or Water Safety instructor trainers can train instructor aides. Follow the *American Red Cross Manual of Administrative Policies and Procedures* (MAPP) for selecting and training instructor aides. MAPP can be found on the Instructor Tools section of Instructor's Corner (*www.instructorscorner.org*).

Lifeguards

An adequate number of lifeguards should be on-duty and conducting patron surveillance during all in-water sessions. Having lifeguards on duty–

- Improves the instruction by letting you concentrate on teaching.

- Increases the safety of participants.
- Provides trained rescuers who can take action in an emergency.

Facilities

To ensure that your course is safe and successful, be sure your swimming facility has the appropriate dimensions. You need to consider the types of classes and the ages of the participants. For example, course requirements may need to be modified when the water is too deep for participants to stand or if the water is not deep enough for safe diving when performing headfirst entries (headfirst entries should not be taught when the water is less than 9 feet deep). If you use a waterfront facility, it should be free of surf and large enough to practice skills. It should have a clearly marked, safe swimming area that is large enough and deep enough for your program. Courses for infants, toddlers and preschoolers should not be conducted in untreated water, which is more likely to carry harmful organisms than sanitized pools. If you are unsure whether your swimming area is appropriate, check local and state regulations or with the health department. Contact your local Red Cross chapter or post a question in the forum on Instructor's Corner (*www.instructorscorner.org*) and check the frequently asked questions for accurate information before offering courses.

Water temperature also may be a key issue for your program. According to the Aquatic Exercise Association (AEA), a comfortable water temperature for swim classes is between 83° to 86° F (28.3° to 30° C) if they are kept on task and active. Ideally, air temperature should be 2° to 4° F above the water temperature.

Be sure you know your facility's policies and procedures related to teaching classes. Be clear on the areas designated for classes. Know and understand the facility's rules and regulations. Teach them to participants and enforce them within your classes. Ensure that qualified lifeguards are on-duty and conducting patron surveillance whenever swim classes are conducted.

Class Safety

As a Red Cross Water Safety instructor, you must make your teaching environment as safe as possible.

Some state and local recreational bathing and health codes require certain standards be met before the course begins. These may include requirements for lifeguards, child supervision ratios, safety equipment and proper water chemistry. You should know the requirements for your state and local jurisdiction. See your facility's risk management policy for specific requirements that are unique to the facility where you are teaching. Regardless of the regulations, you are responsible for the safety of the participants in your classes.

Factors Affecting Class Safety

Safety awareness is necessary for recognizing risks so that conditions can be corrected or controlled. Many other factors also affect the safety of an aquatics program, as discussed in the following sections.

Minimizing Risk

Minimizing the risk of injury is your primary focus while in and around the water. Adopt a "safety-first" attitude and teach this to your participants. Use every possible opportunity to teach participants safe practices in and around the water. Explain safe behavior at your facility and other facilities and aquatic environments during your presentations.

Also consider the participant's developmental level of understanding and maturity when preparing and presenting lessons, examples and demonstrations. For example, you should not present information to children in a manner that might frighten them or have them attempt skills before they are developmentally ready.

Supervision

During your lessons, you are observing participants, providing feedback and evaluating individual performance. It is difficult to keep a watchful eye on everyone at all times. Since any swimming class not properly supervised faces potential hazards, all participants must be accounted for throughout each lesson. There must be lifeguard supervision during swim lessons at all times. See **Chapters 3, 7 and 8** for more information on class supervision.

If you have participants with disabilities, you might want to have a smaller class or obtain additional help. **Chapter 6** provides detailed information to help you better serve individuals with disabilities and other health conditions.

Instructor Preparation

Thorough preparation can improve class safety. Careful preparation includes considering possible risks and managing safety concerns before classes start. Often, you can foresee risks and eliminate or control them long before participants step into the facility. Having co-instructors and instructor aides can help minimize risk by providing additional supervision. Greater attention to individual participants can also enhance participation and learning. Yet, remember: an instructor aide is not a substitute for a Water Safety instructor or having a lifeguard on deck.

Participants

The participants themselves greatly affect how to manage risks in a class. Be sure your participants–and their parents or whoever brings them–know and follow the facility's and program's rules and regulations. Explain and enforce all rules and regulations consistently. Safety should always be your primary concern. Evaluate participants carefully and get to know their tendencies, fears and motivations. Consider the participants' developmental stages and mental and physical abilities when deciding how to safely organize and conduct your class.

Class Organization

Some classes are safe with all participants in the water together, performing either as a group or individually. With other classes, all the participants in the water together may not be safe. See **Chapter 3** for more detailed information on class organization.

Equipment

Chapter 3 provides information on how to use different types of teaching aids. Required and optional equipment are listed in the course outlines. Based on the activities, games and drills you choose, you may need additional equipment. Make sure all equipment is ready and in working order before your class begins. You should request and receive orientation on the location and use of the equipment at any facility where you teach.

Teaching Environment

The teaching environment may involve risks you need to eliminate or minimize. Hazards in permanent or semi-permanent structures cannot be easily altered, such as blind spots and slip or trip areas at lakes, deck areas and around diving boards and other equipment. Be alert for potential hazards that cannot be easily altered. Document and report your concerns to the facility manager and/or program coordinator, and retain a copy for your records. Adjust your class to reduce such risks to your participants if you cannot completely eliminate them.

Healthy Swimming Behaviors

Recreational water illnesses (RWIs) are caused by certain germs, including "Crypto" (KRIP-toe, short for *Cryptosporidium*), *Giardia* (gee-ARE-dee-uh), *E. coli* 0157:H7, and *Shigella* (shi-GE-luh). The germs may spread accidentally when people swallow water that is contaminated with fecal matter. Most germs causing RWIs are killed by chlorine, but chlorine does not work right away. It takes time to kill germs. In addition, some germs, such as Crypto are resistant to chlorine, and can live in pools for days. That is why even the best maintained pools can spread illness.

Healthy swimming behaviors can help protect swimmers from RWIs and help stop germs from getting into pools in the first place. The Centers for Disease Control and Prevention (CDC) offers six "PLEAs" that promote healthy swimming. To the extent possible, you need to ensure the participants in your classes practice these "PLEAs" to stop germs from causing illness at the pool.

For All Swimmers

- Please do not swim when you have diarrhea; this is especially important for children in diapers. Germs can be spread in the water and make other people sick.
- Please do not swallow the pool water. In fact, avoid having water in the mouth.
- Please practice good hygiene. Take a shower before swimming, and wash your hands after using the toilets or changing diapers.

For Parents of Young Children

- Please take children on bathroom breaks or check diapers often. Waiting to hear "I have to go" may mean that it is too late.
- Please change diapers in a bathroom or a diaper changing area and not at poolside. Germs can spread to surfaces and objects in and around the pool and cause illness.
- Please wash your child thoroughly (especially the rear end) with soap and water before swimming. Invisible amounts of fecal matter on their bottoms can end up in the pool.

Facility Policies and Procedures

Besides being prepared to teach, you should be prepared to react appropriately in an emergency. Know the facility's emergency action plan (EAP) to ensure your safety and that of your participants. Know the location of emergency equipment, telephones, first aid supplies and additional personnel. Be sure you know where emergency phone numbers are posted, including police, ambulance, fire, poison control center, security and facility management. You may not have time to find this information when an emergency occurs.

All facility policies and procedures, including how to activate the EAP, should be in writing and available to you. You should have your own copy. It is your responsibility to know how the plan pertains to you and your classes. To avoid misunderstandings, be sure your roles and responsibilities are clearly outlined and documented. If you have exclusive use of the facility, the standard facility EAP may need to be modified. If using a residential pool or other private pool, you need to write your own EAP.

Practice the EAP. If part of a facility program, practice the EAP by participating in regular in-service trainings. If modifications have been made to accommodate exclusive use or when teaching in a private pool, practice the EAP with any individuals who will be involved.

To learn more about EAPs, refer to *American Red Cross Swimming and Water Safety, American Red Cross Lifeguarding* and *American Red Cross Lifeguard Management Manual.*

Records and Reports

Records and reports provide documentation related to your teaching activity and should include–

- Copies of instructor authorizations and related certifications.
- Lesson plans.
- *Course Record* and *Course Record Addendums* or *Water Safety Instructor Activity Reports.*
- Participant attendance records.
- Participant achievement records.

Acknowledging Course Participation

Certification Requirements

Many agencies, organizations and individuals look to the Red Cross for formal training resulting in certification. Red Cross certification means that on a particular date an instructor verified that a course participant could–

- Demonstrate competency in each required skill taught in a course. Competency is defined as being able to perform each skill to meet the objective without guidance. Participants must be able to demonstrate all of the skills listed in the skills outlines in **Chapters 7, 8 and 9** at the level of performance identified in the stroke performance charts, as well as complete the exit skills assessments. Any exceptions, such as headfirst entries, will be identified with an asterisk.
- Pass the final written exam with a minimum grade of 80 percent, if applicable. If the final written exam has more than one section, a minimum grade of 80 percent must be achieved on each section.

Achieving course certification does not imply any future demonstration of the knowledge or skill at the level achieved on the particular date of course completion.

Reporting Procedures

You must complete, sign and turn in the *Course Record* and *Course Record Addendum* or *Water Safety Instructor Activity Report* to your local Red Cross chapter within 10 business days of course completion to receive course completion certificates. Keep a copy for your records and give a copy to the facility where the course was conducted. These forms may be submitted in hard copy, by fax or electronically. Contact your local Red Cross chapter to determine local procedures.

Awarding Certificates

Discuss with your local Red Cross chapter the procedures for obtaining course completion certificates for participants. Be sure to follow local procedures. Sign the certificates before giving them to the participants. If you will receive the certificates after the course is over, arrange to get them to the participants.

Course Evaluation

Receiving feedback from participants is important following any course. Participants and/or parents should have an opportunity to tell you what they thought about the course. This information gives you feedback about the course and its instruction, and it helps you, your facility and the Red Cross maintain the highest quality.

Red Cross Health and Safety Services Resources

Keep updated on the latest instructor information by visiting Instructor's Corner (*www.instructorscorner.org*). Your local Red Cross chapter also may have more information and resources, as well as additional equipment, marketing materials and instructional aids. Before you begin a Swimming and Water Safety program, find out how your local Red Cross chapter can support you.

Part B

Learning Theory

CHAPTER

2

Teaching and Learning Swimming

As a Water Safety instructor, you have one of the most interesting and challenging teaching jobs. You have the responsibility to facilitate all kinds of aquatic learning. For example, you help participants gain new knowledge about swimming and water safety, encourage them to learn and adopt water safety practices and attitudes and teach them to improve their swimming skills and strokes. In this chapter, you will learn principles associated with teaching swimming skills from developmental and learning perspectives. You also will learn related instructional methods that will help you become the most effective swim instructor possible.

Developmental Principles of Learning Motor Skills

Motor skills are motions carried out when the brain, nervous system and muscles work together. Learning motor skills requires coordination of the limbs, as well as the development of strength, posture control, balance and perceptual skills.

Even though all humans change the way they move over the course of their lives, researchers do not agree why motor skills change. But they do agree that movements, including swimming, change progressively. These changes are a result of complex interactions between the characteristics people are born with and their individual experiences. Yet, these changes also can be understood in terms of several natural patterns or developmental principles. For example, swimming skills are gained in much the same way as other fundamental motor skills, such as walking, running, jumping, throwing, catching and even talking. By understanding some basic information about how swimming skills change, you can help participants learn to swim or swim more efficiently.

Types of Changes in Motor Skills

The way motor skills change over time can be measured by using a numeric score as well as by observing the quality of the movement itself. Numeric change can be measured by noting a gradual increase in participants' practice routines–the number of repetitions they can perform, the length of time they can swim or the distance they can cover. For example, when beginners first learn to float on their back, they may only do so for a couple of seconds. But with instruction and practice, they soon can float effortlessly for longer periods of time. When participants gain the coordination and strength to swim a stroke, they may only be able to swim a short distance. But with instruction and practice, they can soon swim longer distances, such as the entire length of a pool one or more times. These are examples of changes that are measured numerically as scores recorded in time, repetitions or distances.

In contrast, use outcome or performance scores to document gradual changes in the type of skills performed or in the way skills are performed. In both cases, people are capable of doing something new and different than they could before. For example, young children or adult beginners may only be capable of moving around in the water by holding onto the side of the pool or walking in shallow water. Gradually, they can move through the water using a glide or rudimentary swimming skill without touching the side or bottom of the pool, thus learning a new skill. Similarly, when novices first try using their legs to kick in the water, they typically perform a distinct leg action that looks like "running" or "bicycling." With instruction, practice and more experience, the leg kicking actions change to a more fully extended position that actually becomes a recognizable flutter-like kick. This change is not simply a gradual increase in speed, range of motion or strength. It is a change into a new and different coordinated muscle action.

Applying the Concepts of Change

The concepts of assigning a numeric score and observing differences in performance patterns are used to illustrate how people learn swimming skills. Swim instructors need to appreciate both ways that swimming skills change while participants are learning new skills. There are several very important reasons for understanding how swimming performance patterns change. First, instructors need to know if participants are making progress. Second, understanding how performance patterns change allows instructors to introduce the most basic skills first. Once participants learn simple skills, they are ready to move on to more challenging skills. It is usually not effective to try to get participants to learn harder skills until they have mastered the earlier, simpler skills.

You should anticipate that some skills, such as breath control or flotation, might improve very gradually or sometimes not at all for some time. When participants' swimming skills are changing slowly, it is important to use outcome or performance scores to document these small, gradual changes. This helps you and your participants stay motivated to continue practicing. At the same time, it is important for you to look for new skills to appear or how the pattern of particular skills changes. When you notice that swimmers' movement patterns, such as the style of kicking, arm stroke or breathing action, begin to change, you can provide additional feedback and reinforcement to your participants.

Predictable Order of Change

Changes in motor skills do not occur randomly, but happen in a predictable order. Some change shows regular increases in number. Other change occurs in ordered sequences or natural progressions. Participants learn easier skills before more challenging skills. Rudimentary swimming movement patterns appear before more advanced swimming patterns. For example, when swimming on the front, beginners will not swim very far, they tend to keep their arms under water during recovery, and they often use a beginner stroke (sometimes called a "dog paddle"). In contrast, with more experience, strength and coordination, swimmers can travel much farther, recover their arms out of the water and use a rudimentary crawl stroke.

Applying the Concept of Predictable Order

Instructors should understand that swimming skills change over time in predictable, natural sequences. Your teaching progressions should always parallel the naturally occurring sequences. You want to help participants move from using simpler and easier skills to practicing more complex and difficult ones. Basic forms of any swimming behavior lead to more advanced skills. Early behaviors, such as using underwater arm recovery, are often prerequisites to later, more advanced skills, such as using above-water arm recovery. Knowing the predictable order of change in aquatic skills allows you to anticipate skills swimmers will use next. For example, before asking participants to submerge their entire head, practice submersion of just parts of the face to help them become familiar with and ready for the more difficult task of full head submersion. The American Red Cross uses predictable sequences, which are based on how swimming skills naturally change, to build the progression of skills within and across all Parent and Child Aquatics, Preschool Aquatics and Learn-to-Swim levels.

Increasing Connections Among Elements

Another principle of learning motor skills is that over time behaviors become more closely connected with other related behaviors. Skilled swimmers doing the front crawl move through the water with apparent ease because they have learned to integrate and time their rotary breathing with their arm stroke and leg kick. In contrast, beginning swimmers often look very different. They may stroke with their arms moving rapidly for a time. Then they either stop their arms or paddle using very short, quick motions while they catch a long breath with their face out of the water. Finally they resume their arm stroke. One key difference between beginner and skilled swimmers is the degree to which they can coordinate their arm stroke, leg kick and breathing.

Applying the Concept of Connecting Skill Elements

The principle of naturally connecting skill elements stresses the importance of encouraging swimmers to practice most aquatic skills as a whole whenever possible. Practicing a stroke using all elements together–the leg kick, arm stroke and breathing–is important because each element influences the performance of the other elements. Some swimmers may have difficulty developing coordinated stroke movements when they practice stroke elements separately. Participants may need to use flotation aids or other instructional devices, such as fins, to practice a stroke pattern safely and effectively.

On the other hand, swimmers tend to learn some skills and strokes easier and effectively when they practice an element of the skill or stroke separately. For example, participants need to learn elements of breath control, such as face and head submersion and rhythmic breathing, before attempting breathing patterns with specific strokes. Additionally, learning the basic patterns of the flutter kick, dolphin kick or breaststroke kick usually is best practiced separately. After this separate practice, you can add other stroke elements, such as the arms then breathing and timing. This method works better in the very early stages of learning skills. At more advanced levels, some skills may be easy to learn as a whole. The teaching method you choose depends upon the specific skills being learned.

Increasing Specialization and Adaptability

As swimmers' skills develop, their skills become more specialized and flexible. Inexperienced swimmers typically move through the water using limited, general patterns such as in a combined stroke on the front. Over time and with greater skill, they may become capable of swimming several different strokes on their front, such as front crawl, breaststroke and butterfly. Ultimately, they are able to select whichever specialized strokes they wish to use and modify them for specific conditions. They also can adapt their arm strokes to the demands of different strokes. For example, swimmers use a similar underwater arm-stroke pattern for both the front crawl and butterfly. But swimmers use one arm at a time when swimming the crawl and both arms simultaneously for the butterfly. Swimmers at this level have become more specialized.

Applying the Concepts of Specialization and Adaptability

You should not worry when your beginning-level participants cannot perform arm strokes and leg kicks like elite swimmers. With instruction, practice and feedback, your participants' arm and leg patterns will change and become more specialized and effective. These changes may occur gradually over weeks, months or years so you and your participants must be patient.

As you read previously, swimmers' first attempts at kicking often look more like "running" in the water than flutter kicking. Novices tend to bend their ankle and push against the water with the sole of the foot as they might while walking or running on land. With instruction, experience and practice, beginning swimmers effectively start using flutter, breaststroke, scissors or dolphin kicks that help them move through the water more successfully and effectively.

As swimmers improve their skills, they can also adapt them for particular situations. For example, a regular breaststroke includes a glide. But if a lifeguard needs to bring a submerged victim to the surface, it is necessary to eliminate the glide and kick continuously and without hesitation. More skilled swimmers can make this adjustment, while also making adaptations as needed to improve their effectiveness in the water.

Age Relationships

Chronological age is often a convenient marker used to understand and measure motor skill development. Unfortunately, many people assume that an increase in age automatically results in improvement or that all children of a certain age have similar skill levels. For example, parents often ask: "Why can all my daughter's friends of the same age swim and she cannot?" The parents assume that there is a cause-and-effect relationship between age and motor skill performance. This leads to the practice of grouping children of similar ages together in the hope of producing similar behaviors and learning. School grades, athletic teams and even swim classes often are grouped solely by chronological age. In reality, people of similar ages vary greatly in their body sizes, knowledge, skills, learning styles, personalities and experiences. Therefore, it is also important to consider ability, level of maturity and mental development when grouping participants. They are only similar in rather general ways. You can read more about childhood development and how it affects children's ability to learn how to swim in **Chapter 5**.

Applying the Concept of Age

Age is only a very general guideline for people's capacity. As a Water Safety instructor, you should carefully consider a variety of personal characteristics in addition to age when determining participants' readiness for various swimming skills and levels. However, learning activities should be age-appropriate. Regardless of actual skill level, most preschool children may learn best when they participate in simple games, songs and activities appropriate for young children. Older children and adults who may have novice swimming skill levels will benefit from more mature learning activities based more on verbal descriptions.

Motor Learning Principles

Like motor development, *motor learning* is a field of study that examines the processes of learning motor skills. Unlike development, motor learning theory presumes that changes in motor behavior result primarily from practice or experience that is controlled by an instructor or coach. As a Water Safety instructor, you can make the process of learning swimming skills more effective by–

- Recognizing participant readiness for learning (i.e., learning stages).

- Setting specific and achievable goals based on that readiness.
- Giving accurate instruction and demonstrations.
- Encouraging active participation and practice toward the goals.
- Giving positive, corrective and timely feedback in relation to performance.
- Using different types of motivation as part of the feedback process.

Motor Stages in Learning

One theory about how motor skills are learned explains that individuals progress through three identifiable stages of learning.

The early stage of learning is marked by awkward, slow movements that learners consciously try to control. People in the early stage have to think before doing movements. Performance in this stage generally does not look like skilled behavior. For example, do you remember the first time you tried to drive a car? Recall the thoughts that raced through your head. "Where is the brake?" "How far before the corner do I put on my turn signal?" Because you had to think through every action, your movements were slow and awkward.

As you gained experience and as your instructor explained things in different ways, your performance improved, but still could vary quite a lot. Your responses were faster and smoother. You developed a general understanding of each movement, but you still did not look like a skilled driver. Once you had the idea of the movement, you progressed to the intermediate stage. In this stage, you spent less time thinking about every detail and began to associate the movement you were learning with other movements you already knew. For example, when you reached the intermediate stage in driving an automobile, you did not have to think so consciously about all the separate tasks of driving, such as using the turn signal, applying the brake and looking both ways when you stopped to turn at an intersection. Your behavior was still variable, but it looked and felt routine.

Finally, with a lot of experience, your driving performance reached an acceptable level. Your movements were accurate and rapid. You seemed

Characteristics of Learning Stages

Characteristics of the early stage of learning include—

- Awkward, slow movements that seem to be consciously controlled by the learner.
- Poor understanding of the task.

At this stage, you need to provide—

- Distributed practice—allowing for frequent rest periods throughout the practice schedule.
- Corrective feedback, especially knowledge of performance.

During this early stage, make sure that participants understand the goal of the task and that their initial attempts at a skill are successful and done properly.

Characteristics of the intermediate stage of learning include—

- More rapid movement.
- Movements that vary with each try.
- Inconsistent movements.
- An increased understanding of the task.
- A lack of understanding of all the fine points that are needed to successfully complete the task.

At this stage, you need to provide—

- Extensive and varied practice.
- Adequate and accurate feedback (both knowledge of results and performance).

People progress to the intermediate stage of learning when they have a general understanding of the goal of the task.

Characteristics of the late stage of learning include—

- Accurate, rapid movement.
- An understanding of skill technique.
- The ability to provide own general feedback.

At this stage, you should provide—

- Minor corrections.
- Specialized feedback.
- Positive reinforcement.

In general, people do not reach the late stage of learning until they are older and more experienced.

to know instinctively what to do in almost every situation. When you did something incorrectly, you realized it immediately and found ways to correct it. You had reached the late stage. In this stage, learning is mostly complete, although the skill can continue to be refined through practice for many years. In the driving example, you no longer depended on the instructor for all feedback about your performance. You did not need to "think" about what you were doing–it was automatic.

Applying the Concepts of Learning Stages

You should be able to observe your participants going through these same stages as they learn swimming skills, especially more complicated ones such as strokes and headfirst entries. It is very likely that people in the same class will be in different learning stages.

The two most important points to take away from the concept of learning stages are that–

- The stages are easily recognizable.
- The role of the instructor is quite different in each stage.

Using Teaching Progressions

The teaching progressions used in Parent and Child Aquatics, Preschool Aquatics and Learn-to-Swim have been designed according to the principles of learning discussed so far. When you lead participants through these progressions, you are using a teaching strategy that is–

- **Developmental.** Motor skills are best learned when skills are broken into steps that are taught logically, each leading directly to the next. In addition, since each new detail or refinement of a skill is added incrementally to what the participants already know, they can integrate the new skill with what they have already learned. The result is a change in the quality of their abilities.
- **Familiar.** The teaching progressions rely on the principle that people learn a variety of skills easier when the skills are taught in a standardized way. The familiarity that comes from this approach helps participants anticipate the next step of a progression, even as they improve the skills they know.
- **Measurable.** Since the teaching progressions are divided into small, measurable steps, you and the participants have a useful standard for setting goals. You can use teaching progressions to assess participants' readiness to attempt new skills (or the next step of a complex skill) and to evaluate their performances after they have practiced certain skills. This approach also helps you deal with any anxiety participants have about attempting skills.

Setting Goals

The first step in the learning process is to present a goal clearly in an age-appropriate way. Methods to accomplish this include–

- Verbal explanations (discussions, descriptions or simple stories).
- Visual descriptions:
  - Instructor or instructor aide demonstrations of the intended skill.
  - Peer demonstrations of the intended skill.
  - Task cards, posters, slides, illustrations, DVDs, videos or films.

Next, participants should set goals to change or improve their performance in a particular swimming skill. You may need to set goals for younger participants. As younger participants advance in experience and skill level, they can participate in setting goals for themselves.

When setting goals for participants, consider these factors:

- Age (children or adults)
- Disabilities and other special needs or conditions
- The level of cognitive and motor skill development
- Language comprehension differences
- Levels of motivation

Applying the Concept of Goal Setting

Each of the above methods is effective with certain learners, situations and skills. With young participants, peer demonstrations can be very effective in helping to set goals. These demonstrations not only show effective or possible ways to perform skills, but also may lead young participants to think, "If she can do it, so can I."

After demonstrating a skill for adults, you might only have to state a learning outcome such as, "By the end of this lesson, you should be able to perform this skill fairly well. We are going to practice it so you can achieve that goal."

Encouraging Practice

Practice is essential for learning and improving motor skills. You should consider various practice factors to swim lessons, including–

- Active practice time.
- Ratio of practice time to rest.
- Variability of practice.
- Structure of how and what is practiced.

Active Practice Time

When planning, make sure that there is adequate active practice time for all participants during each lesson. Wave, stagger, circle and scatter class formations, described in **Chapter 3**, can be used depending on the skill and the level of the participants. Minimize the amount of talking, demonstrating and time participants stand in line, and maximize the time they spend engaged in active practice.

Ratio of Practice Time to Rest

Depending upon the skill being learned and practiced, you should consider how much rest to provide between practice episodes. Gross motor skills that require strength or endurance, such as swimming strokes, require longer rest periods. Less strenuous skills, such as breath control or floating, may allow more repetitions with shorter rest periods. People retain a motor skill longer when instructors provide frequent periods of rest, either to recover from fatigue or to reduce boredom from repetition. When possible, keep participants in the water during rest periods, perhaps engaged in practicing other activities. This helps participants from becoming chilled, which can lessen their enthusiasm for and attention to the lesson.

Variability of Practice

Variability of practice is the most important factor that leads to rapid and effective motor learning. Varying both the skill and the conditions under which people practice the skill improves the quality and rate of learning. This is more effective than practicing the same skill over and over in the same way. For example, learning breath control skills is enhanced when participants practice submersion and rhythmic breathing in a variety of settings, such as while standing at the pool edge, floating or swimming with support, rather than by simply repeating breath holding or blowing bubbles. Frequent changes in the tempo of a stroke can help keep participants interested and improve their feel for the water. Practicing kicking in several situations, such as holding onto the gutter, with instructor support or with a kickboard, can lead to more effective learning of kicking skills than simply practicing the flutter kick at the side of the pool.

Structure of How and What Is Practiced

You should tailor practices to the type of skills you are teaching. For example, simple skills, such as breath control and floating, may be practiced without being broken down into separate parts. But once learners are proficient at the individual elements of strokes–such as the arm action, leg kick and breathing–complex skills will progressively improve with time and should be practiced as a whole. This type of practice works because the elements of strokes change dramatically when performed separately. Practicing each element separately until performing it very well does not necessarily result in an improved stroke. Change in one component often affects all other components. Therefore, all the components should be practiced together as soon as possible to maximize the effectiveness of learning.

It may be easier for people to learn and practice some complex skills when you break them into their component parts. This type of practice is effective for skills that are performed slowly and in a step-by-step fashion, such as putting on and fastening a life jacket, doing an approach for a forward dive from a diving board or performing rotary breathing. Generally, this technique is effective for skills that are not refined over time and that have a single appropriate way to be performed.

Giving Feedback

Giving feedback can help participants learn desired responses and improve execution of skills. Whenever you provide feedback, you give your participants credit for what they have done while providing information about how to improve. This type of corrective feedback enhances learning.

Learning skills without appropriate feedback is like learning by trial and error. Precise feedback is usually more useful to most participants than general feedback. Comments, such as "good" or "nice job," are helpful initial responses for motivation, but are not specific enough to provide participants with a basis for making corrections. For example, such phrases as "good job" should be accompanied by precise feedback, such as "I like how you kept your cheek and ear in the water at the same time" or "That time you kept your knees straighter during the flutter kick."

Participants need both positive and corrective feedback. Remember: when you try to correct participants' mistakes, it may seem difficult to avoid using negative feedback. It may seem natural to say: "Do not bend your knees so much" when participants use a kick that comes out of the water. Unfortunately, this both reinforces what participants have done incorrectly and fails to identify what they should be doing. Fortunately, there are some simple strategies you can use to stay positive. Tell participants what they have done correctly first. Try giving positive feedback before pointing out what participants did incorrectly or what they could have done better. For example, you can say: "I really like how hard you are trying. Great effort. Next time try and straighten your knees so you will make a smaller splash." Another strategy is to rephrase negative comments so they are more positive. Instead of saying, "Do not lift your head" while the participant is trying to learn rotary breathing in the front crawl, you might say: "Can you try turning your chin to the side?" or "If you exhale a little earlier, it will be easier to get your breath while turning your head to the side" or "Can you keep your toes in the water instead of letting them come out of the water so far?"

Applying the Concept of Feedback: Importance of Communication

It is important to communicate at a level appropriate to your participants' level of understanding and skill. There are several ways to check whether you are communicating at the right level. The simplest way is just to ask the participants if they understood what you just said. You can tell how much they understand by asking them to explain it back to you. If your participants seem uninterested or distracted, you may be talking over their heads. Finally, if their movements are nothing like what you explained, you should suspect that you failed to communicate the information at a level appropriate to their knowledge or skill.

It is very easy to give too much information, especially to beginners. The description of even a simple swimming skill involves an enormous amount of information. If you describe (and ask participants to perform) a simple skill broken down in all its parts, you are giving them a large amount of information to absorb all at once. Since they are more likely to remember only the first and last things you say, your communication will be more effective if you give smaller amounts of information. Communicating a single item at a time often works best with younger or beginning participants.

When you are verbally describing a motor skill, you are in a sense painting a picture in the minds of your participants. The challenge is to paint a clear picture using as few words as possible. Choose your words carefully. Develop a vocabulary that describes what you want to see in a skill. If you want a flutter kick with the muscles in the lower leg loose and relaxed, you might tell the participants to use "floppy ankles." Use and reuse those words or phrases so they become part of the participants' vocabulary as well.

When working with older children and adults, it is important to pick words and phrases that are precise and concise. Vague terms such as "in front," "wide" and "long" used in directions, such as "put your hands in front of your body when pulling in the front crawl," "pull wide in the breaststroke" and "pull and glide long in the elementary backstroke" lead to questions about where in front, how wide and how long.

Directional and spatial descriptions should tell exactly where movements should be, and when reasonable, be combined with a physical indication. For example:

- "Your hands should enter directly forward of your shoulders and with the elbow bent slightly. Like this…"
- "Pull to 10 and 2 o'clock before you sweep during the breaststroke pull, from here…to here…"
- "Glide for the count of three or until you are almost stopped when you swim elementary backstroke. One and two and three and four."

Making comparisons is often an effective way to convey information to learners. Saying "kick like a dolphin" paints a clear picture because many people are familiar with how a dolphin propels itself through the water. A direction, such as "stretch like you are hanging from a tree," helps them associate something they already know with something they are learning.

Effective communication may sound spontaneous and unrehearsed, but it seldom is. New instructors should not expect to come up with perfect descriptive phrases or comparisons. It takes time and preparation as well as good mentoring from more experienced teachers. Effective teachers consciously develop a vocabulary that suits their needs. These words and phrases become teaching cues you can use over and over. Think about brief, highly descriptive ways to explain what you want to communicate. Recalling phrases your teachers or coaches used that were meaningful to you may be helpful. It is important to consider the effectiveness of terms for your own style of teaching. What works for one instructor may not be effective for another.

Providing Motivation

Motivation is the internal drive that keeps people moving toward a goal. It can lead people to start, maintain or modify behavior. Reinforcement–anything that increases the likelihood that a person will perform a given task as desired–can help you motivate participants. *Positive reinforcement* is a way of increasing desired behavior by presenting a positive reinforcer after the learner shows the desired behavior. A positive reinforcer is something valued by the learner, such as a fun activity. *Negative reinforcement* is a way of increasing behavior by removing a negative reinforcer after the learner shows the desired behavior. A negative reinforcer is something the learner wants to avoid, like more laps! It is important to remember that negative reinforcers do not have to be mean spirited. Do not confuse negative reinforcement with punishment. Punishment is the process of decreasing undesired behavior by using negative responses.

Most psychologists believe that positive reinforcers provided on a timely basis are far more effective than negative reinforcers in shaping behavior. A good form of positive reinforcement is the personal praise you give when participants perform skills in an appropriate or effective manner. The more participants feel that their efforts are noticed and appreciated; the more likely it is that they will repeat and learn the desired behavior.

It may be tempting to use punishment when participants are behaving inappropriately. But this technique is inappropriate and rarely effective. Instead, examine why participants may be using the inappropriate behavior in the first place. Perhaps directions you gave were not clear or effective in language the participants understand. It may be that the skills being learned are either too difficult or too easy for some of your participants. People may use attention-seeking behaviors to mask fear or insecurity. With some reflection and experience, you will discover that some behaviors are symptoms for other problems. You should address the problems, not the symptoms.

One key to motivation is understanding why your participants want to learn to swim. People come to Swimming and Water Safety classes for many reasons. Participants can range from the fearful child to the self-directed adult. Some may want to learn to swim while others may be required to take the course. To be an effective instructor, you should strive to understand and recognize the variety of motives your participants may possess. Their motivation can come from inside or be externally reinforced by incentives, rewards or challenges offered by instructors or peers. Motivation that comes from participants' own desire to learn is the more powerful and enduring of the two types of motivation because it is under the control of learners. Instructors should be careful not to undermine internal motivation by offering unnecessary rewards or challenges. Sometimes understanding your participants' motivation may simply be a matter of asking each participant, "So why are you here?"

The most fundamental key to positive motivation for everyone, regardless of age, ability or skill level, is to experience meaningful success. Success means that the person must overcome some reasonable challenge rather than simply performing an easily accomplished task. The level of the challenge and criteria for success must always be adapted to each individual learner.

Motivation brings this complex discussion on learning full circle. Participants' motivations can be translated into goals. To be truly motivating, goals must be realistic for participants. If the goals are set too low, they do not challenge people and your participants will not accomplish much. If goals are unrealistically high, participants will likely become frustrated and their motivation will diminish. Your participants' motivation will remain strong if goals are realistic, based upon prior experience, measurable, and above all, meaningful to your participants. Goals also give purpose and direction to practice time. Effective practice involves receiving appropriate feedback. Feedback that allows people to reach goals is a great way to boost fundamental motivation and enthusiasm for aquatics.

Applying the Concept of Motivation: Dealing with Anxiety

Fear and anxiety can lessen participants' motivation and ability to learn. These limiting emotions may come from different sources. Some fears result from real, dangerous experiences, such as a nonfatal submersion (near drowning). Other fears are less concrete and may be referred from other sources, such as the experience of a family member or watching a scary movie, for instance, *Jaws.* Watch for actions suggesting that participants are anxious. The following are the most common avoidance behaviors that may indicate participants are anxious:

- Making excuses (for absences, lateness or not wanting to attempt a skill)
- Huddling (rounding the shoulders too much and making the chest concave, especially when in a prone position)
- Holding the body rigid, particularly the muscles of the shoulders and legs
- Clenching fists
- Pursing or biting the lips
- Shivering even in warm temperatures (someone who is frightened may shiver no matter how warm the water or air temperatures)
- Clinging to supports when practicing skills, especially floating
- Gripping the instructor, especially during floating and submersion skills practice
- Moving unnecessarily (such as kicking when participants should be floating motionless)
- Performing swim strokes with arm actions that are too short, too shallow, too rigid and/or too fast
- Making frequent requests to go to the bathroom (usually in young children)
- The inability to blow air out underwater before returning to the surface
- Breathing in while the face is still submerged

If apprehensive participants are to learn successfully, the following conditions are essential:

- Participants must have a strong desire to learn. Without self-motivation, it is too easy to give up when the task seems difficult or produces anxiety. Remind participants of the goals they have set for themselves and praise them for their effort and the skills they have already acquired.
- Instructors need to maximize opportunities for participant success. You must be extremely patient. Encourage participants at every step. Avoid any verbal or nonverbal signs of exasperation or impatience. Allow participants to practice skills they already can perform successfully to help them gain confidence and to try the next slightly more challenging task in a skill progression.
- Participants should be allowed to own and control their fear. They should never be forced to try something they perceive as threatening, nor should they be criticized for avoiding a fearful situation. Instead, encourage them to take small

steps toward their goals. For successful learning, participants must develop self-confidence and trust in you, the instructor.

You can help participants feel in control and gain self-confidence by taking special care to prepare them for each new experience. Verbalize each new task. Discuss the task and the outcomes. Direct anxious participants to imagine themselves successfully completing the task, a technique called imagery. When the participants feel ready to attempt the new task, encourage and reward each attempt as a success.

Low participant-to-instructor ratios are appropriate for fearful learners of any age. Individual attention allows anxious participants to advance at their own pace rather than fall behind the rest of the class, which can further undermine their self-confidence.

Teaching Principles

Your primary goal as a Water Safety instructor is to enhance participants' aquatic skills and safety in, on and around the water. You will use different teaching strategies to reach this goal. Before choosing a teaching strategy for a particular lesson or skill, you need to consider a number of factors, such as–

- The knowledge and/or skill to be learned.
- The current skill level of the participants.
- How the class will be organized.
- How much practice time you will provide.
- How often and what type of feedback you will provide.
- How you will evaluate participants' performance.

Several different teaching strategies were introduced in *Fundamentals of Instructor Training.* The following section helps you apply several of these strategies to the aquatic environment. It also introduces other teaching strategies that can be effective.

Direct Teaching Strategies

Direct teaching methods are the most common methods used when teaching motor skills, or more specifically, swimming skills. These methods are much more "teacher-centered" because the instructor controls what is being taught, when and how. Most beginning instructors are more comfortable with direct methods because this may be how they learned to swim. Direct methods allow the greatest structure and control of the swim class and are generally very effective. However, they may not always produce effective learning. In the following sections, you will learn the names and descriptions for several types of instruction.

Explain, Demonstrate and Practice

Explain, demonstrate and practice is a commonly used teaching strategy in physical education, coaching and swimming instruction. When using this teaching strategy, instructors control all elements of the class. The participants' roles include being attentive and listening closely to what instructor says to them and ask them to do. Generally the steps in this strategy of teaching are as follows:

- The instructor explains a skill.
- The instructor demonstrates how to perform the skill.
- On the instructor's signal, the participants practice the skill as demonstrated.

When done appropriately, demonstrations may be effective ways to present visual models of motor skills. To demonstrate appropriately, you must be knowledgeable about the subject and proficient at the skills as well. Sometimes you may prefer to have an aide or a class member demonstrate a skill while you comment on the demonstration.

Demonstrations must be at the appropriate level for the participants. If participants are just starting to learn the front crawl, for example, conduct the demonstration with slow and purposeful movements, such as pausing the arms out of the water so participants clearly see the position of the arm during the above water recovery. If participants are just starting to learn the elementary backstroke, demonstrate the stroke with a noticeable hesitation between the recovery phase and the propulsion phase. This way of demonstrating slows down the skill and gives the participants a chance to see all components of a movement. Participants are more likely to learn the skill quickly when they understand the skill you are teaching. If you describe and demonstrate the skills well, you may speed their process of "getting the idea."

As described earlier in the section on feedback, it is important to concentrate on one aspect at a time. For example, to show rotary breathing for the front crawl, you may demonstrate it by standing in waist-deep water and leaning over with just your face in the water. You do not have to perform the entire stroke. Another way to simplify a demonstration is to do it on dry land before you demonstrate it in the water. Some participants may need to be taught how to perform elements of a skill separately. Point out relationships between skill elements whenever you present them. This allows participants to get a better grasp of the total process.

To make the most of a demonstration, first describe what participants are about to see. For example, if you want them to see a starting position for a good breaststroke kick, tell them precisely what to look for: knees approximately shoulder-width apart, feet wider than the knees and the feet pulled up and turned out. You may decide to show a side view and a head-on view.

You must also make sure participants are in a position to see your skill demonstration clearly. In general, participants can see demonstrations better when they are completely out of the water standing on the edge of the deck. Do not let participants stand behind anyone else.

Once you have explained the skill and had participants watch you do it, ask them to picture themselves doing the skill the same way you presented it and duplicate that movement. Then, have participants perform the skill as soon as possible. Give them corrective feedback, if necessary.

Present a skill in as many ways as you can, sometimes by combining methods and teaching strategies. For instance, give a verbal description and a demonstration of a skill at the same time, whenever possible. If you are describing a hand-stroking motion, do the motion while you describe it. Talk with your body as well as your mouth. You can also have a participant or an aide demonstrate while you talk. Learning motor skills is simpler when participants receive information they can see as well as hear. This is a powerful form of communication because it provides more information in the same amount of time and uses multiple senses in the learning process.

While people generally absorb information better when a skill demonstration is immediately followed by skill practice, environmental factors may influence the order of demonstration and practice. In an outdoor setting, a cool breeze in the early morning or on a cloudy day may cause participants to chill if they are repeatedly asked to enter and exit the water to view demonstrations. The advantage to having participants stand to view a single demonstration needs to be weighed against inattention caused by discomfort. In these situations, you should be prepared to adjust the teaching outline so that participants view any demonstrations necessary before they enter the water. Then allow them to remain in the water for the rest of the session.

After a skill is explained, demonstrated and practiced, it is important to review the material. Repetition is a key to learning. If the participants are having difficulty with the skill, consider another demonstration. Participants may be more attentive to and better able to follow a demonstration after trying a skill, particularly if you emphasize the parts the participants found difficult.

TEACHING TIP

If participants are having difficulty, give them reminders of what to think about before practicing. For example, when teaching the front glide, remind participants to take a deep breath, put the head down, get into a streamline position and push. Another way to help participants having difficulty "getting the idea," is to move their body so that they can get a sense of what it feels like to do what you explained and demonstrated. For example, when teaching the front crawl, have the participant perform a front float and then move the arms.

Task Setting

In *task setting*, the instructor assigns the tasks, but allows participants to achieve the goals in their own ways within the structure of the class. Participants are empowered to begin, practice and end assigned tasks according to their own needs and levels of performance. A skilled instructor may even allow variations in the task itself. Task setting can be used in the following ways:

- Assign a single task, allowing participants to achieve the skill in any way. For example, participants are assigned the task of floating on their backs. Some participants may choose to use flotation devices, others may briefly grasp the side of the pool and others may attempt floating without any type of support.
- Set up stations, each involving different tasks. You can verbally describe tasks for each station or create task cards using either words or pictures, depending upon the cognitive level of the participants or use the task cards provided on the instructor's CD-ROM. You may want to organize stations around a theme, such as floating or breath control. Or use each station to feature different tasks within a particular swimming level. If you use a floating theme across all stations, the first station can feature front-floating tasks in shallow water; the second station can feature back floating in shallow water; the third station can involve deep water, front-floating tasks; and the fourth station can encourage back-floating tasks in deeper water. Or, to allow participants to practice different items within a swimming level, the first station can include breath control tasks, the second station can feature water entry and exit tasks, the third station can deal with floating tasks and the fourth station can focus on arm and leg movements.

Reciprocal Practice

Reciprocal, or *partner-style, practice* features the use of partners who practice and learn together. This means participants are given the opportunity to observe their partners' performances. For this to be effective, you must clearly identify the performance criteria. Then, while working in pairs, participants observe each other's performance, help each other and learn together.

To use reciprocal practice–

1. Explain or demonstrate a single task for all pairs to practice and observe.
2. Explicitly identify the performance criteria on which the partners will be observing.
3. Assign several related tasks (see Task Cards on the instructor's CD-ROM).
4. Allow pairs of participants to work on a progression of varied tasks.

Small Group Practice

Small group practice is very similar to reciprocal practice. Rather than simply working in pairs, three or four participants work together. The focus of the small group is on the one participant who is performing a task. The other participants share the role of observer. During each practice session, each participant takes turns as doer and observer. Small group practice may be more appropriate when there are several performance elements to be observed. Each observing peer is assigned to observe a specific element.

Participants work together as a team to motivate and help each other learn.

Teaching Implications for Direct Teaching Methods

Many Water Safety instructors are comfortable and familiar with direct teaching methods. So it may be easier for you to work on mastering these methods before trying indirect techniques. Using a teacher-centered approach, you are responsible for guiding and directing participant learning and providing structure to the class. If you are a beginning instructor, you will need to work diligently to prepare. You should always have a detailed lesson plan that includes more learning activities than you think you will normally need for each lesson. You may even need to rehearse teaching each class until you are comfortable with each activity and the order in which they will work best. Preparation is absolutely critical for success.

Indirect Teaching Strategies

Indirect teaching strategies, also known as "learner-centered" styles, require a vastly different skill set for instructors. Rather than instructors controlling all elements of what they teach, they play the role of "learning facilitator." The methods put the focus on the participants, not the instructors.

Because they are not as commonly used as direct methods, many instructors and participants alike initially experience difficulty with indirect teaching. Often instructors using these techniques are criticized as "not really teaching." It is important to realize that as long as participants are actively engaged in practicing and learning, then "real teaching," in fact, is going on, even if what the instructors are doing are not traditional descriptions and demonstrations.

Swim lessons conducted using indirect methods often are much noisier and chaotic-appearing affairs. Participants may be engaged in a diverse set of practices with their instructors circulating and providing individual guidance and feedback. Indirect teaching should never be confused with instructors who simply let participants have "free time" or allow them to do whatever they wish. Effective indirect instruction requires a great deal more preparation and the use of both teaching-learning progressions and guiding or facilitating questions. These are not easy techniques to master. But instructors experienced with them find that they are rewarding and lead to very effective participant learning.

Active Exploration

The *active exploration* style of indirect teaching is an open-ended, teaching-learning process that draws upon participants' innate curiosity and creativity to investigate ways of using their body to accomplish a task. This teaching style is appropriate for beginners and more advanced swimmers. Appropriate facilitation of the exploration technique requires that instructors are comfortable allowing participants to truly explore and use a wide variety of different tasks and skills to perform any skill. Instructors who feel strongly that there is "only one right way" to perform skills–such as breath control, floating or swimming a stroke–will likely not feel comfortable using exploration and will not be able to take advantage of its potential.

The exploration technique can be used very effectively on the first day of class for children enrolled in swim lessons for the first time. They may be excited and anxious about their upcoming experience. Instructors might conduct a "pool exploration" activity to help reduce children's anxiety while teaching them pool rules, how to identify different parts of the pool and how the lessons will be structured. One way to start is to allow children to follow their partners around the perimeter of the pool. You can ask probing questions that elicit a wide variety of answers from the children. For example, at one of the ladders, you may say "I wonder what this is?" When someone correctly identifies it as a ladder, your follow up question may be "Does anyone know what we use a ladder in the pool for?" You can correct inappropriate answers, such as "jumping from" or "playing on," and reinforce the right responses, such as "climbing in" or "getting out of the pool." You can develop a similar dialogue and set of questions for pieces of equipment and pool rules. Even young children will show a great capacity for identifying appropriate rules and learning the names for new pieces of equipment, such as kickboards, floating toys, rings or life jackets. The key to the learner-centered focus for active exploration is that the participants respond to questions. You do not provide immediate answers.

The power of the active exploration technique is in the "doing" of skills and activities. In the pool ladder example, children tend to learn more effectively when they actually get to experience and explore by using the ladder to enter or exit the pool rather than simply observing or talking about its function. Participants also learn more when they can take a kickboard and explore different ways to use it in the water, including using it as a pillow, pretending it is a flat boat, holding it traditionally as a kickboard or any number of other creative uses that children may discover with a bit of encouragement from the instructor.

SAFETY NOTE

It is not safe to allow anyone to stand on a kickboard (kickboard surfing) or sit on it in the water.

Active exploration is mistakenly considered appropriate only for beginners and children. In fact, it can effectively be used with any age or skill level. For example, older children and adults may find a stroke exploration learning activity to be engaging, as well as challenging. You can ask a class of intermediate or advanced swimmers to identify the different ways one can use their arms (e.g., alternating or simultaneous pulling action or in-water or out-of-water recovery) and legs (e.g., flutter, dolphin, breaststroke, scissors or rotary kicks). Then, the exploration challenge question may be "What different kicks can you use with alternating arms recovered under water?" Your response may be "Show me how you would do that." Questions can be expanded to show the various arm patterns that fit with each kicking style. This is a truly challenging learning activity that provides an opportunity that stimulates active exploration while also encouraging variability of practice (see previous section on Encouraging Practice).

Guided Discovery

While active exploration often produces unexpected results and creative outcomes in an open-ended process, the *guided discovery* indirect style of teaching is more structured. It involves providing learners with a series of tasks and challenges that have several possible, although fairly predictable, solutions. In guided discovery, participants are not expected to perform skills exactly as explained or demonstrated, nor is every outcome always acceptable. Instead you can lead participants step-by-step through a series of tasks, usually using task question "trees," to help the participants explore the achievement of a skill. This method challenges them to use their natural curiosity and excitement to arrive at solutions.

To use guided discovery effectively, you must have a solid understanding of how aquatic skills are learned and be able to design tasks with fairly predictable solutions. The tasks must progress naturally from general to more specific.

Exploring aquatic concepts, such as buoyancy or streamlining, are obvious choices for using guided discovery because these concepts relate so closely to physical principles and laws. When you become skilled at using guided discovery, you can help participants explore buoyancy and floating in a variety of body positions and conditions without telling them exactly how they should perform the skill. Participants are responsible for investigating the various options, and in the process, will start to recognize that the water supports the human body.

Teaching the jellyfish float is another example of how the guided discovery method differs from the direct teaching method. If you use the direct style, you will explain and then demonstrate the right way to perform this skill. Instead, you may want to use guided discovery, which appreciates that floating is a consequence of the density of water in relationship to the human body's density. You can let participants discover these properties for themselves through a structured set of experiences. You might ask swimmers gathered in the shallow end of the pool along the gutter to see what happens if they take a big breath of air and slowly let themselves "sink." Then challenge participants by asking, "Who can keep all of their body parts under water for more than 10 seconds without moving?" Likely none of the participants will be able to do this, since their natural buoyancy will bring them to the surface. Then you might ask subsequent questions, such as "What happens if you take a big breath and make yourself a tight ball?", "What happens if you just let your arms hang down with your face in the water?" or "What happens if you blow out all your air as bubbles?"

Using Task Cards for Active Exploration and Guided Discovery

The use of task cards within a direct teaching station approach was described previously (see Task Setting). An alternative use of task cards can likewise support an indirect teaching style. Instead of being strictly directive, task cards can supplement your exploration and guiding questions. They may be less flexible than you may be when a particularly unique participant response emerges during the process of exploration and discovery. At the same time, task cards can provide an alternative to requiring all participants in a class to do exactly the same thing. Instead, you can set up stations and provide a series of exploration task cards that ask participants to investigate different concepts. Here is how you might teach participants about how streamlining the body helps them move through the water. The task card at one station might ask participants to push off the wall from a face-down position using different body shapes to see which shape allows them to get the farthest away from the wall. Another task may challenge them to do the same from a face-up position. A third station may ask them to modify their bodies to see how high they can jump out of the water. Alternatively, truly enterprising instructors might provide individual exploration task cards for each member of the class. Obviously, this would be a lot of work. But it is an innovative way to provide an optimal challenge for individual swimmers based on their level of readiness or skill.

Problem Solving

The ultimate and most challenging indirect teaching style, for both instructors and participants, is problem solving. Essentially, a problem-solving technique combines the open-ended possibilities of active exploration with some of the structure associated with guided discovery. Since problem solving requires higher-order thinking, it is most appropriate for older children, adolescents and adults. When using this approach, instructors create a particular scenario. Participants, either individually or as a group, need to respond appropriately. The best types of scenarios are those that allow a wide range of appropriate solutions and are not too narrowly defined. Problem solving works best with complex or combined sets of skills, including water safety, rescue and other water-related activities.

For example, you may challenge your class to "swim" across the width of the swimming pool without using their arms, getting their hair wet or touching the bottom. Your participants may come up with a variety of possible solutions. Once the original scenario is accomplished, subsequent and more challenging ones, such as keeping the hair dry and not using either arms or legs, might be added. You will need to develop scenarios in advance and be prepared to modify them as needed, depending upon participants' solutions.

Teaching Implications for Indirect Teaching Methods

Swim instructors who are only familiar with traditional direct style teaching will wonder why they should spend time on such a trivial set of activities as "exploring the pool," "discovering buoyancy" or "problem solving the most effective combinations of arm and leg actions with which to swim." However, when you consider learners' inherent creativity and problem-solving abilities, the use of indirect teaching styles, such as active exploration, guided discovery and problem solving, makes sense. Not all learners are well adapted to follow directions or to learn in step-by-step progressions. By the time children take swim lessons, they have already learned, by trial and error, how to walk, talk and interact with their environment. Although older children, adolescents and adults often suppress their natural curiosity, indirect teaching styles simply take advantage of and structure the method by which people learn best.

Using indirect teaching requires a particular instructional skill set that can take years to learn and master. Swim instructors must be comfortable trading off some "control" in their classes in return for learners accepting more responsibility for their own learning. Instructors who are skilled in using indirect techniques find them particularly rewarding because participants are fully engaged and motivated to continue to learn and master skills. When done well, they produce engaged, active learners who have a strong foundation that allows them to be independent, creative learners long after structured swim lessons end.

Part C

Course Planning and Management

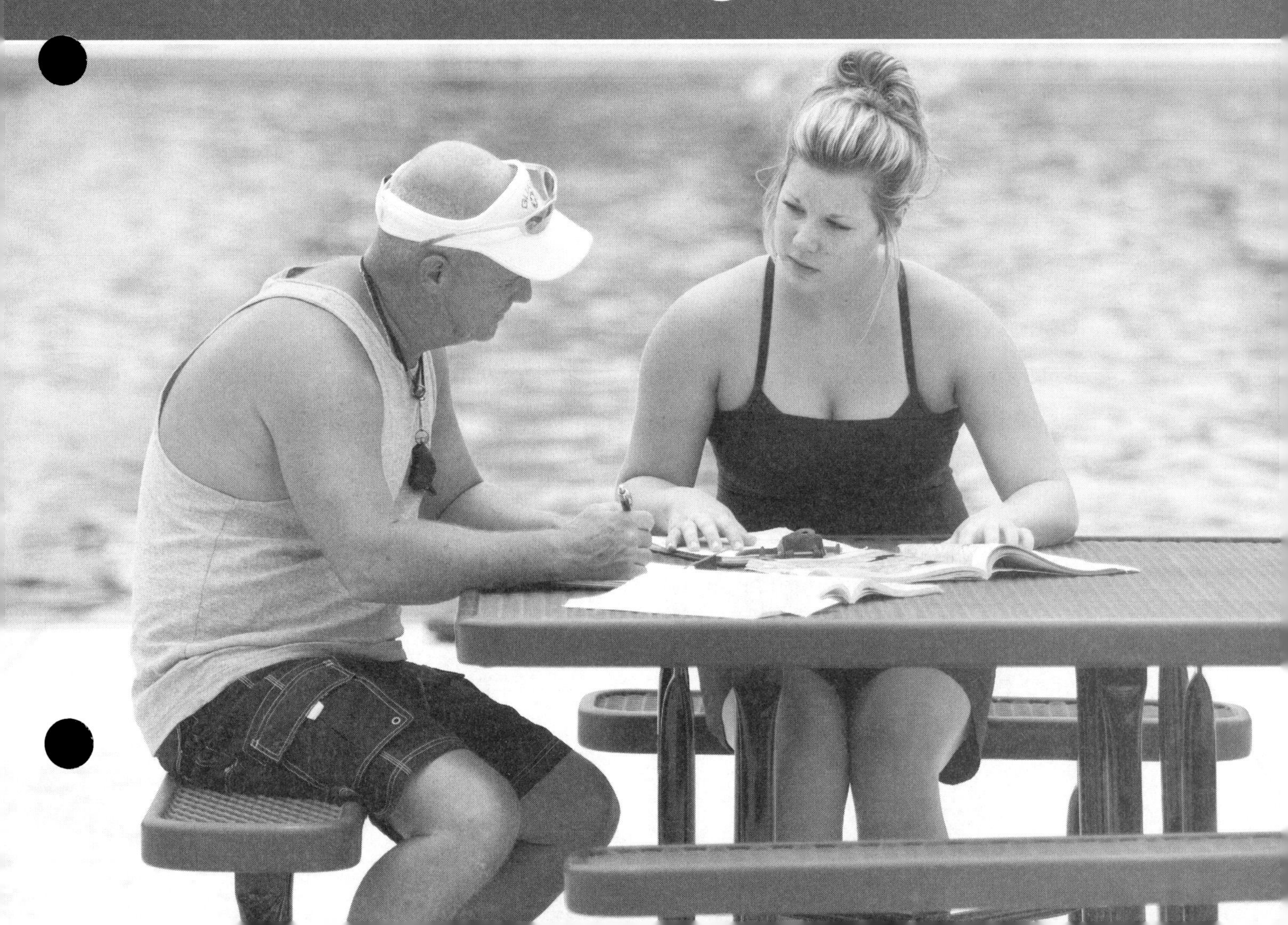

CHAPTER

3

Course Planning

One of your responsibilities as an American Red Cross Water Safety instructor is to make class time as safe, effective and rewarding as possible for the participants. This takes careful planning and preparation, especially when you consider the kinds of activities that take place in a given course:

- Presentation of aquatic and safety skills
- Practice time and learning activities for participants
- Homework or assignments to be given in preparation of the next lesson

In your planning, you must also take the following into account:

- Safety for yourself and the participants
- Requirements for the course
- Differences in participants' age, size and mental and physical development
- Differences in participants' skill levels
- Differences in individual learning styles
- Effective communication based on age, development, ability and language or cultural differences
- Effective strategies for meeting course objectives
- Each participant's goals for the course
- Parents' expectations
- Program-specific procedures and requirements as established by your program coordinator
- The number of classes per session
- The length of time per class
- The availability of equipment
- The potential hazards

As you can imagine, with so many variables, no two classes are ever the same.

This chapter provides you with a framework for course planning. First, there is a discussion of block plans, which you can use to map out a full course. Then there is a strategy for translating your block plan into a day-by-day approach for developing and teaching individual lesson plans. (You can use the templates for block plans, lesson plans and skills checklists found on the instructor's CD-ROM to help chart the progress of your classes.) Techniques for class organization are also provided to help you determine how to set up your classes for learning activities and skill practice. Support and holding techniques are discussed along with how to best use them.

Finally, keep in mind that the most important factor in course planning is the safety of the participants. Make every effort to prevent injuries. Make sure a lifeguard is on duty during instructional periods. Be familiar with the facility's emergency action plan. Explain and enforce safety rules. Never leave the teaching area until all participants are accounted for and have left the area.

Planning a Session

Whether you are preparing a block plan or converting that block plan into your daily lesson plan, you should consider the following:

- Class size. This affects how long it takes to organize drills, practice the skills and give feedback to the group and to individuals. A small class (no more than 6 to 10 participants–and even smaller if your participants are very young or are very fearful) may need less time per activity depending on the amount of time dedicated to individual practice versus group practice. When this is the case, there is time for more activities per lesson. Small classes also allow for greater flexibility with optional skills and other activities. Depending on the participants' background and interests, you can include fitness components or games and water activities in your planning.

  Larger classes tend to be more successful when additional instructors or aides are used. Large classes require more planning to ensure the maximum safety and involvement of all participants. Wave and stagger formations and station teaching can help you use class time wisely and provide more group practice. When individuals need personal attention, make sure that you consider the safety of the entire class. Be sure that all class participants are in front of you, within your view and within quick reach. Be patient, precise and quick with your assessments and directions, then move on to the next part of the lesson. (Information on class organization is described later in this chapter.) Developing your plans is easiest when all the participants are at the same level in prerequisite skills. If they have a wide range of skills at the beginning of the course, try to develop a flexible plan that does not ignore stronger swimmers or frustrate anyone struggling to keep up with the class. Take similar care when you are mainstreaming people with disabilities or other health conditions in your course.

- Participant evaluation. Take the time to evaluate participants' abilities and readiness to determine what skills to teach. Each skill prepares participants for more advanced skills. As participants become comfortable and gain confidence practicing a skill, introduce the next skill in the progression.

  The mnemonic COLA–which stands for Check, Organize, Lead and Assess–can help you plan successful classes at the start of a swim session and throughout the lessons.

  - Check to see what the participants are capable of doing and their willingness to try new skills. See if the participants can perform a few skills in the level that you are teaching. If they are not proficient at those skills, check to see if they can perform any skills from the previous level. This check should take about 1 to 2 minutes for each participant. Ask questions or make the following statements to begin the evaluation process:
    - Can you do ___?
    - Can you try to ___?
    - Show me how to ___.
    - Show me how you ___.
    - Watch me and when you are ready to try, let me know.
    - Watch me and then you try.
  - Organize your lesson plan based the skills the participants showed you or told you that were willing to try.
  - Lead participants by presenting skills that encourage full participation, build confidence and foster a willingness to try new skills.
  - Assess participants' level of progress to help you plan the next lesson. The evaluation process may be performed as a group activity or individiually, depending on the make up of the class.
- Review skills. Red Cross Parent and Child Aquatics, Preschool Aquatics and Learn-to-Swim progress from level to level. Each level builds upon knowledge and skills from previous levels. Reviewing these earlier skills helps build on this progression and reinforces learning. Reviewing skills also helps you introduce new skills by relating them to familiar ones. Teaching from the known to the related unknown is a logical teaching method and helps your participants experience success.
- New skills. Be sure to include all required skills somewhere in your plans. Skills for the various courses are listed in the following chapters:
  - **Chapter 7**: Parent and Child Aquatics
  - **Chapter 8**: Preschool Aquatics
  - **Chapter 9**: Learn-to-Swim
- Performance criteria. Greater proficiency usually results from more practice time and practice with immediate feedback. After you have introduced a skill, participants should review and practice it in subsequent lessons until they have reached the required performance criteria.
- Completion requirements. Be sure you include the skills for successfully completing a course level. Reproduce the appropriate skills checklist from the instructor's CD-ROM for each course you teach prior to the first lesson. List the participants in the row across the top. Keep this checklist poolside as a handy reference and to chart participants' progress.

Developing a Block Plan

The first step in effectively organizing the session is to develop a block plan or template that gives you a day-by-day overview of the session across all lessons (**Table 3-1**). By planning the main parts of your course from the beginning to the end, you set up logical learning sequences to ensure all skills and safety information are included.

One of the easiest ways to develop a block plan is the calendar approach to organization. Each block is one day in the course. The block plan should include some or all of the following basic information:

- Class level
- Day and time
- Number of participants
- Safety topic
- Review skills
- New skills
- Learning activities, including drills and games
- Equipment

The first time you organize the block plan for a course, you may have difficulty determining which skills to review, how to sequence the order of introducing new skills and how much time you will need to introduce a skill. Use COLA at the beginning of a swim course to verify your starting point. One approach you may want to try is to distribute skills across the lessons, allowing several lessons for difficult skills and integrating safety skills throughout the plan. Always plan more activities than you think you will need to avoid running out before the lesson is over. You will also need to allow time for participants to practice and for you to give feedback. Experience is a good teacher. The longer you teach, the better you will be at organizing your block plans.

You may find that after your initial evaluation or after a couple of lessons you have to rearrange the block plan. This happens often, and you should not view it as a failure or lack of organization. Sample block plans for each level of Parent and Child Aquatics, Preschool Aquatics and Learn-to-Swim are on the instructor's CD-ROM. These are examples of block plans and may be used as guides for you to create block plans to meet your own specific needs.

Developing a Lesson Plan

When you have finished organizing the block plan, you can use it to plan detailed daily lessons. An effective lesson plan (**Table 3-2**) usually includes the following:

- Safety topics. It is especially helpful to teach safety issues related to the skill being introduced or practiced. Check the course outlines for cross-references to safety information in *Swimming and Water Safety*. Use key words to remind you of the information you want to include in each day's lesson.
- Equipment. List all the equipment you need. Be sure it is available and in good repair. Note who is responsible for getting it ready.
- Opening. Lessons usually have a formal opening activity. This may be a land drill for a swimming skill, stretch exercises, a water adjustment drill, such as bobbing or rhythmic breathing, or a drill to review a previously learned skill. These activities should last no more than 5 minutes depending on the length of the lesson and the participants' age. Make sure the opening activities are brief and appropriate for the course and the participants. (Information about customizing your lessons for different audiences and individual characteristics is included in **Chapters 5 and 6**. The instructor's CD-ROM also includes activities to consider.)
- Skill review. You can review skills in several ways. You may demonstrate the skill again, verbally present information about the skill (either as statements or as guided questions) or conduct a drill (land, bracket or swimming). You should always give participants time to practice previously learned skills. Choose your methods depending on the complexity of the skill and the past accomplishments of the class. Be sure to plan enough time for providing feedback to the group and to individuals.
- New skill introduction. You may introduce a new skill by asking participants to try something. You may start with the "check" in COLA. This allows you to see what participants can already do and might help apprehensive participants feel less pressure to perform at the pace of others. Be sure your explanations of your expectations are clear. You may also introduce a new skill with a verbal explanation and a demonstration. (For more on demonstrations see **Chapter 2**.) Your class may also benefit from reading appropriate parts of *Swimming and Water Safety* or from viewing the skill as demonstrated in the *Swimming and Diving Skills DVD*.
- New skills practice. You can organize this in many ways. Participants can learn some skills by trying the whole skill immediately. Other, more complex skills should be broken down into small parts that are practiced one at a time. You can review these and other teaching approaches in the *Fundamentals of Instructor Training Participant's Manual*. Plan enough time to arrange the class into an appropriate practice pattern and to give positive corrective feedback to all participants. When using a drill, explain clearly what you want the class to do. Plan more learning activities than you think you will use so you have options. Consider your participants' age and maturity level, as well as the difficulty of the skill, and then determine how long to spend on each skill or part of a skill in each

Table 3-1. Sample Block Plan: Preschool Aquatics Level 1

Note: This block plan is a sample only. Develop block plans to meet your facility's specific needs.

Number of Participants: __________

Instructor Resources: *Swimming and Water Safety manual, Water Safety Instructor's Manual and CD-ROM, Teaching Swimming and Water Safety DVD, Longfellow's WHALE Tales K–6 Educational Packet*

Day 1	Day 2	Day 3	Day 4
Safety Topic			
Recognizing the lifeguards	Staying safe around aquatic environments	Don't Just Pack It, Wear Your Jacket	Too Much Sun Is No Fun
Opening Activity/Review Skills			
Kick legs to make it "rain"	Ease-in, wiggle and splash then blow bubbles	■ Ring Around the Rosie—back float ■ Open eyes under water and retrieve submerged object ■ Front glide and recover ■ Alternating leg action on front ■ Simultaneous leg action on front	■ Follow the Leader ■ Recover from a back float ■ Back glide
New Skills			
■ Enter and exit water safely using ladder, steps or side ■ Submerge mouth, nose and eyes ■ Blow bubbles through mouth and nose	■ Open eyes under water ■ Pick up a submerged object ■ Front glide with support and recover ■ Alternating leg action on front ■ Simultaneous leg action on front	■ Recover from a back float ■ Back glide	■ Alternating leg action on back ■ Simultaneous leg action on back ■ Alternating arm action on front ■ Simultaneous arm action on front
Game			
Blow the Cork	Treasure Hunt	London Bridge	Simon Says
Equipment			
■ ***Raffy Learns to Swim*** booklets ■ Preschool Aquatics Level 1 newsletters ■ Ping-Pong or ball-pit balls	■ Submersible water toys ■ Barbells ■ Noodles ■ Kickboards	■ Submersible water toys ■ Barbells ■ Noodles ■ Kickboards ■ Life jackets	■ Barbells ■ Noodles ■ Kickboards

Table 3-2. Sample Lesson Plan: Learn-to-Swim Level 3—Stroke Development

Note: This lesson plan is a sample only. Develop lesson plans to meet your facility's specific needs.

Instructor: Wilbert E. Longfellow
Location: Municipal Family Aquatic Center
Session Begin Date: June 15 | Session End Date: June 30
Length of Classes: 45 minutes | Total Number of Classes: 8

Day 1

Equipment
- Waddles in the Deep booklets
- Level 3 newsletters
- Foam noodles
- Barbells
- Kickboards
- Different colored balls
- Swim With a Buddy in a Supervised Area poster

Reminders
- Distribute Waddles in the Deep booklets to participants.
- Distribute newsletters to participants and/or their parents.
- Review "Teaching Activities, Games and Drills" on the instructor's CD-ROM.
- Review "Red Ball Green Ball" for set up and directions on the instructor's CD-ROM.

Time	Activity	Key Words/Phrases	Class Organization
Housekeeping			
5 min.	■ Greet participants and parents, introductions ■ Attendance ■ Announcements ■ Policies and procedures		Circle, on deck
Safety Topic			
4 min.	Swim With a Buddy in a Supervised Area		Circle, on deck
Review Skills			
10 min.	Exit skills assessment Level 2		Wave
6 min.	Front crawl ■ Arm stroke drills ■ Kicking drills		Line, stagger or wave
New Skills			
2 min.	Bob (5 times) in chest-deep water	Take a breath and hold it" ■ "Blow bubbles as you come up" ■ "Sweep arms down" ■ "Push off of the bottom with your feet"	Line away from wall

(continued)

Table 3-2. Sample Lesson Plan: Learn-to-Swim Level 3—Stroke Development *(continued)*

Time	Activity	Key Words/Phrases	Class Organization
New Skills *(continued)*			
5 min.	Flutter kick with rhythmic breathing (head up or to the side)	■ "Kick, kick, kick" ■ "Blow bubbles, lift to take a breath, breathe and head back down"	Bracketed on wall
5 min.	Push off on front then begin flutter kicking with kick board (15 yards)	■ "Kick, kick, kick" ■ "Blow bubbles, lift to take a breath, breathe and head back down"	2 lines
2 min.	Tread water using arm and leg actions (15 seconds)		Semi-circle
Game			
4 min.	Red Ball, Green Ball		Line
Closing			
2 min.	■ Thank participants for their attention and participation ■ Offer positive reinforcement of what they did well ■ Review lesson ■ Announcements for next lesson	■ "Good job" ■ "Safe"	Circle, seated on deck

lesson. Include some fun drills or games and use a wide variety of activities to keep participants motivated. Make sure that all participants are challenged and successful.

- Closing. The closing is the "winding down" phase of the lesson. It should include an oral review of what participants learned in the lesson and a look ahead to the next lesson. In some courses, it may include homework or a take-home assignment. This part of the lesson is a great opportunity for individual practice. Let participants practice something they enjoy doing so they leave the lesson remembering the pleasure of the last activity. It is also fun to end with a game that is related to the activity the class just learned or to include optional activities for that course. When participants are reluctant to get out of the water at the end of a lesson, they will remember the experience as a fun activity and come to the next lesson motivated.

Writing the Lesson Plan

Now you are ready to write your lesson plans. The instructor's CD-ROM gives a template you can use for making your own lesson plans and sample lesson plans for each level. As with the block plans, these are examples of lesson plans and may be used as guides for you to create your own lesson plans that meet your specific needs.

For each part of the lesson, you have to decide–

- The assessment criteria you will use to check the readiness and skill level of participants.
- The teaching strategies you intend to use to organize the class.
- How much time each activity requires.
- The key cue words, phrases or question trees you want to use.
- The pattern of organization you will use for participants' practice.

- The methods you use to lead participants' practice.
- The evaluation criteria you will use to assess progress.

The following table is a guide for assigning times for the different parts of a lesson. Classes in Red Cross Parent and Child Aquatics and Preschool Aquatics last 20 to 30 minutes. Learn-to-Swim classes typically last 30 to 45 minutes.

Follow these steps to complete the lesson plan:

- Using your block plan, list the skills on the lesson plan in the section marked "activity." The activity can include any or all of the following:
  - Lecture topic (may include safety information)
  - Review of part of a skill
  - Review of a whole skill
  - Introduction of new skill(s) or parts
  - Practice of skill(s)
  - Transition from one skill or area to another
  - Game or other water activity
  - Assignment for the next lesson
- Arrange the activities in a logical sequence. For instance, if you are using the "explain, demonstrate and practice" teaching strategy, be sure that a review skill appears before the new skill and that the demonstration occurs before the practice.
- Decide what teaching style and practice method are best for this activity. List any equipment you will need.
- For each skill, identify key cue words or questions appropriate for participants' age. Try to think of different ways to say the same thing and write one- or two-word descriptions in the keyword section. For questions, longer descriptions may be needed.
- Use the section on class organization to remind you of additional information at a glance. Describe the pattern of organization or draw a small diagram of the way you want the practice to flow.
- If applicable, decide how to best divide tasks among yourself and any co-instructors or aides.

For every skill or activity, consider how you will safely engage as many participants as possible. The majority of the lesson time should be devoted to the practice (repetition) of skills previously learned and the skills introduced in the current lesson. Each skill introduced should include practice time. You will also need to have additonal ways to practice the same skill. You should be prepared to change activities if the participants are unmotivated or do not grasp a planned activity. Each lesson needs to ensure that all participants are successful as well as challenged. Plan to make the lesson fun for everyone.

	Parent and Child Aquatics and Preschool Aquatics	Learn-to-Swim
Opening/Safety Topic	5 minutes	5 minutes
Review and Practice Previous Skill(s)	10 minutes	15 minutes
Teach and Practice New Skill	10 minutes	20 minutes
Closing/Games and Play	5 minutes	5 minutes

When planning practice time for new skills, list each activity separately in the lesson plan. For example, when you introduce a kick, you may use a drill having all of the participants holding onto the wall and then move to a wave drill using kickboards. Once you have listed the activities, estimate the time required for each one. Use your creativity and that of others to keep the practice time fun by including drills, games and other activities.

The lesson plan should also include transitions from one activity to the next. Consider how long it takes to reorganize your class to begin the next part of the lesson. When planning the lessons, be sure to consider the number of times participants have to get in and out of the water. If they become chilled, they are not likely to make as much progress, nor will the lessons be a positive experience.

Keep in mind that your classes rarely follow your lesson plan exactly as written. You will need to be able to adjust your plan for unexpected circumstances. For instance, some participants may achieve the skills quickly while others may have trouble and need more time.

Adjusting the Lesson Plan

It may be a sign that your lesson plan is not working if the participants are exhibiting negative behavior, appear confused or their skills are regressing. If this happens, you need to adjust your plan or your demeanor. A drill may be too complicated or advanced for the skill level of the group, or participants may need more practice with previous steps in the teaching progression. It may be necessary to address the needs of participants with a wide range of skills, or you may just need to appear enthusiastic and excited about the acivity and your class.

On occasion, you may find that a drill inhibits the learning of the skill. Sometimes participants who can perform the whole skill have difficulty with practicing elements of a skill seperately. Let that person do a variation of the drill to stay with the group rather than risking frustration or failure.

One of the best ways to prepare for needed adjustments to your lesson plan is to write down a variety of methods for practicing the same skill or skill sequence. You may want to include an activity that keeps participants in one place, a drill that requires participants to travel and a game. If a certain method of practice is not working, switch to another.

Evaluating the Success of the Lesson

Evaluation of the lesson plan is an important step for both the participants' success and your own improvement as an instructor. To evaluate your lesson, ask yourself these questions immediately after the class ends:

1. Did I follow my plan?
2. Did the participants have enough time to practice?
3. Did I choose the right activities, or were the drills too difficult, time consuming or easy?
4. Did I use my teaching area effectively?
5. Were the drills I used right for the ages and abilities of the participants?
6. Did I use a variety of methods and equipment to enhance learning?
7. Did I include a variety of skills in the plan so everyone had some success?
8. Did the participants improve?
9. Were my keywords or phrases appropriate and effective?
10. Did I use co-instructors or aides effectively?

Use your answers to these questions to improve the next lesson plan. Analyze all parts of the lesson plan and decide what changes would have made it more successful.

You may find it easier to write the next lesson plan immediately after a lesson ends, while it is still fresh in your mind. Keep in mind that you will need to know your group, how much practice they need and which skills will need only brief review and which need more time in the next lesson. All of the factors discussed previously, including the group's size, age, ability and experience, influence the success of your plans. If you see that you are falling behind, rework your block plan and try to get additional help with your class.

Principles of Class Organization

You need to consider many things to make your lesson plans work. Organizing the class effectively, choosing the best activities and knowing what approach to use in a given situation all take experience. Learning from trial and error, in addition to good planning, can make you a more effective instructor.

To organize a class for effective teaching and learning experiences, always arrange the class so that–

- Everyone's safety is considered and participants can be seen at all times.
- Everyone can be successful and challenged.
- Everyone can hear and see instructions or hear your questions.
- Everyone can hear and see demonstrations.
- Everyone has an opportunity for enough active and effective practice.
- Everyone has an opportunity to be evaluated for skill improvement.

Patterns of Class Organization

Patterns of class organization are formations you use to make sure all participants actively practice skills. Inactive participants may become bored, chilled or restless and may disrupt the class. Some patterns are better than others for observing each participant and providing feedback.

Formations

There are several ways to arrange participants for observation and practice. The most favorable arrangements depend on–

- The task.
- The number of participants.
- The number of instructors.
- The size and depth of the swimming area.
- Whether others are using the facility.

Some of the same formations can be used with participants in the water or at the edge of the teaching area, depending upon whether they are observing or practicing. In an outdoor setting, arrange participants so the sun is behind or partially behind them, if at all possible. It is better if the participants are not facing the sun.

One basic formation is formed by placing the participants in a single line along the edge of the teaching area (**Fig. 3-1, A**). Pay attention to the water depth when you use a single line formation. Be aware of whether the line is along an equivalent water depth or whether the line is along descending depth. Place the more inexperienced and the shorter swimmers in the shallowest water when the depth is descending. You may want to use two parallel lines if the class is large and the teaching area is limited. If participants are on the deck, those in front may sit on the edge to allow better visibility for those behind.

Another option is to arrange the class in an "L" on both sides of a corner (**Fig. 3-1, B**). This type of formation compacts the group for better visibility and hearing, but is best suited for stationary skills, such as bobbing or floating. The corner is an ideal place to conduct classes for participants that are just beginning to swim independently because you can individualize the distance participants are asked to swim. The weaker swimmers can swim half-way across the corner to where you can assist them with the second half. The stronger swimmers can be encouraged to swim the entire distance across the corner. You can adjust the distance by moving the participants along the pool edge to a position that is further from the corner.

You also can form the class into lines perpendicular to the side. The first person in line performs a skill, swims to the side and moves to the end of the line. This pattern is useful for observing individual entries or when the task requires equipment that is of limited supply, such as reaching poles for extension assists (**Fig. 3-1, C**).

INSTRUCTOR'S NOTE

The "buddy system" is often advocated for swimming activities, including instruction. Depending on the formation, "buddies" may be next to, behind or across from one another.

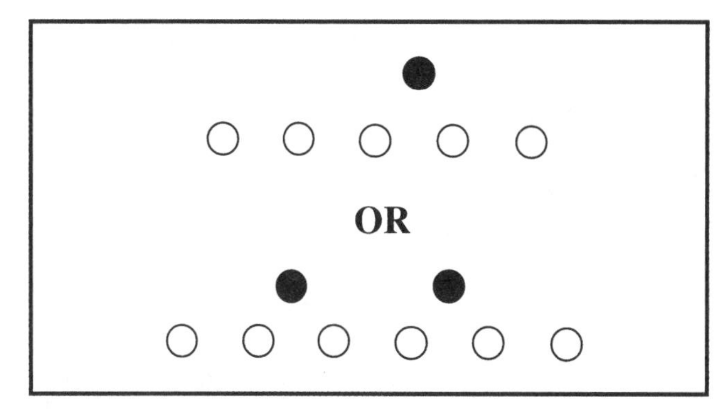

Fig. 3-1, A

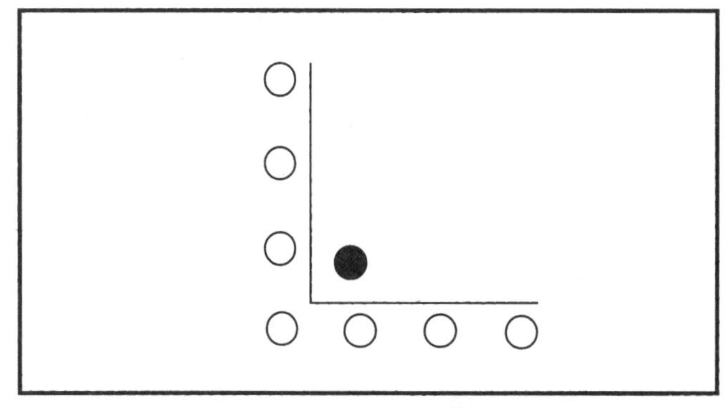

Fig. 3-1, B

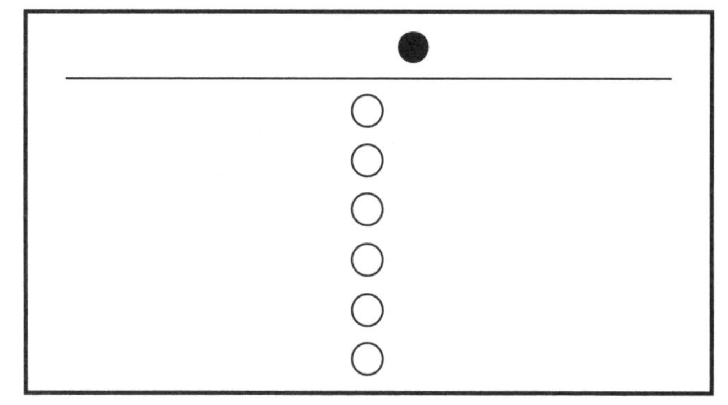

Fig. 3-1, C

Demonstrations

When you demonstrate a skill, be sure all participants are close enough and positioned so everyone can see. You may need to place the class in different formations depending on whether the demonstration is stationary, as in kicking while bracketed to the side, or moving, as in kicking with a kickboard. Some skills should be viewed from the front and back, as well as from the side. If you arrange the class in a line, consider whether it is better to swim up and down the line, across and back perpendicular to the line or both. When using the "L" formation, moving demonstrations may be along each side or diagonally away from and back to the corner.

You can reinforce demonstrations by showing the *Swimming and Diving Skills DVD* or by having a skilled swimmer demonstrate it.

Static Drills

Static drills–when participants practice in one place–are appropriate for certain skills, such as kicking on the wall, treading water and isolating part of a skill to practice it without movement. Participants can be in any safe arrangement along the sides of the pool, standing in lines or randomly scattered. The shape, size and depth of your teaching area are major factors. Be sure to position yourself where you can see all participants at all times. You should be in the water most of the time so that you can readily provide hands-on feedback as well as encouragement and corrections.

Fluid Drills

Use fluid drills–when participants are required to travel–to help participants improve their skills and increase their physical endurance. You also can use fluid drills to evaluate participant performance. Vary the type and formation of drills to keep the practice interesting and help participants meet the course requirements. Consider the following factors when choosing drills:

- The participants' skill proficiency
- The participants' physical condition
- The intensity level of each drill
- The frequency and length of rest periods
- The distance needed for effective practice

Any drill pattern that starts as a line at the edge of the pool also may begin with participants away from the side in shallow water. For beginner swimmers, you may want to take a stance a short distance away from the side and have the participants wade out to you to form a line parallel to and facing the side. Then, participants practice the skill as they go back toward the side. Each subsequent drill can be a bit further out until the participants are comfortable going all the way across the pool. For more advanced swimmers, using a fluid drill allows them to cover a greater distance, such as across the pool for one or more lengths, in a linear or circular pattern. This may not be possible for a beginning activity or drill in a large pool.

Starting away from the side has several advantages over starting at the side–

- Participants have a definitive distance to cover, set by you, that is within their abilities.
- Anxious participants are not facing an open area.
- The drill concludes with everyone at the side ready for the next exercise.

Individual Instruction

Observe your participants one at a time in skills that involve extra safety considerations. Carefully monitor skills such as entering deep water for the first time, diving skills and any other skill that makes participants fearful. Giving feedback to one participant at a time is not very efficient with larger classes since other participants have to wait. So you may want to provide another activity for the rest of the class or have extra instructors available to help. Whenever possible, pick an activity that is related to the skill you are observing individually or one that leads up to it. If you have enough instructors and aides, individualized instruction is a very useful teaching method.

Wave

You may divide a large group into smaller units for maximum supervised practice. In this situation, each group performs as a unit. This method lets you watch smaller groups and give constructive feedback. It also makes better use of a small practice area (**Fig. 3-2**). If you use the buddy system, have participants count off by number to form groups with one buddy in each pair. For example, buddies "1" go first while buddies "2" observe.

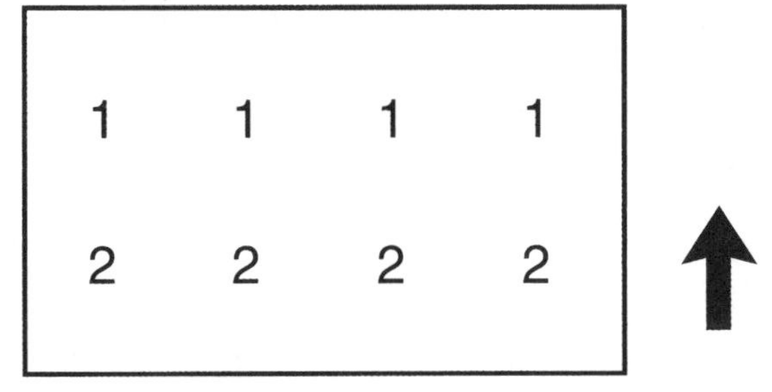

Fig. 3-2

Stagger

In the stagger formation (**Fig. 3-3**), the class remains in a single line. Signal the first person in line to start swimming. The next person in line starts when the person ahead reaches a certain spot. This lets you follow the progress of each participant for a few body lengths. You will also be able to speak to participants individually as they finish the swim and still have time to focus on the next swimmer. With this method, you can provide swimmers with a large amount of practice time and individual feedback. It also gives participants a short rest period while they wait their turns. When using the buddy system, you can structure the stagger in pairs. Then you can track two people at once and still provide individual feedback.

Circle Swimming

For longer-distance swims to build endurance, you may have participants use the pool lanes. One option involves having swimmers keep to the right and swim counterclockwise in one lane. (**Fig. 3-4**). Another option is a circuit swim in which participants first swim in one lane and then move over a lane to swim in the other direction (always keeping to the right side of the lane). You can continue this pattern so participants use all the available lanes.

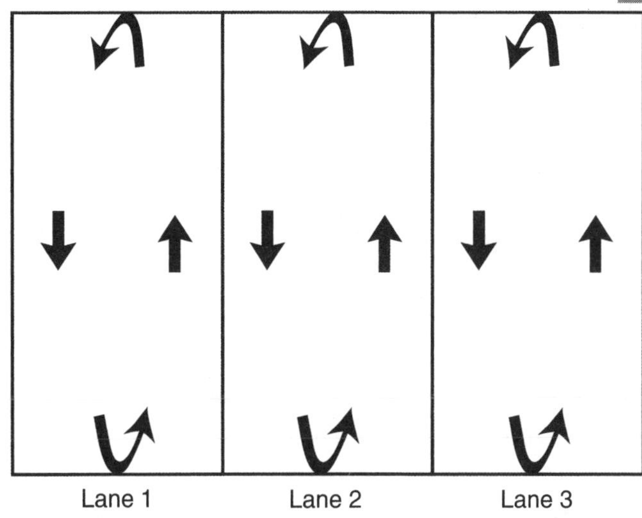

Fig. 3-4

Perimeter Swimming

For smaller pools or pools without lane lines, you can ask participants to swim a circle around the perimeter of the entire pool (**Fig. 3-5**). This works well with reciprocal practice since the coaching buddy can walk alongside the swimmer.

Summary of Other Options

The more flexibility and variety that you build into your lesson plan drills, the more successful and effective the lessons are apt to be. Be creative in using whatever variety of patterns the swimming area permits. You can choose perimeter, circle, stagger or other formation drills.

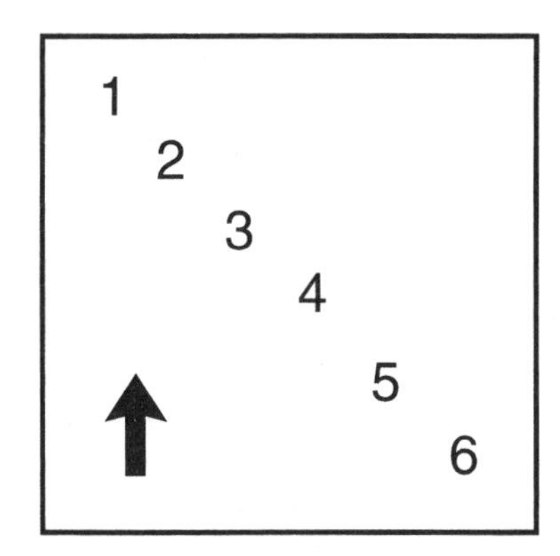

Fig. 3-3

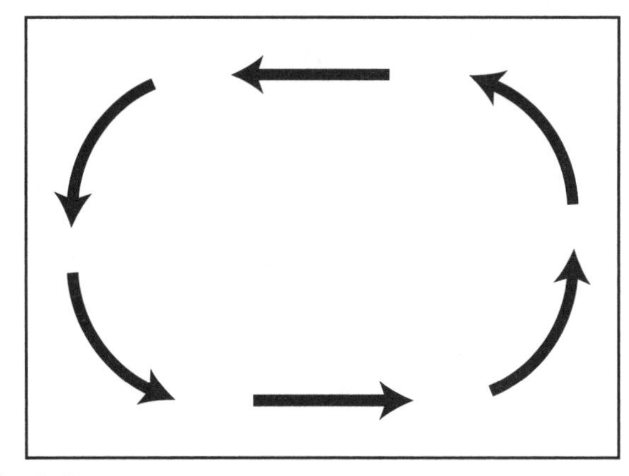

Fig. 3-5

Assembly Lines and Stations

Assembly line teaching is a method of class organization that uses multiple instructors efficiently to help participants more fully. There are many variations on assembly line and station teaching, depending on the numbers of participants, instructors and aides. In your planning, consider the skills at hand, participants' age and experience and the goals of the lesson.

Assembly Line Within One Level

With the assembly line method of teaching, each instructor conducts a particular drill or teaches a specific skill. One way to use this method is to teach the same skill at all the stations, but with different styles, techniques and drills. Another variation is to assign each instructor a different skill. As participants rotate from station to station, they receive a full and varied lesson in groups small enough for individualized attention. Be sure that the activities at the different stations are compatible and that instructors teach the skills they are most proficient at teaching.

Assembly Line With More Than One Level

Another option for the assembly line method is to program the facility with several classes of participants at different, but consecutive Learn-to-Swim levels. This works best if participants are of similar ages. Assign each instructor to a particular station. Participants remain with the same instructor until they perform the required skills well enough to advance. Some participants may move from one level to the next after only one lesson; others may need to remain in the same level for a full series of lessons. This method allows maximum flexibility for participants to proceed at their own speeds, have the chance to experience a variety of instructors and have the opportunity to meet new people as they move through the program.

This method also allows flexibility in class organization. Co-instructors and aides can assist with large groups or they may alter their positions as group structure changes. For example, they can be reassigned if a large group needs to be divided or combined into two small groups.

Station Teaching

Station teaching promotes a high level of participant involvement. It works best when participants take some responsibility for their own progress. Recommended instructor-to-participant ratios should be maintained. Ensure participants' safety when using station teaching by having enough lifeguards on duty to effectively see all activities and respond quickly to any emergencies that may arise.

In the most common use of station teaching, participants form into a single group to receive information about the day's lesson. Then they are directed to stations at various parts of the facility, each with the appropriate equipment and written instructions for practice. The participants perform the skills at that station until signaled to rotate to the next station. You can move from station to station to give as much feedback as possible. Having a co-instructor at each station makes this method more effective. After all participants have completed each station, review the material with the whole group and lead group drills to reinforce or check skills.

Rotating through stations is also an efficient way to review previous skills and to prepare for new skills. This format is also an effective way to teach safety skills.

Holding and Support Techniques

You can use a variety of holding and support techniques to help participants learn skills. Holding provides support and reassurance to participants while they explore the water and learn and practice new skills. With support, participants can assume the correct position for learning and practicing a skill. This helps participants develop confidence. When they know they will not submerge accidentally, they can relax and focus on practicing the skill they are learning.

As a Water Safety instructor, you must teach parents, who primarily provide support to their children during Parent and Child Aquatics classes, how to appropriately provide this support.

Different holding and support techniques are effective throughout the stages of learning. Such factors as participants' age, weight and skill level and your personal preference determine which positions to use. Some techniques are more suited for participants who need individual assistance and practice. Other techniques are more effective for group activities and drills.

These techniques can be a delicate balancing act. You want participants to do as much as possible without support, but also give them the help they need to learn skills in a developmentally appropriate and safe manner. You gradually reduce the support to participants as they begin to relax and perform the skill.

Some concepts to know and apply when providing support to someone who is learning to swim include–

- Establish a relationship with participants based on trust. When providing support, never take that support away unless they are expecting it and have been cued that they are performing on their own.
- Hold participants lightly, not tightly. They should get the impression from you that this is a good experience rather than something of which they should be afraid. Let participants experience as much of their natural buoyancy as possible while also providing enough support to promote confidence.
- Once they adjust to the water, keep the participant at the appropriate level for performing the skill. This is important because it prevents repeated uncomfortable temperature changes between the water and air. For instructors or parents, this often means squatting down to keep the shoulders at or below the surface of the water. For participants, this means keeping them at a level appropriate for the skill. When practicing the back float, for example, your shoulders are beneath the surface of the water, which allows participants to rest the back of their head on the supporters' shoulder in a horizontal position.
- Make your movements smooth and expected rather than jerky and without warning. Whenever participants feel fear or anxiety, hold or support them in a position they find comforting and secure.
- Make direct eye contact with participants whenever possible. This helps keep them focused on what you are asking of them and causes you to focus on them. Sometimes direct eye contact may not be appropriate. Remember to be culturally sensitive and adjust when necessary.
- When movement is called for, smoothly move participants in the appropriate direction of travel. This helps them get used to the sensation of moving forward in a horizontal position. When participants are relaxed, the momentum that you generate by moving will help their body float up to a natural horizontal position.
- Focus on the safety of your entire class even if you are providing support to an individual. Always position yourself so that you can see the other participants. Never turn your back on the other participants in class.

Face-to-Face Positions

Face-to-face holding positions are most effective for children, especially those in the beginning levels of Preschool Aquatics and Learn-to-Swim and with their parents in Parent and Child Aquatics. Use these positions to introduce participants to skills on their front.

Hug Position

Use this position for water adjustment and for teaching and practicing kicking on the front. Position yourself so the water comes up to your shoulders and the participant's upper chest. The participant rests his or her head on your shoulder and places the arms loosely around your neck or over your shoulders. The participant then extends the legs while you support the legs from underneath. You may manipulate the kick in this position (**Fig. 3-6**).

Fig. 3-6

Fig. 3-7

Fig. 3-9

Chin Support Position

Use this position to practice kicking on the front and bubble blowing. Position yourself so the water comes up to your shoulders and the participant's chin. Hold the participant under the upper chest and shoulders with your fingers and palms. Make sure the chin rests on the heels of your palms so his or her face does not accidentally submerge (**Fig. 3-7**).

Hip Support on Front Position

Use this position for water adjustment, practicing kicking on the front, front glide, front float, bubble blowing and learning to kick with the face down unsupported. Position yourself so the water comes up to your shoulders and the participant's chest. Support the participant at the hips and abdomen with your hands from below in a horizontal position. The participant's arms should be nearly fully extended and rest on top of your arms (**Fig. 3-8**).

Fig. 3-8

Shoulder Support on Front Position

Use this position for water adjustment, practicing kicking on the front, the front glide, bubble blowing, underwater exploration and rolling over. Position yourself so the water comes up to your shoulders and the participant's chin. With your arms nearly fully extended, hold the participant under the armpits (**Fig. 3-9**). Grasp a heavier or fearful participant underneath the arms and upper chest with your thumbs up.

Back-to-Chest Positions

Use the back-to-chest holding positions to introduce participants to skills on the back. Most participants feel less confident on their backs so introduce these positions gradually and be sure to give firm support initially. Do not continue any holding position if participants become distressed. You may want to let them start with their ears above the surface to help them adjust to the position.

Cuddle Position

Use this position for back float, back glide readiness, kicking on the back and rolling over. Position yourself so the water comes up to your neck and the participant's ears. The back of

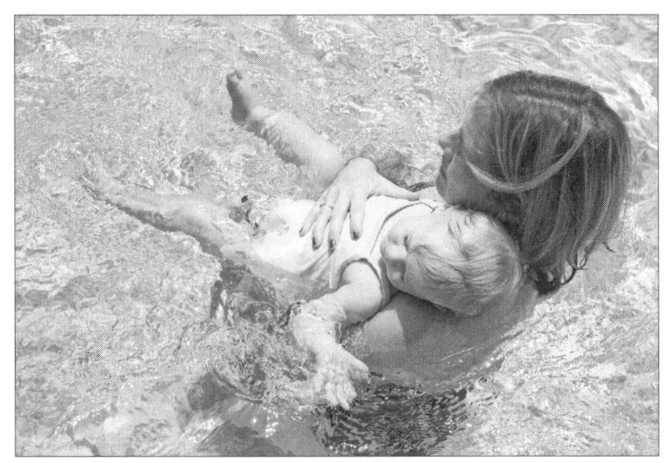

Fig. 3-10

the participant's head rests on your shoulder, with the participant's cheek or side of the head touching or right next to your cheek. Place one hand on the lower back and the other on the chest. The participant's legs point away from you. Hold the participant horizontal by "sandwiching" the participant between your hands (**Fig. 3-10**).

Hip Support on Back Position

Use this position for back float and back glide readiness and for kicking on the back. Position yourself so the water comes up to your neck and the participant's ears. The back of the participant's head rests on your shoulder, with the participant's cheek or side of the head touching or right next to your cheek. Hold the participant with both hands on the back to bring the body horizontal (**Fig. 3-11, A**).

Your exact hand position on the participant's back depends on his or her ability to relax. Hands on participants' lower back lends the most support; hands on the upper back give less support but more freedom of movement. As participants becomes more comfortable, their legs will relax, and they will lay their heads back and let their ears submerge. Once the participant relaxes, you may reach down to the participant's legs and manipulate the kick (**Fig. 3-11, B**).

Back Support Position

Use this position when participants are comfortable on their backs and maximum freedom of movement is desired, yet support is still necessary. Position yourself so that your shoulders and the participant's ears are in the water. Position yourself behind the participant. Support the base of the participant's head near the neck with one hand, and place the other hand in the middle of the back to lift and stabilize him or her in a horizontal position. Tilt the participant's head back. Extend your arms to separate the participant's head from your body. Start moving backwards smoothly to help them float to a

Fig. 3-11, A

Fig. 3-11, B

Fig. 3-12, A

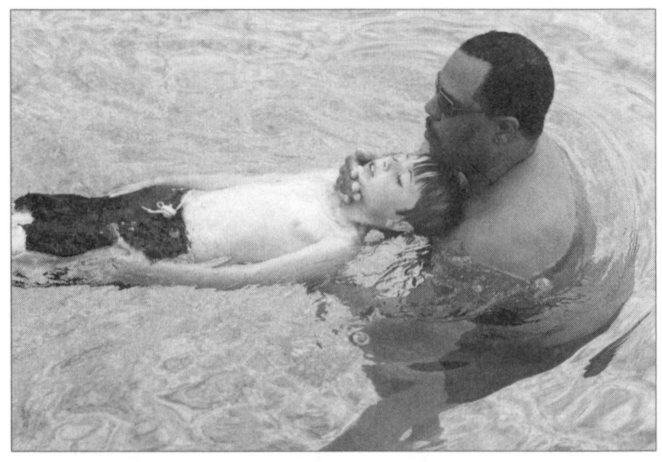

Fig. 3-12, B

horizontal position (**Fig. 3-12, A**). The momentum that you generate by moving helps the body rise up to the surface.

If participants have trouble relaxing and lift their head, you can vary this holding position. Pull the participant close to you and position the head on your chest or shoulder for more support. Place one hand in the middle of the back and the other hand around the chin or lower jaw (**Fig. 3-12, B**). Gently tilt the head back. Resume the back support position when the participant relaxes.

SAFETY NOTE

Do not push on the fleshy part of the participant's throat.

Arm Stroke Position

Use this position to help young participants explore arm movements in the water. Brace your back against the side of the pool or sit on the steps or kneel on one knee in shallow water. The water comes up to your shoulders and the upper chest or armpits of the participant.

Sit the participant on your knee, facing away from you. Use one of your arms to circle the participant's chest and keep him or her upright. With the other hand, hold the participant's same side wrist from underneath and place your hand on top of participant's hand (**Fig. 3-13, A**). Pattern an alternating or simultaneous paddling motion.

You can balance a more secure participant on your knee and guide both arms in an alternating or simultaneous paddling motion (**Fig. 3-13, B**).

Fig. 3-13, A

Fig. 3-13, B

Fig. 3-14

Side-to-Side Positions

Use these positions for water adjustment, bubble blowing, kicking on the front, front glide, front float, beginning stroking, passing and practicing combined skills.

Hip Straddle Position

Use this position for water adjustment, bubble blowing and water entry and exit. This position is most appropriate for young participants and can be used in various depths of water depending on the skill the participants are learning. Have the participant face you and straddle your hip while your arm supports the back by reaching around to hold the upper thigh (**Fig. 3-14**). Your other hand may hold the participant's hand. Position yourself so the water level is appropriate for the participant. If the participant is cold or afraid of the water, begin by immersing the lower part of the participant's body. As the participant becomes comfortable, gradually immerse yourself and the participant until the water reaches the participant's chest.

Shoulder Support on the Side Position

Use this position for water adjustment, bubble blowing, kicking on the front, front glide, front float, beginning stroking, passing and practicing combined skills. Position yourself comfortably so the water line is between your waist or shoulders and the participants' chin or neck. This position gives maximum mobility in a support position.

Start with you and the participant facing the same direction. Hold the participant at one side using your hands to hold him or her at the armpits, keeping the head up. You should be able to see the participant's face. The arm or elbow of the arm going across the back can rest against the buttocks and legs to keep them under water (**Fig. 3-15, A**).

For more support, use this same arm to encircle the participant by placing your palm on the chest. Your other arm should support the participant from the back near the armpit (**Fig. 3-15, B**). As the participant becomes more confident and skilled, hold him or her with both hands on the waist.

Fig. 3-15, A

Fig. 3-15, B

Flotation Devices and Teaching Aids Used in Red Cross Programs

Flotation devices serve different roles in aquatic experiences. Some are safety devices, some are teaching aids. You should know the differences, benefits and dangers associated with each of them and how to use them appropriately. The following section highlights the flotation devices recommended for use in Red Cross Parent and Child Aquatics, Preschool Aquatics and Learn-to-Swim classes.

Free-Floating Supports

Free-floating supports can prop up the body to help participants practice skills with or without: using the arms only, breathing and/or using various kicks. Participants can hold these supports with one or both hands or arms, or between the thighs or lower legs. Common free-floating supports include barbell floats, kickboards, foam noodles and pull buoys. Maintaining correct body position using a leg support, such as a pull buoy, can be difficult, and only advanced swimmers should use these devices.

Kickboard

The most common and one of the most useful teaching aids is the kickboard. You can use kickboards at all levels with varying degrees of assistance. Kickboards are available in different sizes so ensure each participant uses the appropriate size. Kickboards may not be safe or appropriate for participants who are too small, not coordinated enough to maintain a stable body position or who risk unintentional submersion while using this equipment.

As participants mature and develop size and strength, they can hold the kickboard while they practice kicking. The kickboard helps to simulate proper body position so that they can concentrate on kicking only or kicking in the streamlined position and rhythmic breathing. To practice kicking only on the front, participants should hold the kickboard on the sides near the top with their arms extended. This allows the arms to rest on the kickboard and keeps the participant's head up to breathe normally (**Fig. 3-16, A**). To add rhythmic breathing, participants should hold the kickboard on the sides near the bottom with the arms extended. The face is down in the water and participants only lift the head to breathe, and then return to the streamlined position.

To practice floating and kicking on the back, participants should hold the kickboard on the sides in the middle of the kickboard. Squeezing the kickboard against the chest and stomach helps participants float up to a horizontal position (**Fig. 3-16, B**). Sometimes it may be easier for beginners to hug the kickboard while pressing it against their chest and stomach. More skilled swimmers can manipulate the kickboard in the water overhead in the streamlined position on the back (**Fig. 3-16, C**). If the kickboard alters body position or is too cumbersome, discontinue use.

Fig. 3-16, A

Fig. 3-16, B

Fig. 3-16, C

Fig. 3-17, A

Fig. 3-17, B

INSTRUCTOR'S NOTE

Smaller kickboards are available that are easier for young participants to use. Also, some kickboards are available in shapes that are attractive to children, such as teddy bears and fish.

Barbell Floats

Barbell floats are comprised of a bar with floats on each end. This equipment is available in different sizes and materials. Use the appropriate size for each participant. Participants should hold the barbell in front with the arms stretched straight and use it much like a kickboard (**Fig. 3-17, A**). Because the bar is easier to grasp than a kickboard, these aids are most useful with smaller children or participants who have problems with kickboards. You can place the barbell under participants' armpits for support, so they can kick and stroke ahead of it without fear of sinking (**Fig. 3-17, B**). When using barbell floats, face participants, offer encouragement and stay close enough to support them if the barbell float slips away. Barbells also can be used to practice on the back by holding it against the chest or over the head.

Foam Noodles

Foam noodles are available in different sizes. While widely sold as toys, foam noodles are useful instructional aids. They can be used much like a barbell float, but they are less stable so you should closely supervise their use. As a teaching aid, participants can hold the noodle in front with arms stretched straight and use it much like a kickboard or barbell (**Fig. 3-18**). Participants may place the noodle under the armpits for support so they can kick and stroke ahead of it without fear of sinking. Foam noodles can also be used to practice on the back by holding it under the armpits against the chest or over the head.

Pull Buoys

Foam devices, such as pull buoys, are commonly used in the upper levels of Learn-to-Swim and in competitive training. The pull buoy can be placed between the thighs, knees or ankles to provide buoyancy and allow participants to concentrate

Fig. 3-18

Fig. 3-19

Fig. 3-20

on their arm strokes (**Fig. 3-19**). The placement of the device depends on how much buoyancy swimmers need. Be sure participants remain in good body position when using a pull buoy; never allow participants to tie this device to their legs.

Life Jackets

Life jackets have limited usefulness as teaching aids because their bulk makes it difficult to perform skills effectively. They also can promote poor body position. Additionally, if life jackets do not fit correctly, they can slip or slide off, which can turn panicky children face down and put them in danger.

However, Red Cross aquatics programs strongly advocate that all participants, including parents, know how to choose, use, wear and swim in properly fitted U.S. Coast Guard-approved life jackets (**Fig. 3-20**). So while you should not use life jackets to teach participants to swim, you should teach them how to enter the water and swim while wearing this important life-saving device.

Stationary Supports

Stationary supports include the deck or the side of a pool or a dock, the ladders or steps leading into the water, and the bottom of shallow water. Participants can use these devices to support the body as they practice leg movements. For example, participants should learn to bracket themselves to practice leg actions in proper body position. Bracketing is a technique in which participants balance and control their body position while holding onto the side of the pool or the dock. Practicing in this position helps participants develop correct form. Participants may also find ways to bracket themselves other than those described here.

Bracketing in the Front Position

When bracketing in the front position, participants should grasp the gutter with one hand and bend the elbow slightly. They should press the other hand against the pool wall below the water line with their fingers pointing down and their elbow straight (**Fig. 3-21, A**). The submerged hand should be deep enough to support correct body position. Participants keep their head in the water to the ears and breathe rhythmically to let the hips and legs rise toward the surface naturally. When participants keep their heads up, the hips and legs are lowered. Participants may breathe normally in this position but will need to work harder with their legs to keep the body near the surface. If this hand position is too difficult for participants, they may try holding the gutter with both hands while keeping both elbows locked into a straight position (**Fig. 3-21, B**).

Bracketing in a Side-Lying Position

Participants grasp the gutter with the hand of the upper arm while the elbow is slightly bent. They should place the palm of the lower hand against the wall directly under the top hand, with the fingers pointing toward the bottom and at a comfortable distance beneath the surface. Participants should try to keep the elbow of the lower arm straight and the body

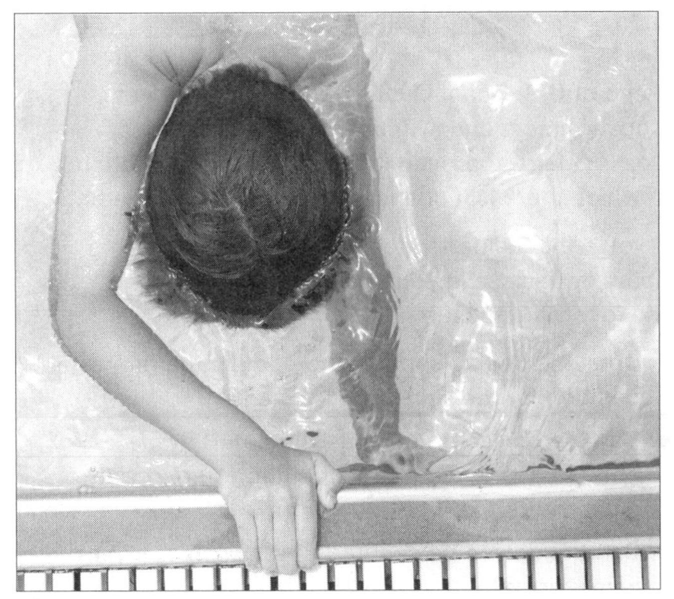
Fig. 3-21, A

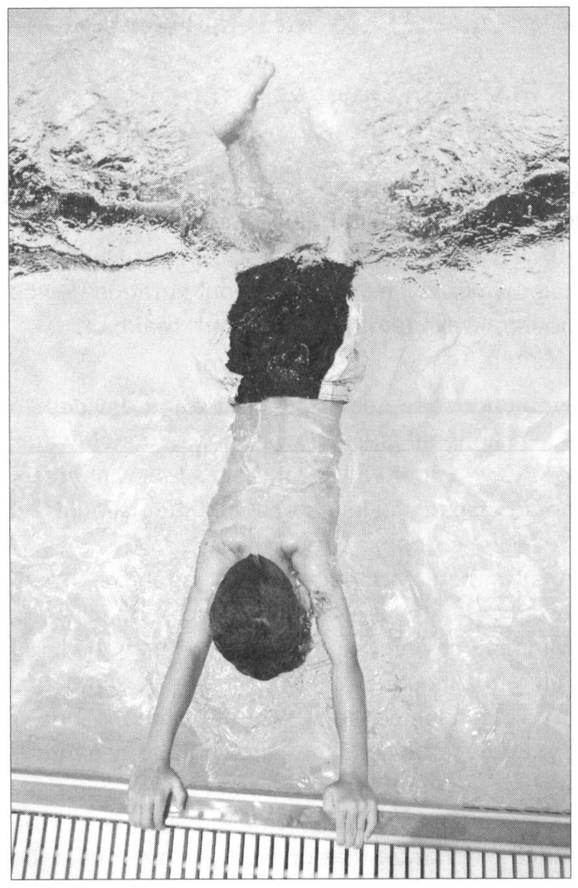
Fig. 3-21, B

straight, stretched and perpendicular to the wall with the lower part of the ear in the water (**Fig. 3-22**).

In this position, the lower hand gives most of the support and control for the body. If participants sway forward or backward, they can slide the lower hand in the direction of the sway and exert pressure against the wall to push the body back into position. In this position, participants have stable support while they practice the scissors kick.

Fins

Fins can help swimmers move faster and kick with less effort. Wearing fins can be especially helpful for developing a fluid flutter kick and dolphin kick. They also allow swimmers to concentrate on arm stroking patterns, timing and breathing. Be sure to have various sizes available so participants can use fins that fit correctly. The fins should fit well enough that they stay on swimmers' feet but do not cause the feet to cramp.

SAFETY NOTE

Do not allow participants to walk on the deck in fins. Have participants sit on the edge of the pool while they put on and take off the fins.

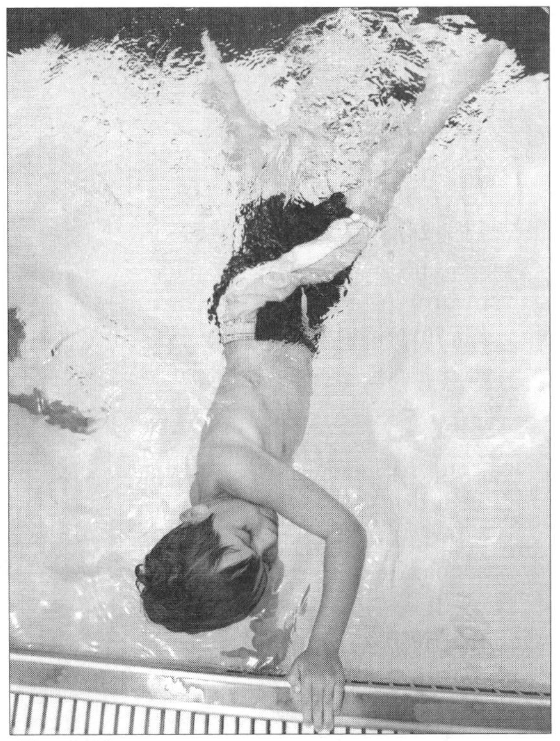
Fig. 3-22

All Flotation Devices Are Not Created Equal

A flotation device is not a substitute for close adult supervision. All children up to about the age of 5 or 6 years, no matter how well they can swim on their own or swim with or without flotation devices, should always remain within arm's reach of an adult.

If you choose to use attached floating devices as instructional aids, allow nonswimmers in your classes very limited use of them. Nonswimmers should stay in shallow areas, and they should not become dependent on these aids. Teach nonswimmers and their parents about the potential hazards of using these aids for recreational swimming or practicing skills without supervision from a qualified instructor. Children, in particular, may get a false sense of security. Children who rely on these devices may drown if they go into the water without them or if the devices come loose when they enter or paddle in the water. You should emphasize that these aids do not take the place of U.S. Coast Guard-approved life jackets. Nonswimmers and swimmers alike should wear Coast Guard-approved life jackets in any situation in which there is a chance of falling into the water.

If you are considering the use of attached flotation devices in your classes, ask yourself the following questions—

- Does the device support the body in the proper position for the skill to be learned?
- Can the device be placed on the part of the body requiring support without interfering with movements of other body parts?
- Can the device be secured so it does not slip or come loose?
- Is the device constructed so it cannot deflate accidentally?

If you answered "yes" to all of these questions, proceed with caution.

The following information describes some of the potential uses and highlights the disadvantages of two different types of attached flotation devices.

Inflatable Arm Bands

This equipment, sometimes called "muscles," "wings" or "swimmies," is used primarily for very small children. It may also be used as adaptive devices for aquatic participants and some older, less confident participants. Inflatable arm bands are used to keep participants' heads above water and permit them to move independently. This gives parents and/or instructors time to assist with the manipulation of the limbs. Keep in mind, however, that arm bands restrict proper arm movement. They may be useful for water adjustment, but they tend to reinforce a false sense of security in children who may not realize that the artificial device is providing the flotation. These devices often develop leaks and tend to slip off. They raise the center of buoyancy and actually impair progress if participants become accustomed to kicking in a vertical position.

Styrofoam Floats

Styrofoam floats also called floatbelts are attachable devices that come in a variety of shapes and provide enough buoyancy to support small children. They can help build strength and endurance because children can typically practice longer in water over their head. Styrofoam floats can be useful when practicing combined skills. For example, placing these devices on the back can help children float on the stomach, or the children can float on their back when the device is placed on the stomach.

The disadvantages often outweigh the advantages as parents and children alike may become overconfident of the children's ability and safety. Poorly positioned devices can submerge children's faces. Warn parents that they should not depend on any artificial devices for their children's safety other than U.S. Coast Guard-approved life jackets.

CHAPTER

4

Integrating Water Safety Into the Courses

Wilbert E. Longfellow, the father of American Red Cross water safety education, once said: "Water can be a good friend or a deadly enemy." Wherever there is water, there is a risk for drowning. In fact, people can drown in less than 1 inch of water. Each year, young children tragically die because parents and caregivers do not realize the danger posed by bathtubs, toilets, kiddie pools, ditches and even buckets of water. Importantly, the great majority of these deaths are preventable. It is vital that parents and caregivers recognize the risks associated with all types of aquatic activities and environments and follow and enforce the basic rules of water safety.

It is the mission of the Red Cross to prevent, prepare for and respond to emergencies. The Swimming and Water Safety program helps fulfill that mission by teaching people to be safe in, on and around the water. Water safety is an integral part of Red Cross Parent and Child Aquatics, Preschool Aquatics and Learn-to-Swim courses.

Water safety is more than a set of rules and swimming tips. It is a combination of attitude, knowledge, practices and skills. As a Water Safety instructor, you have a responsibility to teach participants at all levels and their parents what it takes to be safe in, on and around the water. You should always promote a "safety-first" attitude.

Putting Water Safety into Practice

The concept of water safety should be central to every part of an aquatics program. Parents and participants should feel confident that water safety is being practiced at all levels of the program. Anyone should be able to walk into the facility and see a well-supervised program. An adequate number of lifeguards should be on-duty and conducting patron surveillance during all in-water sessions. Visitors should see appropriate signage. Safety and rescue equipment should be clean, working and available during swim lessons. All facility staff should be consistent role models for safe behavior. This means they should always follow the rules and do the right thing. Instructors should practice water safety in all they do.

Water Safety as Part of Learning to Swim

Water safety should be a major focus when participants learn to swim. Throughout all levels, and especially at the early levels, nearly every skill participants learn is a safety skill. Entering the water, controlling breathing, floating for extended periods, making forward progress and exiting the water are skills that can make a life-and-death difference when participants are in, on or around the water.

Instructors are required to address certain safety topics at each level. As you plan your courses, set aside some time during each class to teach water safety knowledge and skills. You can teach participants to have fun and stay safe in the water. You should encourage them to be prepared and think "safety first." You can help participants focus on safety by teaching them to–

- Look out for themselves and others.
- Know what to think about before entering the water.
- Know what hazards to look for and how to be safe in different aquatic environments, such as oceans, lakes, rivers, home pools and waterparks.
- Know general safety guidelines.
- Know how to stay healthy in the sun and the water.
- Know how to help themselves in an emergency.
- Know how to help others in an emergency, such as calling 9-1-1 and performing nonswimming rescues.
- Know how to choose, properly put on and swim in a life jacket.

You should teach safety information to parents in Parent and Child Aquatics and to parents of Preschool Aquatics and Learn-to-Swim participants. The following are just some benefits from teaching parents about water safety:

- Parents who are educated about water safety can more safely supervise children around aquatic environments.
- Parents who know what safety information their children are learning can reinforce the lessons with their children.
- Parents will be exposed to your "safety-first" attitude. This will give them confidence that your classes are safe, and their children are learning good safety habits.

In addition to the planned safety topics, take advantage of "teachable moments." Take every opportunity to impart safety-related knowledge and practices whenever situations arise within lessons. Use spontaneous situations as examples to teach or reinforce safety practices. (Make sure you do not embarrass anyone or create fear in these situations.) Keep in mind the developmental age and maturity level of participants when presenting your safety messages. Discuss information in ways that participants can understand. Have them clearly repeat your messages back to you.

Encourage participants and parents to teach others about safe aquatic behaviors.

Water Safety Resources

Many safety resources are available through the Red Cross. You can use these resources in class and as "take-home" materials to reinforce safety messages. Be sure to choose materials designed for the ages you are targeting.

Newsletters

Newsletters are available for each level of Parent and Child Aquatics, Preschool Aquatics and Learn-to-Swim. These newsletters highlight what participants learn at each level, including the safety topics and skills. They also feature safety tips that parents can use when supervising children around aquatic environments and to help their children progress and learn about general water safety. You should send these newsletters home with participants early in each session.

Raffy Learns to Swim and Waddles in the Deep

There are two booklets available to help teach young children about aquatics safety in a fun and informative way. *Raffy Learns to Swim* is designed to support Red Cross Preschool Aquatics Levels 1 and 2 and Learn-to-Swim Level 1, while *Waddles in the Deep* is designed to support Preschool Aquatics Level 3 and Learn-to-Swim Levels 2 and 3. These booklets reinforce the content learned during the lessons and provide a way for instructors and parents and participants to communicate. Each booklet contains the following:

- An overview of Red Cross Preschool Aquatics and Learn-to-Swim, including descriptions of the three Preschool Aquatics levels, six Learn-to-Swim levels and the skills taught within each level
- A story line that supports and reinforces the knowledge and skills that participants gain from Red Cross swim lessons
- Achievement cards that indicate participants' progress toward passing the levels
- Information to help parents reinforce knowledge and skills with their children
- Water safety information to help keep families safe in, on and around the water

Consider providing the booklets to participants as they register for classes or on the first day of class. Take time to point out the features of the booklets to parents. On the first day, read the story to the class to get them excited about what they will be learning. About halfway through the session, have participants bring their booklets to class so you can fill in their achievement cards. This is a great opportunity to remind parents of how they can help their children progress and talk "water safety" as a family. On the last day of the session, be sure to update achievement cards and encourage parents to continue the Learn-to-Swim experience. Remind parents and participants that water safety is not just about knowing how to behave around the water. It is also about having an arsenal of skills they can use to handle themselves in aquatic environments and situations.

Longfellow's WHALE Tales

Longfellow's WHALE Tales K–6 Educational Packet provides easy-to-follow information to help children learn safe behavior in, on and around the water. WHALE (Water Habits Are Learned Early) Tales is designed for participants in kindergarten through the sixth grade. It is intended to be taught in a classroom, but you can take advantage of the information and resources as part of your classes on the pool deck. *Longfellow's WHALE Tales K–6 Educational Packet* includes the following lessons:

1. Swim With a Buddy in a Supervised Area
2. Be Cool, Follow the Rule–the reasons behind water safety rules
3. Look Before You Leap–choose safe places to swim and dive
4. Think So You Don't Sink–what to do when things go wrong
5. Reach or Throw, Don't Go–safe ways to rescue a swimmer in trouble
6. Don't Just Pack It, Wear Your Jacket–the importance of wearing a life jacket
7. Think Twice Before Going Near Cold Water or Ice–knowing the hazards of Cold Water
8. Learn About Boating Before You Go Floating
9. Do Your Part, Be Water Smart–how to minimize water hazards around the home

10. Too Much Sun Is No Fun–how to protect yourself from sun exposure
11. Wave, Tide or Ride, Follow the Guide–learning to be prepared for different aquatic experiences, such as going to a waterpark

There are many ways that you can use the *Longfellow's WHALE Tales K–6 Educational Packet* to teach the required safety topics or include additional safety information and/or topics. You may want to begin each class throughout the session using a different topic. You can also expand on one or more of the topics already introduced in the level. However you choose to use the topics from Longfellow's WHALE Tales, consider using the color posters as you facilitate the discussions. Think of ways to relate what they learned at the start of the class to any safety skills you will be teaching for the day. As participants leave class, you may want to provide them with worksheets to take home so they can talk about safety topics with their families. You may be surprised at how many children bring back their completed worksheets for your approval and praise! You can find more detailed information on the *Longfellow's WHALE Tales K–6 Educational Packet* in **Chapter 10**.

Swimming and Water Safety

This comprehensive reference manual is the complete guide to swimming, diving and water safety. **Chapters 1**, **2** and **3** of *Swimming and Water Safety* include information about the attraction of water and the associated dangers. They also provide details about safety issues to consider when swimming or participating in aquatic activities that take place in, on and around water and ice. In addition, these chapters discuss the procedures involved in responding to an aquatic emergency, including tips and information about self-rescue and helping others.

Use *Swimming and Water Safety* to help you learn more about being safe in, on and around the water. The more you know, the more you can pass on to participants. This resource can also provide content to help you customize your safety messages to meet regional and local needs. Your older participants or parents of participants may be interested in owning a copy of *Swimming and Water Safety* as they explore different types of aquatic activities and become more aware of water safety. Direct people who are interested in buying a copy of *Swimming and Water Safety* to the local Red Cross chapter.

Safety Equipment During Lessons

As part of successfully completing the Red Cross Parent and Child Aquatics, Preschool Aquatics and Learn-to-Swim courses, participants must learn about certain safety equipment and how it is used. From the earliest levels, you will teach participants and their parents the importance of life jackets. Train all participants so they know how to enter and exit the water and swim while wearing a life jacket. Parents in Parent and Child Aquatics and participants in Preschool Aquatics and Learn-to-Swim also learn how to choose and put on life jackets and when they should wear them.

You will also need to teach participants an important concept–"reach or throw, don't go." Let them know that they should never place themselves in danger. Instead, they should learn how to use reaching and throwing equipment to help people who are in trouble in the water. For example, teach them how to use equipment to reach out and pull someone who is about their size to safety. In addition, participants should learn to throw certain items to a person in trouble to hold onto until qualified rescuers can reach him or her. Some of the items participants will use when learning these skills include reaching poles, shepherd's crooks, ropes and ring buoys with lines attached. They should also practice reaching and throwing assists using improvised equipment.

Keep Water Safety Active

When parents register their children for swim lessons, they expect that their children will be in the water learning aquatic skills. Some observers may not understand why you spend time on the deck teaching water safety. Be creative in your approach to water safety, especially when the topic is not an active one. Here are some steps you can take to minimize concerns and complaints about spending time out of the water. Also included are examples of how you can integrate a water or sun safety topics into each step:

- Remind parents daily that water safety is a part of the routine. As you greet participants and their parents, let them know the safety topic of the day.
- Limit the amount of time you spend out of the water just talking to participants. Gather the participants in a circle around you. Use a poster from *Longfellow's WHALE Tales K–6 Educational Packet* as a visual aid as you briefly highlight some of the relevant safety messages in terms they can understand. Spend no more than a few minutes with participants on the deck.
- Get participants active as soon as possible. For example, prior to entering the water, have participants simulate putting on sunscreen. Have them "rub lotion" onto their arms and legs while they stretch and bend.
- Consider other ways to relay the information or get participants thinking about the topic. You can ask questions and reward appropriate responses by letting them go first. As examples, ask "What can you do to prevent a sunburn?" or "Why is it important to wear a life jacket when you are boating?"
- At the end of the lesson, distribute any take-home information on the safety topic. For example, give participants copies of any worksheets from the *Longfellow's WHALE Tales K–6 Educational Packet* that support the safety topic of the day. Make sure the worksheet is age-appropriate.
- Speak with parents at the end of the lesson to give them brief updates about what participants are learning. This brief update should highlight new skills participants are learning as well as the safety topic. Point out that you have given their children some safety information to take home.

Key Water Safety Topics

The chart on the following page outlines the main points of the key water safety topics associated with Parent and Child Aquatics, Preschool Aquatics and Learn-to-Swim. Each level requires that certain water safety topics be covered. Arranged by topic and recommended level, use this section to integrate water safety into your classes.

Because this information is extremely important, many of the topics are repeated through several levels. The repetition of these messages also helps ensure that participants who are new to Red Cross Parent and Child Aquatics, Preschool Aquatics and Learn-to-Swim or who are absent from class still learn this critical information. It is strongly recommended that you have a safety topic every time your class meets and that you add topics to meet specific needs of your participants, facility or region.

When teaching water safety topics, strive to keep the learning as active as possible and present the information in new ways throughout the levels. Try using open-ended questions or scenarios so the topics stay fresh and increase participants' understanding. For example, you could ask participants, "Why is it important to swim with a buddy in a supervised area?" or "What should you do first if you see someone in the water who is having trouble?" For the higher levels, you could simulate different types of behaviors in the water, such as swimming, distressed swimmer, passive drowning victim or active drowning victim, and have participants say if help is needed or not. Also, consider using resources from the appropriate lessons in the *Longfellow's WHALE Tales K–6 Educational Packet* to reinforce those specific topics.

Water Safety Topics	Recommended Levels
The Importance of Wearing a Life Jacket	Parent and Child Aquatics Levels 1 and 2 (parents)
Don't Just Pack It, Wear Your Jacket*	Preschool Aquatics Levels 1–3 Learn-to-Swim Levels 1–4
How to Call for Help	Preschool Aquatics Levels 1–3 Learn-to-Swim Levels 1 and 2
How to Call for Help and the Importance of Knowing First Aid and CPR	Parent and Child Aquatics Levels 1 and 2 (parents) Learn-to-Swim Levels 5 and 6
Basic Water Safety Rules	Parent and Child Aquatics Levels 1 and 2 (parents)
Basic Water Safety Rules Review	Parent and Child Aquatics Levels 1 and 2 (parents)
General Water Safety Around the Home**	Parent and Child Aquatics Levels 1 and 2 (parents)
Recreational Water Illnesses	Parent and Child Aquatics Levels 1 and 2 (parents) Learn-to-Swim Levels 4–6
Sun Safety	Parent and Child Aquatics Levels 1 and 2 (parents)
Too Much Sun Is No Fun*	Preschool Aquatics Levels 1–3 Learn-to-Swim Levels 1–4
Reaching Assists	Parent and Child Aquatics Levels 1 and 2 (parents)
Reach or Throw, Don't Go*	Preschool Aquatics Level 3 Learn-to-Swim Levels 3–6
Safety at the Beach and the Waterpark**	Parent and Child Aquatics Levels 1 and 2 (parents)
Wave, Tide or Ride, Follow the Guide*	Learn-to-Swim Levels 4–6
Water Toys and Their Limitations	Parent and Child Aquatics Levels 1 and 2 (parents)
Staying Safe Around Aquatic Environments	Preschool Aquatics Levels 1–3 Learn-to-Swim Levels 1 and 2
Recognizing the Lifeguards	Preschool Aquatics Levels 1 and 2 Learn-to-Swim Levels 1 and 2
Swim with a Buddy in a Supervised Area*	Learn to Swim Levels 3–6
Recognizing an Emergency	Preschool Aquatics Levels 1–3 Learn-to-Swim Levels 1 and 2
Look Before You Leap*	Preschool Aquatics Level 3 Learn-to-Swim Levels 1–6
Think So You Don't Sink*	Preschool Aquatics Level 3 Learn-to-Swim Levels 1–6
Think Twice Before Going Near Cold Water or Ice	Learn-to-Swim Levels 3–6
Learn About Boating Before You Go Floating	Learn-to-Swim Level 6

*Lesson in the *Longfellow's WHALE Tales K–6 Educational Packet*

**Supporting information in the *Longfellow's WHALE Tales K–6 Educational Packet*

The Importance of Wearing a Life Jacket

Tell participants:

- **Life jackets are not just for boats, but everyone should wear a life jacket while boating. In addition, young children and anyone who cannot swim well should wear a life jacket whenever they are in, on or around the water.**
- **Even in public pools or waterparks, people who cannot swim well should wear a life jacket.**
- **Life jackets are not a substitute for close supervision. Young children and poor swimmers need close supervision at all times. Whenever children are in, on or around the water, a responsible individual should be designated to provide constant supervision and stay within arm's reach if the child is young or a poor swimmer, even if the child is wearing a life jacket.**
- **There are several types and many styles of life jackets, and they are rated for their buoyancy and purpose. The type of activity and water conditions help determine which type to use.**
- **For any type, be sure it is U.S. Coast Guard-approved and in good condition.**

Activity:

- Point out the U.S. Coast Guard marking on the life jacket and highlight the weight guidelines in the label.
- Emphasize the importance of selecting the correct size life jacket and wearing it properly, including fastening all zippers, ties or snaps.
- Guide parents in selecting and putting appropriately-sized U.S. Coast Guard-approved life jackets on themselves and their child.
- Have parents enter the water first, then help the child enter the water and move around the teaching area. Give light support as needed.
- Have the parent hold the child in a face-to-face position, then cue him or her to roll over onto the back then float for a brief period. Cue the child again to roll over onto the front then return to the wall.
- Cue the child to jump into the water then return to the wall using the combined stroke on front.
- Working with one parent and child pair at a time, hold the child while the parent experiences buoyancy, such as by lifting his or her feet off the bottom or floating on the back.
- Optional: Have the child wear lightweight clothes under the life jacket (e.g., T-shirt and shorts; no jeans or sweatshirts or pants) and back float in water. Start in shallow water then move to deeper water. Limit this activity to a few minutes.

INSTRUCTOR'S NOTES

- *Provide U.S. Coast Guard-approved life jackets in various styles and sizes.*
- *Ask anyone who has a life jacket at home to bring it to class so the child can practice in his or her own life jacket. Not all will have them, so have life jackets available also. Children can take turns if your supply is limited.*

Don't Just Pack It, Wear Your Jacket

Tell participants:

- **A life jacket helps you stay afloat if you fall into the water.**
- **Whenever you go boating wear a life jacket. Put on your life jacket before going out on the dock and do not take it off until you return.**

- **Life jackets are not just for boats. You should wear a life jacket whenever you are in, on or around the water. The only time you should be near the water without a life jacket is when you are at a swimming area and a grown-up is watching you.**
- **Even if you are at a swimming pool or a waterpark, if you cannot swim well then you should wear a life jacket and stay near the person who is watching you.**

Add for Learn-to-Swim Level 3 and above:

- **Even if you are a strong swimmer, you should wear a life jacket whenever you are in, on and around water if it is cold.**
- **Always wear a life jacket in any situation where there is a chance of falling or being thrown into the water, such as being towed on water skis or tubes or while riding personal watercraft.**

Activity for All Levels:

- Point out the U.S. Coast Guard marking on the life jacket and highlight the weight guidelines in the label.
- Emphasize the importance of selecting the correct size life jacket and wearing it properly, including fastening all zippers, ties or snaps.
- Guide the children in selecting and putting on an appropriately sized U.S. Coast Guard-approved life jacket.
- Help children enter the water then move around the teaching area. Give light support as needed.
- Working with one child at a time, have the child in a face-to-face position, then cue him or her to roll over onto the back then float for a brief period. Cue the child again to roll over onto the front then return to the wall.
- Cue the child to jump into the water then return to the wall using the combined stroke on front.
- Optional: Have the child wear lightweight clothes under the life jacket (e.g., T-shirt and shorts; no jeans or sweatshirts or pants) and back float in water. Start in shallow water then move to deeper water. Limit this activity to a few minutes.

INSTRUCTOR'S NOTES

- *Provide U.S. Coast Guard-approved life jackets in various styles and sizes.*
- *Ask anyone who has a life jacket at home to bring it to class so the child can practice in his or her own life jacket. Not all will have them, so have life jackets available also. Children can take turns if your supply is limited.*

How to Call for Help

Tell participants:

- **When you see someone who is in trouble, stay calm and tell the lifeguard or a grown-up right away.**
- **If a lifeguard or a grown-up is not nearby, use a phone and call 9-1-1 or the local emergency number.**
- **Tell the person who answers the phone what happened. Do not hang up. The person who answers the phone might be able to tell you how you can help.**

- **You should only call 9-1-1 or the local emergency if there really is an emergency. Never call this number unless emergency help is really needed.**

Activity:

- Use a toy or non-working telephone and have participants simulate calling for help. Do not have them actually place the call!
- Tell participants to memorize the phone number "9-1-1," their address and telephone number, the color of their house or the car in the driveway. After class, speak to parents and remind them to help their children practice this task.

SAFETY NOTE

Take appropriate measures to ensure that 9-1-1 or the local emergency number is not accidentally made. Do not let participants actually place the call. If using a mobile phone, ensure that it is turned off or the battery is removed.

Tell participants:

- **When you call 9-1-1, the person who answers the phone might want to know–**
  - **Your name.**
  - **The telephone number from where you are calling.**
  - **What happened.**
  - **Where you are.**
  - **How many people are hurt or in trouble.**
  - **What is wrong with the person.**
  - **What help (first aid) is being given.**

INSTRUCTOR'S NOTE

When dealing with young children, concentrate on the first five sub-bullets.

How to Call for Help and the Importance of Knowing First Aid and CPR

Tell participants:

- **Drowning is the second leading cause of death for children ages 1 to 4. Anyone watching children who are in, on or around a pool or any other body of water must understand that drowning happens quickly and suddenly.**
- **When you recognize an emergency, stay calm and call or have someone call 9-1-1 or the local emergency number. Every second counts.**
- **If the child is unconscious, send someone else to call emergency medical service (EMS) personnel while you care for the child. If the child is conscious, first try to safely get the child out of the water and then determine the help and care needed.**

- The following conditions and situations are serious and require a call to EMS personnel:
  - Any drowning or nonfatal submersion situation
  - Injury to the head, neck or back
  - Difficulty breathing
  - Persistent chest or abdominal pain or pressure
  - Unconsciousness
  - Severe bleeding, vomiting blood or passing blood
  - Seizure, severe headache or slurred speech
  - Poisoning
  - Possible broken bones
  - Multiple injuries
- Do not hang up first when calling for help. In many cases, the dispatcher may need more information or may be able to help by giving first aid directions.
- The American Red Cross recommends that at least one person in every household be trained in lifesaving first aid, cardiopulmonary resuscitation (CPR) and automated external defibrillator (AED) skills.
- Anyone who has a home pool or lives near a body of water, such as a canal, pond, river or ocean, should ensure that anyone who cares for their children know first aid, CPR and how to use an AED.

Basic Water Safety Rules

Tell participants:

- Only swim in designated areas and whenever possible under the supervision of a trained lifeguard. Be sure to follow all posted rules.
- Designate a responsible individual(s) to watch over children whenever they are in, on or around any body of water, even if a lifeguard is present. This individual should not be distracted or drinking alcohol and should know how to respond to an aquatic emergency.
- A great number of aquatic emergencies involving young children happen as a result of a lapse in supervision, which is why it is paramount to keep your eyes on your child at all times.
- Stay within arm's reach of weak swimmers and young children regardless of their swimming ability. Have young children or inexperienced swimmers take extra precautions, such as wearing a U.S. Coast Guard-approved life jacket.
- Do not rely on substitutes. Water wings, swim rings, inflatable toys and other items designed for water recreation cannot replace parental supervision, nor should they be counted on as lifesaving devices. These devices can suddenly shift position, lose air or slip out from underneath, leaving the child in a dangerous situation.
- Children should only enter the water after they have received permission. Help them learn to ask first.
- Know each child's swimming ability and set specific rules for each child based on swimming ability.
- Make sure children enter the water feetfirst.
- Be prepared. Know how to prevent, recognize and respond to emergencies. Whenever possible have a telephone or mobile phone nearby.

Basic Water Safety Rules Review

Tell participants:

- As the parent, you are always primarily responsible for the supervision of your children, both in and out of the water, no matter where you are.
- Only swim in designated areas and whenever possible under the supervision of a trained lifeguard. Be sure to follow all posted rules.
- Designate a responsible individual(s) to watch over children whenever they are in, on or around any body of water, even if a lifeguard is present. This individual should not be distracted or drinking alcohol and should know how to respond to an aquatic emergency.
- Knowing and enforcing what is safe and unsafe behavior in and around aquatic environments is a part of good supervision–set specific rules for each child based on swimming ability.
- Facilities should have their rules posted in clear view. You should read and follow the rules and teach them to your children. The following are some basic rules and tips to make your child aware of for all aquatic environments:
  - Always swim with a buddy. Never swim alone.
  - Swim only in supervised areas.
  - Always walk, never run or skip.
  - Check the depth of the water before jumping or diving in the water.
  - Look for potential hazards and make sure no one is in front of you before jumping or diving.
  - Do not engage in rough horseplay, such as dunking.
  - Do not eat or chew gum while swimming.
  - Shower before and after swimming in a pool, river, lake or ocean.
  - Watch out for the "dangerous too's": too tired, too cold, too far from safety, too much sun and too much hard play.
- If you have a home pool, be sure to post rules for the pool and enforce them without exception.
- Teach your children always to only enter the water after they have received permission. Help them learn to ask first.

General Water Safety Around the Home

Tell participants:

- Water safety and steps to prevent drowning are needed around any body of water, not just the swimming pool or spa.
- Any water deep enough to cover the mouth and nose can cause drowning.
- Drowning can occur in the home in a bathtub, toilet or any other container of water.
- Use physical barriers and prevent unsupervised children from entering any source of water.
- Provide constant and vigilant supervision whenever children are around any source of water (such as pools, rivers, lakes, bathtubs, toilets and even buckets of water) no matter how well the child can swim and no matter how shallow the water.

- For anyone who has the responsibility of a home pool, the best way to keep children safe from drowning is to provide layers of protection. This includes placing barriers around your pool to prevent access, installing pool alarms, making sure everyone in the home knows how to swim, closely supervising your child and knowing how to respond to an aquatic emergency.
- The following tips can help reduce the risk of drowning in and around the home:
  - Never leave a young child unattended in a bathtub. Do not trust a child's life to bathtub aids that help a child sit upright in the tub–they do not replace constant supervision.
  - Keep bathroom doors closed, use safety locks on toilets and keep toilet bowl covers down to prevent toddlers from reaching the toilet.
  - Empty buckets, kiddie pools, bathtubs and any other containers of water immediately after use.
- Identify potential water hazards within the community and make certain that children stay away from them. For example, prevent access to community and landscape water features, such as small ponds and waterfalls.
- When visiting another home, check the site for potential water hazards and always supervise children.

Recreational Water Illnesses

Tell participants:

- A recreational water illness (RWI) is an illness that comes from contact with contaminated water.
- RWIs can be transmitted in waterparks, swimming pools, hot tubs and spas, rivers, lakes and oceans. Diarrhea is the most common symptom of a RWI, but they also can cause infections in the skin, ears, eyes, chest and lungs.
- These illnesses are most commonly spread through swallowing or breathing in water particles containing germs.
- The Centers for Disease Control and Prevention (CDC) recommends that all swimmers follow the "PLEAs" that promote safe healthy swimming:
  - Please do not swim when you have diarrhea. You can spread germs in the water and make other people sick. This is especially important for kids in diapers.
  - Please do not swallow the pool water. In fact, avoid getting water in your mouth altogether.
  - Please practice good hygiene. Take a shower before swimming and wash your hands after using the toilet or changing diapers.
  - Please go on bathroom breaks often. Waiting until you have to go may mean that it is too late.

Add for Parent and Child Aquatics:

- Please take kids on bathroom breaks or check diapers often. Waiting to hear "I have to go" may mean that it is too late.
- Please change diapers in a bathroom or a diaper-changing area and not at poolside. Germs can spread to surfaces and objects in and around the pool and cause illness.
- Please wash your child thoroughly (especially the rear end) with soap and water before swimming. Everyone has invisible amounts of fecal matter on their bottoms that ends up in the pool.

Sun Safety

Tell participants:

- Overexposure to the sun's ultraviolet (UV) rays is a problem for everyone, regardless of age, location or skin color.
- Sunburns in childhood can result in health problems later on in life, so children are especially at risk.
- The consequences of overexposure are severe. Too much sun can lead to eye damage, cataracts, immune system suppression, premature aging of the skin and, most seriously, skin cancer.
- Protect your and your children's skin in the following ways:
  - Seek shade and limit the amount of time in direct sunlight between 10 A.M. and 4 P.M. This is the time of day when UV rays are most harmful.
  - Always make sure you generously apply sunscreen to children about 10 to 15 minutes before they go out into the sun. Apply sunscreen to all exposed skin using a sun protection factor (SPF) of at least 15 that provides broad-spectrum protection from both ultraviolet A (UVA) and ultraviolet B (UVB) rays. Reapply every 2 hours, even on cloudy days, and after swimming or sweating.
  - Have children wear protective clothing, such as a long-sleeved shirt, pants, a wide-brimmed hat and sunglasses, whenever they are exposed to UV rays.
  - Watch for the UV Index. The UV Index provides a daily forecast of the expected risk of overexposure to the sun, using a scale of 1 to 11+. On a day with an intensity level of 1, there is a low risk of overexposure and on an 11+ day there is an extreme risk.

Too Much Sun Is No Fun

Tell participants:

- Some of the light that comes from the sun is bad for you. That is why you need to protect your skin whenever you go outside in the sun. If you stay in sun without protecting your skin, you can get a sunburn.
- Every time you go outside, protect your skin.
  - Try to stay in the shade. Play in the shade or stay inside between 10 A.M. and 4 P.M. This is when light from the sun is most dangerous.
  - Put on a lot of sunscreen before you go outside. Put it on again every 2 hours and put it on again after you go swimming or if you are sweating.
  - Wear clothes, like a long-sleeved shirt and pants to protect your skin from sunlight. You also should wear a hat with a brim and sunglasses. These things will help protect your skin from getting burned.
  - You have to be extra careful when you are by water, sand or snow. When sunlight shines on water, sand or snow, it bounces off and can burn your skin.

Add for Learn-to-Swim Level 4:

- Energy from the sun is called solar radiation. UV rays are a type of solar radiation. Overexposure to UV rays can cause sunburns and lead to serious illness later on in life.

- **UV rays are invisible, so you need to take steps to protect your skin whenever you go outside in the sun.**
- **Seek shade if possible. Remember that the sun's UV rays are strongest between 10 A.M. and 4 P.M. Follow the shadow rule when in the sun: Watch your shadow, no shadow, seek shade!**
- **Pay attention to the UV Index. The UV Index provides important information to help you plan your outdoor activities in ways that prevent overexposure to the sun. Stay inside when the UV Index is high.**

Reaching Assists

Tell participants:

- **Sometimes parents and others watching children around water fail to recognize that a swimmer is in trouble.**
- **Most people who are in trouble in the water cannot or do not call for help. They spend their energy just trying to keep their heads above water to get a breath.**
- **A swimmer in distress may be too tired to get to the side of the pool or may be trying to swim, but making little or no forward progress. If not helped, a swimmer in distress may soon become a drowning victim.**
- **If you notice a swimmer in trouble, tell a lifeguard. If no lifeguards are present, the next step is to help get the swimmer out of the water, if it can be done safely.**
- **If the distressed swimmer is close enough, use a reaching assist to help him or her out of the water.**
- **Perform a reaching assist simply by extending your arm or any object to the victim. If you are already in the water, hold onto something secure and extend your free hand or one of your legs to the victim.**
- **If any object is available, use it to extend your reach, such as a foam noodle, kickboard, shirt, belt, stick or towel.**
- **Community pools, recreational areas and many hotel and motel pools have reaching equipment, such as a reaching pole or shepherd's crook, near the water.**

Activity:

- Lead parents through the reaching assist without equipment and the reaching assist with equipment. You should demonstrate the steps yourself and then let the parents try (if they are able to do so while keeping the children safe.)
  - Reaching Assist with Equipment
    1. Brace yourself on the pool deck, pier surface or shoreline.
    2. Extend the object to the victim.
    3. When the victim grasps the object, slowly and carefully pull him or her to safety. Keep your body low, and lean back to avoid being pulled into the water.
  - Reaching Assist without Equipment
    1. Brace yourself on the pool deck, pier surface or shoreline.
    2. Reach with your arm and grasp the victim.
    3. Pull the victim to safety.

Reach or Throw, Don't Go

Tell participants:

- **If you see that someone needs help, call an adult and/or the lifeguard.**
- **If no adult or lifeguard is present or capable to help and the victim is close enough, without going into the water yourself, use a reaching assist to help him or her out of the water.**
- **Perform a reaching assist simply by extending your reach to the victim.**
- **If any object is available, use it to extend your reach, such as a foam noodle, kickboard, shirt, belt, stick or towel.**
- **Community pools, recreational areas and many hotel and motel pools have reaching equipment, such as a reaching pole or shepherd's crook, near the water.**
- **If you cannot help quickly, call or have someone else call 9-1-1 or the local emergency number.**

Activity:

- Lead children through the reaching assist with equipment and the reaching assist without equipment that the children can handle. You should demonstrate the steps yourself and then let the children try.
  - Reaching Assist with Equipment
    1. Brace yourself on the pool deck, pier surface or shoreline.
    2. Extend the object to the victim.
    3. When the victim grasps the object, slowly and carefully pull him or her to safety. Keep your body low, and lean back to avoid being pulled into the water.
  - Reaching Assist without Equipment
    1. Brace yourself on the pool deck, pier surface or shoreline.
    2. Reach with your arm and grasp the victim.
    3. Pull the victim to safety.

Add for Learn-to-Swim Levels 4–6:

Lead participants through the throwing assist.

- Demonstrate the steps yourself then have participants practice.
  - Brace yourself on the pool deck to ensure you cannot be pulled into or fall into the water.
  - Hold the coil of line in the open palm of the nonthrowing hand and grasp the side of the ring buoy with the throwing hand.
  - Step on the nonthrowing end of the line.
  - Hold the buoy vertically, step back with the leg on the throwing side, swing the buoy backwards and then forwards for an underhand toss. Let go of the coiled line and keep your foot on the end.
  - Aim the throw so that the ring buoy lands just behind the person's shoulder. Tell the person to grab the buoy.
  - After the person has a firm grasp on the ring buoy or line, drop any remaining coil and pull him or her to safety. Keep the body low and lean back to avoid being pulled into the water.
  - Slowly pull the person to safety by reaching out and grasping the line with the thumb inward. Pull the line in to the side with that hand while reaching out with the other hand. Continue the alternate pulling and reaching action until the person is at the side or is able to stand in shallow water.

Safety at the Beach and at the Waterpark

Tell participants:

- Whether it is a community pool, lakefront beach or a waterpark, only allow children to swim in clean, supervised and designated aquatic environments.
- Many of the same basic water safety rules for pools apply to beaches, waterparks and other designated aquatic environments, but these environments also require some additional considerations.
- Even when a lifeguard is present, swimming at a designated swimming area that is part of a natural body of water requires more caution. In an ocean, river, lake or other natural body of water, swimmers may encounter potentially dangerous conditions, such as aquatic life or inclement weather, which do not exist in a pool. It is important to recognize that in many of these swimming areas, conditions can change from hour to hour.
- If you are at a natural body of water, make sure you know about the water environment so you can avoid any potential hazards, such as cold water, deep and shallow areas, currents, depth changes, obstructions and the locations of entry and exit points.
- Due to the exciting environment of a waterpark, it is easy for children to forget the rules and run up stairs and between attractions. Be sure to remind children not to run.
- Many waterpark attractions have special rules; read and follow all posted rules.
- Young children or inexperienced swimmers should wear a U.S. Coast Guard-approved life jacket whenever they are in, on or around water, although some waterparks may prohibit the use of life jackets on some attractions.
- As is true whenever children are in, on or around water, make sure a responsible individual maintains constant supervision.

Wave, Tide or Ride, Follow the Guide

Tell participants:

- Waterparks are great places to swim and play.
- A waterpark is a lot different than a pool. Some waterpark attractions have big waves and others have currents. The water at the bottom of a slide can be deep and have a current as well. You have to know what to expect before you get in the water.
- Whenever you are at a waterpark, follow these guidelines:
  - Follow all posted rules. Be sure to ask the waterpark staff if you are unsure about any rules or procedures.
  - Remember that water depth and procedures change between attractions.
  - Get into the correct position before starting down a waterslide–face-up and feetfirst. On speed slides, cross the legs to help prevent injuries.
  - Shower before entering a waterpark attraction and do not go in the water if you have diarrhea.

Water Toys and Their Limitations

Tell participants:

- It is important to know the difference between a toy and a lifesaving device.
- Inflatables, such as water wings, swim rings and other flotation devices, are not substitutes for U.S. Coast Guard-approved life jackets. Some of the materials used in many of these devices deteriorate in the sun and through contact with rough pool surfaces, resulting in leaks.
- These devices enable swimmers to go beyond their ability and may lead to a drowning situation, if the device fails or they fall off.
- Never use a flotation device or a U.S. Coast Guard-approved life jacket as a substitute for close supervision.
- Also follow this advice:
  - Inspect your child's toys to make sure they are safe and working properly.
  - Read the manufacturer's instructions and make sure that children follow the instructions.
  - Be sure that children do not play with toys that have parts or strings in which they can become entangled.
  - Use common sense. If a toy seems unsafe, it probably is unsafe.
  - Make sure that children play with toys that are age appropriate.

Staying Safe Around Aquatic Environments

Tell participants:

- Playing in, on and around the water can be a lot of fun, but it also can be dangerous. There are special rules to follow whenever you are near water.
- Only swim in areas where swimming is allowed and only when a lifeguard or grown-up is watching you. A grown-up should know where you are and what you are doing at all times.
- Every swimming area has rules; be sure to follow all the rules. If you do not know the rules, ask your parents or the lifeguards to explain them to you.
- Always ask permission before going anywhere near water. If your home has a pool or there is one near by, stay away unless you have permission and a grown-up is with you. Stay away from any other source of water like a pond, a fountain or even a bucket of water.
- Stay within an arm's reach of the grown-up who is watching you. If you are playing with an inflatable toy, you still need to stay by a grown-up. If you fall off or the toy loses air, you could get into trouble.
- Pool decks are for walking only, no running or other horseplay. They are very slippery and you could fall.
- Only go in the water after a grown-up has given you permission.
- Make sure that you go to the bathroom before entering the pool and ask to go to the bathroom whenever necessary.

Recognizing the Lifeguards

Tell participants:

- It is the lifeguards' job to watch all of the swimmers in and around the water.
- If the lifeguards see someone who is hurt or who is in trouble (drowning), they will help.
- You can tell who the lifeguards are by looking for the people wearing uniforms and holding rescue equipment (rescue tube).
- Only swim in areas where the lifeguard can see you. If you can see the lifeguard, then the lifeguard can see you.
- If you are having trouble or if you see something you think is dangerous, let a lifeguard know.
- Do not try to play with or talk to lifeguards when they are on duty.

Swim with a Buddy in a Supervised Area

Tell participants:

- No matter how old you are or how strong of a swimmer you are, always swim with a buddy in a supervised area.
- Even if you are at a pool where there is a lifeguard or at a waterpark, never swim alone.
- A buddy is a person, like a friend or a brother or sister who can get help if you get in trouble.
- Make sure that you and your buddy can both see each other at all times.
- Stay close enough to hear one another at all times.
- Never leave the swimming area without your buddy.
- Remember; always ask for permission before you go near any source of water and only swim if a lifeguard or an adult is watching.

Add for Learn-to-Swim Level 6:

Tell participants:

- Many people enjoy swimming in natural bodies of water, including lakes, rivers and oceans.
- Such environments can be safe when under the supervision of a lifeguard or designated as a swimming area by the proper authorities.
- However, if these elements are not in place, always assume that these areas are too dangerous for swimming.

INSTRUCTOR'S NOTE

The Water Safety Handbook *and* ***Chapter 2*** *in* Swimming and Water Safety *contains additional information on these topics. Consider making these resources available for participants.*

- The water in rivers, streams and creeks is constantly flowing downstream.
- Take great care around these currents, which are often unpredictable and fast moving.

- Currents can abruptly change in direction and intensity due to changes below the surface.
- The current may not be visible on the water surface even though it may be strong below the surface.
- Because the water is moving, anyone caught in a current may have a difficult time getting to shore, be carried downstream or get caught between the force of the water and an immovable object. Anyone accidentally caught in a current should–
  - Roll onto his or her back and float downstream feetfirst.
  - Back paddle with the arms and try to steer away from the main current.
- Once out of the main current, the goal is to swim or wade directly toward shore. Because of force of the current, this will result in a slightly downstream path.
- Lakes and ponds are common features of many communities. Because lake and pond water is murky–
  - It may be difficult to see below the surface. In such murky conditions, it may be hard to notice a distressed or submerged swimmer.
  - It may be difficult to determine the depth of the water or safety of the bottom surface.
  - The bottom of lakes and ponds often contain hidden hazards, such as rocks, plants or weeds, sunken logs or broken glass that can cause serious injury and/or entrapment.
  - Conditions in these bodies of water change constantly.
- Ocean waves and currents are always a safety concern. Even at beaches with lifeguards, wave activity can be dangerous.
- Do not swim at ocean beaches that are not protected by lifeguards or in areas not designated for swimming.
- Be aware of the various actions of the waves and currents and how to remain safe in the ocean.
- Breaking waves are tremendously powerful and capable of moving large objects and can knock anyone down.
- Differences in bottom conditions and wave height create changes in how waves break. In some situations, the weight of the wave and power of the crashing water can hold a person underwater.
- Breaking waves near rocky shores are especially dangerous. Slippery conditions nearby can make it easy to fall into the water.

Recognizing an Emergency

Tell participants:

- Anyone who falls into water and cannot get back to shore or the side of the pool is in trouble and needs help. Tell the lifeguard or a grown-up right away.
- Never try to go into the water and help someone who is in trouble. They could grab onto you and pull you in the water.
- Sometimes a person who is in trouble cannot call for help, which is why you should tell the lifeguard or a grown-up right away if you think someone is in trouble.
- A person who is face down and has not moved or is on the bottom of the pool and not moving is in trouble and needs help. Tell the lifeguard or a grown-up right away.

Look Before You Leap

Tell participants:

- Swimming in a safe place is very important. That is why you should only swim in areas where swimming is allowed and only when a lifeguard or grown-up is watching you.
- Check with a lifeguard to see if it is okay to jump in the water. If it is allowed, make sure that you can see what is in front of you before you enter the water.
- When you are ready to go in, stand at the edge and curl your toes over the edge. Do not run and jump or dive. Do not jump or dive on people or objects.
- If you cannot see the bottom and you are not sure what is under the water, do not jump or dive in.

Add for Learn-to-Swim Levels 1 and 2:

- Jumping into a pool can be great fun, but it is important to make sure the area is safe before you jump in.
- It might be hard to see the bottom at some swimming areas, like a beach at the ocean or a lake.
- Only jump into the water at a pool, beach, waterpark or other designated swimming area and only do so if it is allowed. Because you cannot tell what is on the bottom or how deep it is, never jump in the water unless you are at a designated swimming area. There may be rocks, weeds, sunken logs, broken glass or other things that could cause injuries.

Add for Learn-to-Swim Levels 3 and 4:

- Whenever entering the water in a headfirst position, follow safety rules at all times–never make exceptions. This includes when learning from different positions, including the sitting, kneeling, compact and stride positions.
- Be sure the water is at least 9-feet deep and ensure that nothing is in the way in the water every time you enter the water in a headfirst position.
- Never dive or enter the water headfirst into an above-ground pool, the shallow end of any in-ground pool or at a beach.
- Never dive or enter the water headfirst into cloudy or murky water.
- Check the shape of the pool bottom to be sure it is safe for diving or headfirst entry.
- Pools at homes, motels and hotels might not be safe for diving or headfirst entry.
- When performing a headfirst entry from a deck, the area of entry should be free of obstructions (such as lane lines, kickboards and other pool users) for at least 4 feet on both sides and a clear, safe distance in front.

Add for Learn-to-Swim Levels 5 and 6:

- The following are rules to keep in mind when diving from a diving board:
  - Use the ladder to climb onto the diving board or tower. Climbing in any other way is not allowed.
  - Only one bounce on the end of the diving board, unless supervised by a coach.
  - Only one person on the diving board at a time.
  - No other swimmers in the diving area when the diving board or tower is in use.
  - Only dive or jump straight out from the end of the diving board or tower.
  - Look before diving or jumping to make sure no one is in the diving area.

- Swim to the closest ladder or wall immediately after diving or jumping.
- The hands must enter the water first when performing a headfirst entry.
- The tower can be used only with supervision from a qualified instructor or coach.
- Learn or practice twisting, somersaulting, inward and reverse dives only under the close supervision of a qualified instructor or coach.

Think So You Don't Sink

Tell participants:

- **Even if you are following the rules, accidents and emergencies can still happen.**
- **If you are swimming and an emergency happens, remember to think so you don't sink. If you get tired and cannot make it to safety, do not panic and think about what you can do.**
- **You can lean back or roll over on your back and float.**
- **That way you can rest. You can stay on your back and wait for help or start swimming when you have had enough rest.**

Add this Activity to Learn-to-Swim Level 2:

Activity:

- Have participants swim 3 body lengths on the front then roll to the back and then float on the back for 5 seconds.
- Have participants swim 3 body lengths on the front then roll to the back and float on the front for at least 5 seconds. Then, have participants roll to the front and swim another 3 body lengths then roll to the back and float on the back again. Have participants repeat these steps until they make it back to the side of the pool.
- Have participants swim 5 body lengths on the front then roll to the back and float on the back for 10 seconds. Then, have participants swim back to the side on the back.

Add for Learn-to-Swim Level 3:

- **You can bob toward safety if you get into water that is a little over your head.**
- **Take a breath and submerge to the bottom then push off toward shallow water or the side of pool. Just keep bobbing until you reach safety.**

Add for Learn-to-Swim Level 4:

- **You can use survival swimming to reach safety.**
- **That way you can save energy. You can stay on your front and make forward progress.**

Add for Learn-to-Swim Levels 5 and 6:

- **For many people, waves are part of what makes swimming in an ocean fun. Even at designated beaches, waves can be dangerous.**
- **When the waves crash onto shore, they create currents. One type of current created by wave action is a rip current, sometimes referred to as a *rip tide*.**
- **Rip currents often form narrow strips of choppy water that moves differently than the water on the other sides of it. Rip currents move very fast, and if you get caught in one, they can take you away from shore.**

- **If you get caught in a rip current it is important to remember to think, so you don't sink.**
- **You can try to swim parallel to shore until you are free of the current. You can also just let the current take you away from shore.**
- **Rip currents weaken a little way from shore, once the current weakens you can begin swimming back to shore. If you are too exhausted to swim to shore, signal a lifeguard by calling and waving for help.**

Add for Learn-to-Swim Level 6:

Activity: *Self-Rescue Techniques While Clothed*

Have participants inflate a shirt or jacket by blowing air into it in the following way:

1. Tuck the shirt in or tie the shirttail ends together around the waist.
2. Unbutton the collar button, take a deep breath, bend your head forward into the water, pull the shirt or jacket up to the face and blow into the shirt.
3. Keep the front of the shirt or jacket underwater and hold the collar closed.
4. Repeat the steps above to reinflate the shirt or jacket if necessary.

Have participants inflate a shirt or jacket by striking air into it in the following way:

1. Fasten the buttons or close the zipper up to the neck.
2. Hold the bottom of the shirt or jacket out with one hand, keeping it just under the surface of the water and lean back slightly.
3. From above the surface of the water, strike the water with the free hand (palm down) and drive it down, pulling air to a point below the shirttail or jacket.
4. Keep the front of the shirt or jacket underwater and hold the collar and the shirttail closed.
5. Repeat the steps above to reinflate the shirt or jacket if necessary.

Have participants inflate pants in the following way:

1. Take a deep breath, lean forward into the water and reach down and remove your shoes.
2. Loosen the waistband and belt.
3. Take another deep breath, lean forward and reach down and take off your pants one leg at a time without turning them inside out. Bring your face out of the water and take a breath whenever necessary.
4. Once the pants are off, tie both legs together at the cuff or tie a knot in each leg as close as possible to the bottom of the leg then zip or button the pants to the waist.
5. Hold the back of the waistband underwater with one hand and, while keeping the pants on the surface of the water, strike the water to force air into to the open waistband with the other hand. Strike the water with the palm of the free hand and follow through into the open waistband below the surface. You can also inflate the pants by submerging them and then blowing air into the open waistband below the surface of the water.
6. Once the pants are inflated, gather the waistband together with your hands or by tightening the belt and then slip your head in between the pant legs where they are tied together. If the pant legs are tied separately, reach one arm over and between the two pant legs for support.
7. Repeat the steps above to reinflate the pants if necessary.

Think Twice Before Going Near Cold Water or Ice

Tell participants:

- **Cold water is dangerous, even if you do not intend to go in. Whenever you are in, on or around cold water, wear a life jacket.**
- **People cannot swim as far in cold water as they can swim in warm water. That is why it is very important to decide if you should try to swim toward safety or float in place and wait for help in a cold-water emergency.**
- **Anyone who falls into cold water should try to swim to safety if it is possible to do so with only a few strokes.**
- **Strokes with an underwater arm recovery can help maintain heat when swimming in cold water.**
- **Floating in place until help arrives is the best way to survive a cold-water emergency in open water or when a great distance from the shore.**
- **If you fall into the water while wearing a life jacket–**
  - **Keep your face and head above the surface. In the event of a boating accident, try to climb onto the capsized boat to get more of your body out of the water.**
  - **Keep all your clothes on, especially a hat. Even wet clothes help retain body heat.**
  - **If you are caught in a current, float on your back and go downstream feetfirst until your breathing slows. Breathe normally for a few seconds before starting to swim to shore. Immediately try to swim to safety if the current is carrying you toward danger.**
  - **Stay still and let the life jacket provide support until help arrives if you are not in immediate danger but far from shore. To stay warmer, assume the heat escape lessening posture (HELP).**
- **Treading water chills the body faster than staying still with a life jacket on in the water. In cold water, tread water only if it is necessary.**
- **If you are going to be by water and it is cold outside, be sure to wear rain gear, a warm hat and layers of clothes or insulated clothes to help you stay warm in an emergency.**

Heat Escape Lessening Posture (HELP)

Activity:

- Have participants get in the water wearing life jackets and–
  1. Draw the knees up to the chest.
  2. Keep the face forward and out of the water.
  3. Hold the upper arms at the sides and fold the lower arms against or across the chest.

INSTRUCTOR'S NOTE

Tell participants that they should not use the HELP position in swift river currents or whitewater.

Huddle Position

Activity:

- Have participants get in the water wearing life jackets and–
  - With two people, put their arms around each other so that their chests are together.
  - With three or more people, put their arms over each other's shoulders so that the sides of their chests are together.

Learn About Boating Before You Go Floating

Tell participants:

- **Recreational boating includes, but is not limited to, the following types of vessels:**
  - **Open motorboats**
  - **Personal watercraft**
  - **Cabin motorboats**
  - **Sailboats**
  - **Canoes/kayaks**
- **Boating can be a safe and enjoyable pastime, but it is important to know the dangers. Follow the basic rules of boating safety:**
  - **Always wear a life jacket.**
  - **Take a boating safety course.**
  - **Do not drink alcohol.**
  - **Make a float plan and have a way to communicate.**
  - **Pay attention to weather forecasts and understand local water conditions and hazards. If you are caught in severe weather–**
    - **Slow down and maintain enough speed to steadily move forward and still stay in control.**
    - **Make sure everyone onboard is adequately dressed and wearing a properly fitted life jacket.**
    - **Turn on the boat's navigation lights.**
    - **Head into waves at a 45-degree angle. Personal watercraft should approach waves at a 90-degree angle.**
    - **Have passengers sit low in the boat or on the floor of the boat near the centerline.**
    - **Anchor the boat, if necessary and it is safe to do so.**
- **To prevent yourself or passengers from falling overboard–**
  - **Do not lean out. Keep centered in the boat with your center of gravity low in the boat. Always keep your shoulders between the gunwales on small boats.**
  - **Do not move about the boat. If you must move, maintain three points of contact.**
  - **Sit only where appropriate. Do not sit on the gunwales, bow, seatbacks or any other area not designed for seating.**
  - **Do not stand up in small boats.**

- Riders should wear U.S. Coast Guard-approved life jackets when using personal watercraft.
- A personal watercraft is a type of boat. Know the local laws and regulations. Some states have special laws governing the use of personal watercraft that address operation, life jacket use, registration and licensing requirements, education, environmental restrictions, required safety equipment and minimum ages.
- Operate personal watercraft with courtesy and common sense. Pay attention to surroundings and follow the traffic pattern of the waterway. Obey no-wake and speed zones.
- Use extreme caution around swimmers, surfers and other boaters. Run personal watercraft at a slow speed until the craft is away from shore, swimming areas and docks. Avoid passing close to other boats and jumping wakes. This behavior is dangerous and often illegal.
- Ride with a buddy. Always ride in groups of two or three. You never know when an emergency might occur.
- Riders should always attach the engine cut off lanyard to themselves and the personal watercraft during operation.
- Develop a float plan before leaving the shore.

CHAPTER

5

Customizing for Your Audience

Many aquatic facilities organize their Learn-to-Swim classes by large age categories, such as preschool age, school age, adults and senior citizens. Many significant differences among these age groups affect how they learn and how you should teach them to swim. Some of the differences you may notice include participants' ability to communicate, their developmental readiness, their desire for achieving personal goals and their physical capabilities. As a Water Safety instructor, you should have a basic understanding of these differences and know how to customize lessons for your audience. This chapter describes some major characteristics of large age categories. It also offers techniques for maximizing the aquatic experience at each level. Chapter 6 discusses individual characteristics, such as disabilities and other health conditions, to help you further customize lessons to meet the needs of each participant.

Characteristics of Child Learners

Infants and children from birth through age 5 undergo rapid and remarkable changes. Their ability to think, feel, move and play all change dramatically. Because children's behavior greatly differs from adult behaviors, it is crucial that instructors and parents understand some of the complex learning and developmental changes that take place at various stages.

Factors that Influence Learning in Young Children

Many factors that influence young children's learning are largely under the control of their parents and instructors in the home or teaching environment. During swim lessons children usually learn more effectively when the focus is on their learning rather than on the teacher's instruction. Instruction is just one way to improve learning in young children. Some other methods include setting a goal, practice, observing and imitating others and providing feedback and motivation. You can read more about these other methods in **Chapter 2**. You may need to make some adjustments when using these methods to help children. For example, to help children accomplish goals, you may need to use the same principles that work for adults but may also need to provide physical assistance and reinforce their movements. Keep in mind that–

- Infants and young children may respond better to demonstrations or physical manipulation than to verbal descriptions and commands.
- Preschool age children may understand fairly complex verbal instructions.
- Crying or fearful children may require soothing yet playful verbal descriptions that attract their interest.
- Shy children may respond better to a more enthusiastic and challenging presentation of skills along with regular praise of what they do correctly.

Practice

Practice is essential for improving both the learning and performance of motor skills. (See **Chapter 2** for more information about different types of practice.) In general, however, infants and young children seem to benefit most from distributed practice in which they get frequent rest periods throughout the practice schedule. A distributed practice schedule has three important advantages:

- It prevents fatigue.
- It allows more time for assimilation of learning.
- It maintains motivation and interest in the learning activity.

Feedback, Reinforcement and Motivation

Feedback should be used as positive reinforcement to motivate and encourage the repetition of desired responses. Positive feedback is crucial to motivating children to try their best. If children are not motivated to try their best, they may experience little improvement in swimming or other motor skills. (See **Chapter 2** for more on the importance of feedback and how you can provide the precise and positive feedback to motivate people learning to swim.)

Stages of Learning

As people's experience and skill levels shift, they may differ in how skills are learned. One reason for the learning difference relates to stages of learning (see **Table 5-1**). Understanding these stages can help you work more effectively with beginners and help you tailor your goal setting, practice and feedback to your participants. (See **Chapter 2** for more information on these stages.)

Children's Development

Developmental changes in movement, thinking, feeling and play are especially pronounced and rapid during childhood. Children's age, heredity, experiences and other individual differences influence these developmental changes. With most young children, learning progressions clearly relate to increasing basic skills and developing motor function. Older children can do more things and do them in a more coordinated fashion than younger children can. Therefore, learning progressions for older children relate to improving basic skills and learning advanced skills.

It is important that both you and participants' parents understand the general sequence of changes as the child develops. When you

Table 5-1. Characteristics of Motor Learning Stages

Stage	Movement Characteristics	Providing Assistance
Early	Slow, awkward, step-by-step, rigid	Getting the idea of movement using demonstrations, physical manipulation, verbal descriptions and commands.
Intermediate	Variable, faster, flexible and consistent	Encouraging practice and repetition and providing feedback and motivation.
Late	Consistent, rapid, accurate, flexible	Refining skills by continuing to practice while providing feedback and motivation.

understand this, you can anticipate the next task or motor pattern that children should reach and can tailor your classes accordingly.

Early Childhood Development

Young children change in many different ways from birth through age 5. **Tables 5-2 through 5-5** list some examples of the changes that occur during this time. **Table 5-6** summarizes some of the changes as they relate to swimming and the water. The changes are arranged into areas of movement, thinking, feeling and perceiving, and play and socialization. They are also subdivided into three age groupings.

INSTRUCTOR'S NOTE

The age groupings are only guidelines. Red Cross Parent and Child Aquatics and Preschool Aquatics participants are placed based on experience, maturity and ability in addition to age. For the sake of simplicity, we use age groupings with the understanding that the previously mentioned factors may alter the developmental time lines of children.

The Fearful Child

One challenge you may face with young children is dealing with their fears about water. Infants and young children may be reluctant to approach the pool, work with instructors or any adults other than their parents, go into the water itself or submerge. When you understand children's learning and development processes, you will be better able to teach fearful children.

Some fears are related to children's developmental level. At about 8 months, infants start to express stranger or separation anxiety. As they recognize the difference between parents and others, they may react by crying, screaming or becoming withdrawn. Some infants react with anger often marked by the stiffening of their bodies. One way to reduce their fears is to be consistent in your lessons. If you start, end and organize each lesson the same way, children become familiar with the routine and may participate more easily.

After about 2 years of age, children's emerging memory and active imagination may trigger fears of the unknown. Their fantasies can be distressing to both adults and children. They may imagine monsters, scary animals and other fearful images. Sometimes their fears make them less willing to try new skills.

Other fears come from experience. For instance, children who previously had unpleasant experiences with water react with fear when adults encourage them to enter the water or try new aquatic skills. Coach parents to be patient and not to force their children to progress before they are ready. Remind parents that their children's moods often reflect the parents' feelings. If parents maintain a positive attitude toward swimming, their children will likely be less afraid.

There are ways to reduce or eliminate fearful behavior in young children. First, you can reduce the impact of learned fears by anticipating possible problems. Be aware of those developmental stages when children are most likely to have fears. If you anticipate infant separation anxiety, avoid activities that separate infants from parents. You can reduce

Table 5-2. Changes in Young Children's Movement from 6 Months to 5 Years

6 to 18 months	
Characteristic	**Change**
Posture and equilibrium reactions	Gradually appear (4 to 8 months)
Voluntary motor milestones	Acquired during first 2 years
Fine motor skills	Sequentially able to reach, grasp and splash water with the hands.
Toy play	Use of toys that make noise to grab attention of infant in the pool or something bright. Infant is working on grasping skills but can hold on to some objects.
18 months to 3 years	
Characteristic	**Change**
Voluntary gross motor skills	Begins with awkward rudimentary skills; gradually acquires smoothness; pattern improves (blow bubbles, kick, walk, bounce, gallop and run)
Fine motor skills	Grasps items, such as a railing to maintain balance, a fork for feeding or a crayon for scribbling
Fundamental motor skills	Rudimentary, awkward and unskilled; little control over force or accuracy (throw, strike and kick)
Toy play	Can use several toys to throw, squirt water or hold. Pretend play with objects. For example, a kickboard is a spaceship.
4 and 5 years	
Characteristic	**Change**
Locomotor skills	Improved walking, running, jumping and galloping; rudimentary acquisition of hopping, skipping and sliding
Fundamental motor skills	Gains competence in throwing, striking and kicking; begins catching, swinging and climbing
Fine motor skills	Improved drawing and coloring (pictures may be recognizable); use of scissors; can begin writing letters of the alphabet
Toy play	Can use both small and large toys in movement; lies on a boogie board with or without support and kicks, rides three-wheel bike and may begin riding a two-wheeler after 5th year

other problems related to fears by presenting progressions carefully, giving enough time in the lesson to play and paying attention to the individual needs of the children in your courses.

To reduce the impact of learned fears, plan carefully and give a lot of positive reinforcement. Children enjoy the water more when they can take their time, experience success, practice repeatedly and receive praise for their efforts. For example, when young children go underwater for the first time, they need to understand what is going to happen, be ready and agree to go underwater.

Table 5-3. Changes in Young Children's Thinking from 6 Months to 5 Years

6 to 18 months	
Characteristic	**Change**
Memory	Gradually shifts from immediate events to some recent occurrences
Knowledge	Slowly links events together without action; begins to know that one event causes another event
Object permanence	Existence of object out of sight is understood; stranger/separation anxiety results
Language	Sounds and babbles evolve into monosyllabic words; knows own name and names of family and common objects
18 months to 3 years	
Characteristic	**Change**
Memory	Greatly expanded beyond infancy; begins to remember past; dependent upon oral memory
Knowledge	Can understand abstract concepts; very egocentric (self-centered) and animistic (thinks all things are alive)
Language	Can say more than 20 words by the 2nd birthday, but often is hard to understand; loves repetition of stories; uses sequences of two words or more
4 and 5 years	
Characteristic	**Change**
Memory	Sense of past and future, but not as established as adult memory; remembers through oral means; can recite jingles and rhymes
Knowledge	Intelligence becomes more active and relevant; fears and worries are based on primitive thinking patterns
Language	Vocabulary includes all commonly used words, sentences and questions; can count; begins letter and word recognition; very practical and literal; may not understand humor or sarcasm

Table 5-4. Changes in Young Children's Feelings and Perceptions

6 to 18 months	
Characteristic	**Change**
Feelings	Global, general and without specific stimulus
Perceptions	Linked directly to action and stimulus
Expressions	Crying, smiling and laughing
18 months to 3 years	
Characteristic	**Change**
Feelings	Rudimentary, but linked to increasing language skills; uses movement to communicate some feelings
Perceptions	Limited discrimination of stimuli; poor selective attention; inability to integrate different senses. Some integration of senses by age 3: touch with smell; touch with hearing.
Expressions	Somewhat empathetic as young as 2 years. Embarrassment which comes on between 2 and 3 years.
4 and 5 years	
Characteristic	**Change**
Feelings	Egocentric, but sometimes empathetic with others; can express some feelings vocally
Perceptions	Increasing discrimination of stimuli levels; limited ability to attend to adult-specified tasks; begins to associate relationships across senses
Expressions	Highly empathetic by 4 or 5. Will attend to adult instructions and many become frustrated, some embarrassed when they cannot live up to standards. This is why it is important for instructors to set acceptable standards for their level.

Table 5-5. Changes in Young Children's Play and Socialization

6 to 18 months	
Characteristic	**Change**
Socialization	Limited to smiling and vocalizing through the first 6 months
Play	Manipulates objects; solitary exploration; singing can be soothing. By 12 months enjoys social feedback and reciprocal play although patience on adults end is needed. May explore on own for a bit then return back to the adult.
About 18 months to 3 years	
Characteristic	**Change**
Socialization	Increases with language development; self-centered behavior slowly declines during this period.
Play	Solitary or parallel with children; difficulty in sharing toys with others; simple drills can be enjoyable; "games" in strict sense are beyond ability; enjoys songs and rhymes.
About 4 and 5 years	
Characteristic	**Change**
Socialization	Very good at socialization most of time and enjoys being with other kids more than with adults. Learning basic rules for interacting with adults and peers.
Play	Major avenue for learning and development; small groups often use dramatic and expressive play; can use simple games effectively for learning and practice.

Table 5-6. Changes in Young Children's Swimming Behavior

6 to 18 months	
Characteristic	**Change**
Breath control	Reflective holding of the breath; changes to imitation of breathing and submerging
Leg actions	Few spontaneous leg movements, such as both legs pushing straight back; "pedaling" or "running" actions
Arm actions	Arms held passively at side or overhead; splashing or weak paddling movements
Body position	Body position in the water is controlled by adults as children learn to walk on land; children hold the body vertically in the water; some children can learn to enjoy floating on the back with support
18 months to 3 years	
Characteristic	**Change**
Breath control	Active submersion, bubble blowing possible; dislikes adult to control submersion
Leg actions	Pedaling action shifts to rudimentary alternating flutter kick or frog kick action
Arm actions	Paddling movements become alternating pulling actions with most of the force downward and mostly ineffective
Body position	Maintains largely vertical positioning in the water; often dislikes the back position
4 and 5 years	
Characteristic	**Change**
Breath control	Experienced preschooler can submerge for several seconds, swim under water and open eyes to recover objects; most children still raise head straight up out of the water to get a breath; inexperienced preschooler shows fear and dislike for water in the face
Leg actions	Alternating kick varies in effectiveness depending upon the body position; individual differences between rudimentary flutter and frog kick actions are often evident
Arm actions	Increased proficiency of arm actions is evident; experienced children are capable of using over-water recovery for rudimentary crawl, but the beginner stroke may be preferred
Body position	Experienced children can use semi-horizontal position when head is submerged; when head is raised, the position is more vertical

Common Health and Safety Concerns for Infants and Young Children

There is some controversy about the health and safety of young children who participate in aquatic programs. Some concerns, summarized in the following text, have not been completely resolved.

Risk of Drowning

Statistics show that children under 6 are at greater risk for death by drowning than any other age group except young adults. Most fatal and nonfatal drowning incidents of young children occur in unsupervised water situations involving bathtubs, residential pools and hot tubs. Nevertheless, as an instructor, you must give careful attention to the safety of all participants during lessons. Remind parents that even if their children have learned to move in the water, they still lack the judgment to recognize dangerous situations and the strength, stamina and ability to swim to safety if necessary. The American Academy of Pediatrics (AAP) has issued the following policy statement:

> "Infant and toddler aquatic programs provide an opportunity to introduce young children to the joy and risks of being in or around water. Generally, children are not developmentally ready for swimming lessons until after their 4th birthday. Aquatic programs for infants and toddlers have not been shown to decrease the risk of drowning, and parents should not feel secure that their child is safe in water or safe from drowning after participating in such programs. Young children should receive constant, close supervision by an adult while in and around water."

Disease and Infection

Infections usually spread among children by direct contact and not through the water, particularly when correct pool water chemistry is maintained. However, pediatricians recommend that children with fevers, rashes, diarrhea or any symptoms of an infection not participate in an aquatics program.

Aquatic programs for infants and young children should have a clear, well-defined policy restricting participation by children or parents with any contagious illnesses. It is also essential to maintain proper water chemistry to prevent the spread of infections.

Make sure that every child in diapers uses specifically designed swim diapers or snug-fitting rubber pants that are less likely to leak. Because these are not leak-proof, parents must change their children's diapers often.

Ear Infections

Ear infections are a very common reason that children are restricted from participating in aquatic programs. Exposure to water has been blamed for causing ear infections. Some pediatricians keep children with tympanotomy tubes in the ear canal from participating in swim programs. Because medical professionals disagree about swimming, ear infections and tympanotomy tubes, advise parents to follow their health care providers' instructions.

The following are suggestions to limit the risk of ear infections:

- Avoid swimming in polluted water.
- Use earplugs when swimming, showering or bathing.
- Dry the outer ear thoroughly after exposure to moisture from swimming, showering or bathing with a clean towel.
- Drain the water from the ears after swimming or bathing. The following are suggestions that may work to drain the water from the ear. Try any or all of the following methods:
  - Tilt the head down to each side and gently push and pull the tragus (the gristle-like flesh near the opening of the ear).
  - Tilt the head down to each side and gently pull the ear lobe.
  - Tilt the head to each side and dry with a towel.
- Never insert a finger or any sharp or hard object into the ear.
- Dry the ears using a hair dryer set on the lowest heat and speed. Be sure to hold it several inches from the ear.

Other Water-Related Conditions

As discussed in **Chapter 1**, recreational water illnesses (RWIs) are caused by certain germs including *Cryptosporidium*, *Giardia*, *E. coli* 0157: H7 and *Shigella.* As a reminder, the Centers for Disease Control and Prevention (CDC) offers the following six "P-L-E-As" that promote healthy swimming.

For All Swimmers

- Please do not swim when you have diarrhea; this is especially important for children in diapers. Germs can be spread into the water and make other people sick.
- Please do not swallow the pool water. In fact, it is best to avoid having water in the mouth.
- Please practice good hygiene. Take a shower before swimming, and wash your hands after using the toilets or changing diapers.

For Parents with Young Children

- Please take children on bathroom breaks and check diapers often. Waiting to hear "I have to go" may mean that it is too late.
- Please change diapers in a bathroom on a changing table if one is available and not at poolside. Germs can spread to surfaces and objects in and around the pool and spread illness.
- Please wash your child thoroughly (especially the buttocks) with soap and water before entering the pool. Invisible amounts of fecal matter on their bottoms can end up in the pool.

Another condition, called *hyponatremia* (better known as "water intoxication"), occurs when there is an imbalance of electrolytes, especially sodium, in the bloodstream. Hyponatremia is extremely rare. To help prevent this condition, do not let young children submerge more than 3 times in a lesson during the initial learning phase.

Characteristics of School-Age Children

Two youths of a similar age can be developing normally yet appear and act distinctly different. This diversity can be present among participants in areas such as–

- Thinking abilities, which may range from thinking in concrete terms to abstract terms.
- Relationships with adults, which may be important to some but not to others.
- Communication, decision making and critical thinking, which differ from person to person.
- Peer relationships, in which some participants find peer approval extremely important, while others have no difficulty making individual decisions.

School-age children need structure and discipline. Many school-age children are accustomed to organized activities, such as attending school or participating in scouting groups or athletics. Swim lessons represent another organized activity. They expect you to be prepared and knowledgeable. In classes for this age group, you may have to take steps to maintain discipline. See **Table 5-7** for more information on the learning characteristics of school-aged children.

The first step toward maintaining discipline in class is to be thoroughly prepared as described in **Chapter 3**. Let participants know the goals at the start of each class, and let participants and their parents and/or caregivers know the swim lesson rules. Make sure the participants understand the terms that you are using and exactly what you are asking of them. Also remember that this age group likes activity. You must keep them active and working toward their goals. Plan all parts of the lesson to prevent unoccupied time. If there is down time between participants' turns to practice, big gaps between activities or a wait while you organize equipment, you could be setting yourself up for discipline problems.

Tips for Working with Youth

- Avoid assumptions based on appearance. You cannot always tell what young people are like by the way they look (e.g., dress, earrings or overall appearance).
- Respect their opinions. Participants may come from families that handle discipline or communication in a different manner than the way you teach the course. Show respect by maintaining an atmosphere of openness to differing points of view.
- Stay current with the youth culture. When you stay informed of the ever-changing interests, styles and even music preferences of youth, you are choosing to be more connected to their world and will have more avenues for communication with them.

Table 5-7. Learner Characteristics of School-Age Children

	Ages 6 to 9	Ages 8 to 13	Ages 12 to 17
Common characteristics	Highly imaginative; activity is important; enjoys working, learning and accomplishing; follows the instructor as a leader	Interested in developing skills and looking good	Peer group opinion becomes more important than the opinion of the instructor; self-conscious in front of peers; wants to "look good"
Social characteristics	Individualistic but becoming interested in the group	Interested in the group; best pals with only a few friends; challenges authority	Develops more personal relationships; enjoys more independence and responsibility
Physical characteristics	Coordination of large muscle activity (such as kicking) improving; endurance improving; primarily short-distance swimmers	Growth spurts may affect coordination and endurance; generally good coordination; better endurance	Interested in perfecting each skill; growth spurts may be continuing; excellent coordination and endurance
Learning emphasis	Ready to follow instructions to learn basic skills; reacts well to praise	Can think more abstractly, but can benefit more from concrete examples; greater attention span	Adult-like thinking
Teaching water safety knowledge	Needs rules but requires reasons and examples	Requires reasons and is interested in exceptions	Challenges authority and must see that rules are reasonable

- Model effective decision-making skills. Whenever possible, ask participants questions that guide them in decision making and problem solving. Avoid giving answers without providing the participants an opportunity to think critically.
- Be insightful when organizing skill practices. Organize the skills and activities based on the personalities in the group to minimize concerns individuals may have about working with one another. For example, you may want to pair males with males and females with females.

Characteristics of Adult Learners

Adults differ from children in their attitudes, values, aspirations, anxieties, self-regard, responsibilities and physical characteristics. Adults also differ from children in their approach to learning. When children learn a skill, they are also learning *how* to learn the skill. Adults already have many strategies they rely on when learning new things. They also have more extensive learning histories–a combination of experiences, what they have already learned and how they acquire information and skills. Thus, even though children and teens may learn motor skills faster because of their physical abilities, adults bring more developed learning strategies to what they want to accomplish.

Not only are older participants different from younger participants, they frequently are very different from each other. They enter the learning environment with an incredible diversity of interests, needs, concerns and habits. The

Table 5-8. Learner Characteristics of Adults

	Young Adults (18 to 25)	Adult (21 to 50)	Older Adult (50 plus)
Common characteristics	Well motivated and independent; usually prepared to take a leadership role	Often motivated by watching their children learn to swim or desire for fitness	Often interested in fitness; many have deep-rooted fears
Social characteristics	Self-reliant; adjust to groups readily	Initially may be uncomfortable joining a group; often participate for social benefits	Often self-conscious; may be motivated by social interest
Physical characteristics	Growth tapers off; endurance increases quickly; coordination depends on previous experiences, resulting in great variety of abilities and speeds of learning	Endurance is slowly declining; flexibility is also declining, but can be developed through practice	Endurance diminishing; coordination and flexibility may be deteriorating; reaction time may be slow
Learning emphasis	Motivation and attention span tend to be high	May be hesitant to attempt new skills and strokes; prefers private feedback	Requires a great deal of reassurance and positive feedback
Teaching water safety knowledge	Adventurous and active; emphasize precautions in water sports	For swimmers who are parents, emphasize the safety of children and preventing injuries	Common sense approach is appropriate

characteristics of adult participants can influence what and how you teach them. Moreover, because adults often differ from one another in strength, size, functional ability and general health and fitness, teaching them is an exciting challenge. See **Table 5-8** for more information on the learning characteristics of adults.

Chronological Age Versus Physiological Age

Aging is truly a highly individualized process. We mark our progress through life by counting the years we have lived (chronological age). However, chronological aging by itself rarely produces a dramatic physical change. Most of what affects the ability to learn results from changes in physiological function. The extent of these changes depends greatly on how active people stay throughout adulthood. Current research suggests that as much as 50 percent of the physiological changes attributed to the aging process actually result from inactive lifestyles. Therefore, do not consider chronological age the primary factor when you assess the needs of adults. Instead, classify both younger and older adults in terms of physiological function.

Physiological Changes

Physiological changes occur in everyone at various rates over time. Yet, all sorts of people can be successful at aquatics. The following section discusses some considerations when customizing your course.

Most people reach physical maturity by age 18, when many physiological functions (strength, physical ability, motor control and reaction time) are near peak levels. By age 30, physical capacity has begun a slow decline that continues through the rest of life.

During most of adulthood, the percentage of body fat gradually increases and lean body mass decreases. This is especially true for inactive adults. Although adults in middle years may be quite buoyant because of their percentages of body fat, people of advanced age tend to be thinner and less buoyant. Bone density changes may also affect buoyancy and balance in the water.

Overall strength declines little throughout life, especially in muscle groups used in daily activities. This means that most people have enough strength for aquatic skills. However, inactive individuals of advanced age may have much less strength, especially in the legs.

One of the greatest changes that occurs with aging is the gradual loss of flexibility, especially in joints and muscle groups not used regularly. The saying "move it or lose it" has great meaning as we grow older. Stretching and range of motion are important for maintaining flexibility as we age.

Most adults are affected to some extent by gradual degeneration in the joints. Healthy, active adults at any age also may have injuries from sports or other causes that affect their mobility. Joint pain and swelling may limit their ability to swim certain strokes. For example, the breaststroke kick might not be possible or desirable for people who have undergone knee surgery.

The older people are the more likely it is that other changes will influence their ability to learn new tasks. For example, how people process information changes with age. The speed of the nerve impulse as it conducts a message from one point to another slows. This affects the speed of problem solving and may lead to slower response or reaction times. As a result, people may need more time to plan and start actions. Past learning also affects the way adults process information. Their learning history may make it easier or more difficult to master new skills. Sometimes adults take longer to start an action because they are trying to take advantage of past learning.

Hearing, vision and how the body regulates temperature may also become impaired as people age. Older adults are particularly susceptible to heat- and cold-related illnesses. They may chill easily in average water temperatures and be unable to generate enough heat to stay comfortable through a lesson. Instructors need to make sure programs for older adults are safe.

As they age, adults become more vulnerable to heart disease, osteoarthritis, diabetes, hypertension and osteoporosis. These diseases may seem to speed up the aging process, limit functional ability and reduce the ability to learn motor skills. It is often hard to draw a line between the normal aging process and chronic degenerative diseases. You should not keep adults from a program just because of their age. Instead, their age should only remind you to make a few adjustments, if needed, in your teaching approach.

Psychological Changes

Healthy, active adults have psychological needs just as younger people do. They need security, recognition, a sense of accomplishment and a feeling of belonging. However, self-confidence and perceptions of self may change through the aging process. Some adults want to succeed in new tasks but lack the self-confidence to do so. They learn best in a positive environment that promotes trust and a sense of accomplishment and self-worth.

Reasons for Participating in Aquatics

A very important benefit when working with adults is that nearly all adults take swim lessons because they want to take them. Some adults may not have had the time or opportunity to learn to swim when they were younger. They may want to learn or improve aquatic skills or perhaps to join their children in aquatic activities. Many adults pursue new activities to help stay functionally independent as long as possible; regular physical activity has quite an impact on lifestyle. Some adults may have strong skills but desire certification. Others may want to improve their skills to compete.

Adults also frequently learn to swim to improve their health and fitness. Those with an injury may need swimming for rehabilitation. Their health care providers or physical therapists may have advised them to take up aquatics as therapy. In your planning, consider fitness-swimming alternatives, such as lap swimming.

Another reason adults give for joining an aquatics program is enjoyment and social contact. Swimming attracts adults because it feels good, helps improve their body and allows them to meet new friends and have social contact during the day. Thus, you should include recreational aquatic games in your program.

Finally, do not overlook the importance of safety. Adults who own a home pool and plan aquatic activities with family and friends, especially children at home, want safety information to help them prevent aquatic emergencies and respond to them, if necessary. Make information on water safety an integral part of each program.

For many reasons, adults are determined to learn. Understanding their motivation helps you establish objectives and plan lessons that address their needs.

Techniques to Enhance Adult Learning

Planning with the Participants

The most significant benefit to working with adults is that you can enlist them in the planning process. All adults like to pursue their own interests and make their own decisions about what they want to learn or accomplish. By discussing motivations, interests and needs with participants, you can make lesson time as productive as possible. By involving them in this way, you plan *with* them rather than *for* them. You also help ensure their motivation to follow the mutually designed plan of learning.

The critical step in planning is to consider the participants' experiences, current goals and physical characteristics. Ask them the following questions:

- "What are you comfortable with in the water and what would you like help with?" (past experience and current goals.)
    - Participants with experience may want just a few "coaching" tips to help them improve. In this case, it is easy to analyze their existing skills and work toward more efficient movement.
    - Some participants may have no experience in the water. They may have the same fears and anxieties as youngsters who are learning to swim. In this case, you may want to reorder your usual progressions to teach strokes, such as the sidestroke, elementary backstroke or a modified breaststroke that let participants keep their face out of the water. Then slowly work on submersion and rhythmic breathing.
- "What do you want to know?" (current goals)
    - When working with adults, you should not have rigid plans or expectations. Consider participants' individual needs and desires. Stroke choices should reflect participants' wants. If adults want to learn only the front crawl, plan an approach that sets up gradual successes and builds endurance along the way. Encourage participants to try all strokes to learn which they do best, but remember that personal desires provide a very strong motivation to learn. Never underestimate the ability of older adults to learn skills and accomplish goals. You need to be flexible in your lesson plans regardless of the course you are teaching. Plan to introduce all the required skills, but customize them to meet the goals of your participants as well as the objectives of the course.
- "Do you have any limitations that I should know?"
    - Because physical abilities change with age, physical characteristics and abilities may determine how successful participants are in learning certain strokes. One objective of your planning should be to help the participants adapt strokes to their physical capabilities.

Individualizing the Approach

The ideal teaching situation for any activity would be a group that is completely alike in interests, previous experience, physical characteristics, goals and motivation to learn. Unfortunately, limitations in programming, facility or staff may not permit scheduling separate classes for such homogeneous groups.

As mentioned earlier, adults greatly differ from each other. These differences may require an individualized plan. Within a single group, you may have as many lesson plans as you have participants. In some cases, all participants may attempt the same skills, but your expectations may differ from person to person. Although this may seem a complicated task, certain learning characteristics of adults actually help this style of teaching. For example–

- Adults want a lot of freedom. They like to practice on their own with minimal interruption. A combination of a carefully chosen, logical teaching progression and a less formal approach in organizing and conducting the class can make learning as self-directed as possible.
- Adults, regardless of age, can learn new motor skills. However, the pace at which they learn may be faster or slower than that of young people. Some adults can use their past learning strategies to master new skills quickly. Others need more trials for mastery and may improve slower than younger learners. Allow participants the freedom to try new skills their own ways first.
- Most adults in an aquatics class are eager to be there. However, some may have serious doubts about their abilities to succeed at new tasks. Some may also suffer from perfectionism and be impatient to learn. They have a tendency to worry more about the accuracy of a skill than the speed with which it is performed. While young participants may work quickly through drills just to finish, adults may take time to do each part correctly. Be sure to allow adequate practice time and give positive and corrective feedback.

Adapting Teaching Methods

The Fundamentals of Instructor Training course introduced you to several teaching methods for motor skills. The following guidelines may help you adapt these methods for adult participants:

- The whole approach works well with skills that are simple and for which individuals can transfer past experience (i.e., relate existing skills to the new learning). Even though adults may need to practice skills in parts, they are interested in the end result, not the parts. They often want to try the whole thing on their own first.
- The part-whole approach may be better when you want to focus the attention of adults on key concepts rather than whole skills. It gives an opportunity for many small successes. In the early stages of learning, people often forget some information. Therefore, learning key concepts in parts might help with learning strokes. Then combine the parts to make the whole.
- The progressive-part approach limits some of the forgetting that can occur in the part-whole approach. It provides more trials from the start to finish of the skill and may minimize the frustration of trying to master a more complex stroke or activity.

Other teaching methods are reviewed in the *Fundamentals of Instructor Training Participant's Manual* and in **Chapter 2** of this manual. Remember always to give positive, corrective feedback to your adult participants. People can improve a skill only with feedback. Adults need to know how they are doing and are just as affected by feedback in the learning process as younger participants.

Adjusting the Learning Environment for Adults

Physical Elements

Several aspects of the learning environment may affect adults more than children or teens. Adults are more sensitive to the whole physical environment. Children might not notice a dirty locker room or swimming area because of their excitement to get into the water. Adults, on the other hand, may consider dirty locker rooms, cold showers or cluttered swimming areas reasons to stop coming to lessons. Check locker rooms, the deck and swimming areas regularly for cleanliness and safe conditions. Refer any potential problems to the facility management.

Another issue is safe access to the water. People with physical disabilities cannot participate in a program if they cannot safely enter and exit the buildings or swimming area. You should know how to use any access equipment in your facility.

Water temperature may also be a key issue for your program. According to the Aquatic Exercise Association, a comfortable water temperature for swim classes is between 83° to 86° F (28.3° to 30° C). Most participants are relatively comfortable learning in water between these temperatures. This temperature is only slightly above that enjoyed by serious lap swimmers. Infants, toddlers, preschoolers and older adults may have difficulty regulating their body temperatures and may chill easily. If you cannot adjust the water temperature to accommodate them, you may have to adjust to shorter lessons to reduce discomfort. You may want to let participants wear additional clothes for warmth as long as they do not interfere with learning skills. For instance, a sweatshirt is too heavy in the water, but a rash guard shirt or a T-shirt might help. A swim cap may also minimize heat loss. You should be alert to the early signs of hypothermia and take precautions to prevent it.

Ideally, air temperature should be at least 2° F warmer than the water temperature. Because this cannot be regulated in outdoor settings, encourage students to bring additional towels that can be used as needed.

Most school-age children, teens and adults who can stay focused on a task will not be bothered by minor distractions. Infants, toddlers, preschoolers and older adults may be more easily distracted by background noise. Be alert to any distractions in the setting. Follow these guidelines:

- Minimize interfering background noise. This may be especially critical for participants who are hearing impaired.
- Move the class to a quiet area or offer the course at a time when there is less activity in the facility.
- Minimize interruptions in the learning process by being prepared and having equipment ready before the lesson starts.

Psychological Elements

Everyone needs a relaxing, positive environment for learning. The following are ways to prepare the psychological environment to give the best opportunities for success:

- Start practice sessions with a good review that includes some previously learned skills, especially those related to skills in that day's lesson.
- In each lesson, include skills that participants can do reasonably well.
- Remind participants that few people do everything right the first time.
- Take breaks from hard and/or complex skills before participants become frustrated.
- Create an atmosphere in which participants feel safe and confident that they will not be ridiculed and are not afraid to make mistakes.
- Provide privacy as much as possible. Even curious onlookers can seem threatening.
- Be enthusiastic and reward each step toward success. Let participants feel your desire to be there, or you will lose the interest and respect of the group.
- Develop trust by always being prepared. Organize the course effectively so participants do not feel that their time is being wasted. Prepare participants for each new experience.
- Provide a social atmosphere.
- Give participants more time to respond to the information you give them. You can help them be more successful by slowing down the presentation of skills and giving them enough freedom to work at their own pace.
- Say just enough to communicate what is needed. Most adults can understand the principles involved in aquatic skills. You should know and be able to explain basic physical principles and how they apply to swimming. Do not over-explain a skill.
- Use vocabulary appropriate for the age and capabilities of the participants in the courses.

Working with Apprehensive Beginners

A certain amount of fear and anxiety is normal among people who cannot swim or who swim poorly. However, intense fear can keep them from learning a new skill or make them reluctant to try it.

Adults in your courses may have avoided learning to swim for some reason. The most common reasons are fear of drowning, anxiety about not being able to breathe and fear of not being able to get back to safety. Adult beginners may fear deep water or being forced to do something that they perceive to be personally threatening. They may simply be afraid of failure and humiliation. Fear may be strongest when people have seen or experienced a nonfatal submersion (near drowning). Apprehensive beginners often exhibit the avoidance behaviors listed in **Chapter 2** in this manual.

Issues of Scheduling

A program orientation helps prepare participants. This is critical for apprehensive beginners. Orientation reduces the fear and anxiety of the first lesson because adults know where to go, how to find the swimming area, what the first-day procedures are and whom to ask for help. Even if they are rushing from a job, they may arrive for the lesson more relaxed because they are familiar with the setup of the program.

Schedule the orientation at a separate time and publicize it well. Make the orientation meaningful. If possible, invite former or current participants to share success stories. The orientation may seem like a waste of time unless you treat it as an important part of the program.

A typical lesson lasts about 45 minutes, but this depends on the needs and comfort of the participants. Since older adults need warmer water, you may need to shorten their lessons if the water is too cold for them. For some adults, there never seems to be enough practice time. You might schedule a course before a recreational swim time so that participants can stay as long as they want after the lessons.

Another scheduling issue is the number of lessons per course. It may be useful to have an "ongoing" program and let adults participate until their needs are satisfied. If a course offers a set number of lessons, individual planning and goal setting in the first lesson should help you determine whether certification is the goal of any participants. Determine how much material is covered in each lesson to meet group and individual needs. You may find yourself with many goals within the same course. Capitalize on the learning characteristics of adults to help you plan your lessons.

You may find that participants respond better when you give more individual practice time and less guided group practice. When incorporating more individualized practice in your lesson plan, follow these guidelines:

- Plan for frequent rest periods throughout the lesson.
- Watch for signs of fatigue.
- Assess whether participants are making more, rather than fewer, mistakes in a new skill.
- Look to see if participants have difficulty with a skill that had been mastered. (This means that it is time to rest or change to a different skill.)
- Include skills that need additional work for mastery when you plan for individualized practice. People often practice only those skills at which they are successful.
- Prepare more material than you think you will need for each lesson. This helps you to accommodate differences in the speed of learning.

CHAPTER

6

Customizing for Individuals with Disabilities and Other Health Conditions

As a Water Safety instructor, you will often teach people without disabilities or other health conditions. Some individual characteristics such as physical size, age, stages of intellectual and physical development, and other health conditions may require adaptations or special accommodations to make learning to swim in conventional swim classes successful. Participants in the American Red Cross Water Safety Instructor course learn to recognize and respect all people regardless of their individual characteristics, disabilities, or health conditions and integrate them into conventional swim lessons whenever possible.

People with individual characteristics that affect their ability to swim may have a wide range of disabilities or other health conditions. The causes of those disabilities or other health conditions can vary. It is important that you do not treat participants with disabilities and other health conditions differently because that may limit their ability to learn to swim. It is equally important to be respectful and sensitive to their physical needs and emotional state. Many people, who developed their health condition between birth and 5 years of age, adapted early in life. Others, such as those experiencing a traumatic injury, may still be adjusting to their health condition. In addition, people are living longer, and those over age 65 are more active than ever before. With age comes an increase in chronic diseases and degenerative conditions. Coping with these problems can be difficult at times for people who may have been strong and active when they were younger.

This chapter describes specific etiquette and teaching methods for helping participants with disabilities reach their goals.

Teaching Swimming to Individuals with Disabilities

Mainstreaming, integration, inclusion–these words all mean the same thing: people with disabilities joining in activities or programs originally designed for people without disabilities. Although there will always be a need for a variety of programming opportunities, you should try to include people with disabilities and other health conditions in conventional programming whenever possible. Few people with disabilities want or need adapted aquatics courses.

Mainstreaming people with disabilities into your courses can be tremendously rewarding. Much of the reward comes from watching participants succeed. As the instructor, you are helping them learn and improve skills, maintain and increase their physical fitness, achieve success and recognition and experience self-actualization in a regular aquatic environment.

As a Water Safety instructor, you are obligated to treat all people with respect and consideration. For this reason, mainstreaming is usually possible and not difficult. Sometimes it simply requires a bit more patience. Oftentimes, the additional consideration comes in the form of allowing a little more time to catch on, experimenting or building the strength and kinesthetic awareness to perform swimming skills with proficiency. If you are interested in working with individuals with severe disabilities, you should seek more training. Some American Red Cross chapters, colleges, universities and professional organizations offer specialized training.

Assessing Participant Needs

As a Water Safety instructor, you are trained to teach aquatics to the general population, including people with disabilities and other health conditions to the greatest extent possible. A typical swim class might include participants with disabilities and other health conditions. Having a particular medical condition does not automatically mean a person has an impairment and having an impairment does not automatically mean they have a disability. People who have an impairment or a disability usually do not need special or separate aquatics programming. For example, a disability that limits a person's range of motion on land might not limit their function in the water. Do not make general assumptions about abilities or limitations. Present the task or skill and let participants decide what they can do or are willing to try.

In **Chapter 3**, you learned to use the mnemonic COLA–which stands for Check, Organize, Lead and Assess–to help evaluate the abilities of your participants early in a session. If you are aware that people have certain limitations, it is often a good idea to conduct the evaluation prior to the start of the session. In addition, you should respectfully speak with them or their parents about their abilities and limitations. Some participants may not be able to learn and perform swimming skills as traditionally described. Participants may need certain skills broken down into easier, more manageable steps. Those who are not able to learn and perform particular swimming skills should be taught skills that they are able to perform.

Pay attention to the needs of all your participants as you plan your classes. Often you only have to modify your teaching a little to include people with disabilities or other health conditions in your courses. Specific recommendations for such changes are discussed later in this chapter. Sometimes you will need to modify the program itself. Whether you adjust your teaching strategy or change the program, you must be aware of the needs of participants with disabilities or other health conditions and the many ways you can meet those needs.

Sometimes, participants, caregivers or parents may not initially share information about disabilities and other health conditions. You may have situations arise during lessons that cause you to suspect that participants have impairments. After consulting with your swim program coordinator, ask participants, caregivers or parents questions to help you understand the impairment to gain information on the best way to teach participants. Tact and discretion are needed to discuss health issues that may affect your ability and/or methods to teach participants. It is essential that you have all the information so you can create the best learning environment for participants who require special consideration.

Obesity

Overweight children are more likely to face social problems and develop serious health problems, such as high blood pressure, high cholesterol, type 2 diabetes, sleep apnea and asthma. In addition, overweight children and teens are more likely to become obese adults. Some people who are obese may not be very mobile or may have decreased range of motion. However, there are some advantages to being in the aquatic environment, including–

- They can use their natural buoyancy to remain upright or in a horizontal swimming position with less effort.
- When effort is applied, they can get a good workout.
- They are able to exercise without putting weight on the knee and ankle joints.

For people who are obese, you can improve how they learn aquatic skills in these ways:

- Do not make assumptions about their abilities or limitations.
- Stage and divide practice into smaller chunks with frequent breaks.

Aging

Reduced function occurs with aging. Older adults who want to learn to swim or who want to resume swimming again after not exercising for some time should talk to a health care provider before starting any exercise program. They should also begin gradually. Some conditions that are common with older adults are cardiovascular disease, arthritis and osteoporosis, asthma, cancer, diabetes and obesity. If any of these conditions are associated with older adults, you can improve learning aquatic skills in these ways:

- At first, teach the strokes without modifying them unless there are obvious limitations, such as no or very limited use of a joint.
- Stage and divide practice into smaller chunks with frequent breaks.
- Concentrate on what participants are able to do well and improve swimming abilities using their strengths.
- Communicate directly with older adults, not through a third person.
- Offer assistance, and if accepted, ask how you can best assist them.
- Avoid using the word "elderly" because it implies frailty and helplessness, which most older adults are not.
- Be patient.

More information about teaching older adults can be found in **Chapter 5**.

Needs of Individuals with Disabilities

People with disabilities and other health conditions have many of the same needs as everyone else. Being sensitive to the emotional state of individuals with disabilities and other health conditions is an important characteristic for Water Safety instructors to possess. Two factors affect their emotional states:

- Adjustment to the conditions. With most impairments present from birth, most people are already adjusted to their health condition before entering an aquatics program. For impairments that are acquired, consider how long people have had to adjust to the health condition and learn to function with existing capabilities. People with progressively deteriorating health conditions need to have accepted their ever-decreasing ability. You must accept people as individuals. This will help you both adjust. Because situations and people may change, you should continue to monitor participants' progress and adjust your teaching as needed.

- Instructor-participant relationship. Participants must be confident that you can provide emotional security as well as teach skills. All participants, regardless of their abilities, need to feel your interest in them as individuals. A consistent, patient approach helps build their confidence.

Canine Companions

Service animals are animals that are individually trained to protect and perform tasks for people with disabilities, such as guiding people who are blind, alerting people who are deaf, pulling wheelchairs, alerting and protecting people who are having a seizure or performing other special tasks. Service animals are working animals, not pets. The most commonly recognized assistance animals are dogs. Canine companions are very comfortable in aquatic environments. Many of them are "water dogs" who love to swim. However, when they are on duty, they will remain alert, out of the water and ready to assist their master as needed.

Under the Americans with Disabilities Act (ADA), businesses and organizations that serve the public must allow people with disabilities to bring their service animals into areas of a facility where customers are normally allowed to go. Usually, owners of canine companions will explain their needs and etiquette for their dog. The following are some important things to consider when canine companions are present:

- Be sure that participants and their dogs have a clear line of sight to each other.
- Do not let people pet, tease, feed or play with canine companions.
- Offer fresh water for the canine companions.
- Educate lifeguards and other participants of the presence and etiquette of canine companions in the facility.
- Post a sign or signs in your facility that clearly states that canine companions are welcome.

The Range of Programming

Aquatics programming ranges from participation in regular programming (mainstreaming) to one-on-one instruction in an adapted aquatics program given by a Water Safety instructor trained to teach individuals with disabilities and other health conditions. Between these extremes are many possibilities. However, with creativity and patience these possibilities are endless.

Instructor Responsibility

Many factors affect how successful individuals with disabilities will be. When people with disabilities are interested in your course, you have a responsibility to provide the best possible opportunity. Meeting this responsibility may require you to–

- Give basic information about the course.
- Fairly and consistently screen all potential course participants. Any age or height requirements should apply to all participants. If there are no restrictions for applicants, individuals with disabilities should be able to register.
- Discuss the course with the individuals to determine suitability.
- Get more information from individuals to ensure their safety. This might include asking about–
  - The specific nature of the disability.
  - Whether individuals have seizures.
  - Whether individuals can control their bladder.
  - Whether individuals are on medication.
- Have people with disabilities get a health care provider's statement indicating fitness level to participate in your course.
- Give a preassessment or a trial lesson if they have medical approval, but you are unsure whether participation in your course is appropriate.
- Consider all aspects of programming and individual characteristics before making any final decision. These might include–
  - Class size.
  - Instructor-to-participant ratio.
  - Size and depth of swimming area.
  - Air and water temperature.

- The individuals' abilities to control behavior.
- The individuals' previous aquatic experience.
- The individuals' degree of independent functioning.
- The individuals' cognitive level.
- Peer group sensitivity.
- Instructor training, background and experience.

- Give individuals specific reasons if admission to a particular course must be denied.
- Help them find a different suitable aquatics course, if needed.

Designing the Right Course

There is no one method that is always successful for teaching aquatic activities to individuals with disabilities. However, you can use many different methods, either alone or in combination. Keep in mind the following when working with anyone in aquatics courses:

- Individualize the approach. Regardless of the grouping of participants or the approach you use, your teaching should focus on individual performance standards and should emphasize individual abilities. When working with individuals with disabilities, remember that the best programs strive to meet individual needs and focus on all participants' abilities, not disabilities. The following section, "Techniques to Enhance Learning," presents ways to vary your teaching strategies and the etiquette to use when individualizing the approach. You can use these techniques with individuals with disabilities in any setting. It can also be helpful to have assistance, such as a co-instructor or aide, if possible when teaching.
- Modify the course. In addition to teaching techniques, you sometimes have to modify the course itself. A section later in this chapter discusses how to change the course to accommodate participants' needs. When modifications are made to a course, inform the local Red Cross chapter and indicate it on the *Course Record.*
- Adjust expectations. Although most individuals with disabilities are successful in regular courses, some are not. Sometimes you can predict lack of success; sometimes you cannot. When adaptations to mainstream programming fail to meet the needs of some people, these individuals should be referred to an adapted aquatics program. The final section of this chapter, "Exploring Alternative Programs," discusses related issues and resources.

Techniques to Enhance Learning

No two participants with the same type of disability function in exactly the same way. For one person, a medical condition may result in severely restricted functioning. For another, the same condition may only be a minor disability. Your sensitivity to individual differences is the key to helping each person succeed.

- Do not hesitate to ask participants, in an appropriate, considerate manner, about their capabilities, range of movements and ways of doing motor tasks. A questionnaire is available on the instructor's CD-ROM.
- Give participants with disabilities as much independence as possible. Do not do anything for them that they are able to do themselves. Often, giving people just a few extra minutes lets them do the skill independently.
- Make sure you and any assisting staff read any medical clearance sheets for participants, if they exist, noting any special conditions.

Factors That Affect Learning

The environment, participants and the instructor all interact in the learning process. Some factors influence learning for all participants in varying degrees. Other influences can positively or negatively affect learning for participants with disabilities. These include–

- The degree to which the disability inhibits intellectual, motor and/or sensory function.
- The degree to which participants have adjusted to the impairment and/or disability.
- The instructor's acceptance of participants.
- The group's acceptance of participants.
- The participants' prior experience.
- The accessibility of the environment.
- Environmental conditions, such as air and water temperature.

See **Chapters 3 and 5** for more on factors that affect learning.

Sensory Impairment

Individuals with impairment of one sense do most of their sensory learning through the other senses. Try to capitalize on the senses that give the most information to them. Sensitivity and respect should be understood and practiced at all times. Examples are given in the following sections.

Hearing Impairment

Hearing impairments vary greatly from mild hearing loss to profound deafness. Hard-of-hearing describes people who have moderate hearing loss. Mild hearing loss describes people who are able to hear everything except high-pitched sounds. Moderate hearing loss describes people who are unable to hear a conversation without amplification. Deaf describes people with severe to profound hearing loss who are unable to hear anything but the loudest sounds, such as a jet airplane.

Participants with hearing impairments usually have no observable characteristics. They may seem inattentive if they cannot hear. Be careful not to mistake a hearing impairment for lower intelligence. Participants with hearing impairments usually have normal intelligence and are very attentive, especially visually. Most participants with hearing impairments are quite successful in a regular aquatics program.

For participants with hearing impairments, you can improve learning in the following ways:

- Give most information visually. Increase demonstrations.
- Decrease auditory distractions.
- Be sure the area is well lit.
- Minimize glare on the water by repositioning the participants or blocking the direct light.
- Make sure you have participants' attention before you speak. You may need to lightly tap them on the shoulder or wave to get their attention.
- Do not talk through a third person. Speak directly to participants.
- Give clear verbal directions. Do not exaggerate your speech. Be sure participants can see your face when you are speaking because many individuals with a hearing impairment are good at speech-reading (lip-reading).
- If necessary, keep items to write on nearby to help communicate.
- Move participants' arms or legs in the desired pattern of movement. This enhances kinesthetic awareness.
- Use pictures and charts as tools to reinforce a demonstration.
- Supplement your instruction with the *American Red Cross Swimming and Diving Skills DVD*, which is subtitled.
- Be aware that people with a hearing impairment who wear a hearing aid are at a disadvantage in swimming programs because they cannot wear hearing aids in the water.
- Remember that wearing a swimming cap and/or putting the head under water decreases hearing ability.
- If possible, learn to sign the terms used in aquatics instruction so you can communicate with participants who use signing. Consistent, clear gestures also aid communication.
- Use an interpreter, if possible, in classes that require extensive verbal information, such as lessons on safety.
- Be aware that people with a hearing impairment may also have impaired speech. Impaired speech does not indicate impairment in intelligence.
- Listen attentively to participants who can speak (most individuals with hearing impairments can) so you learn to understand their speech. Do not pretend to understand when you do not.
- Advise participants to keep their eyes open to stay in visual contact with their environment.

SAFETY NOTE

Establish clear gestures for emergencies. Use printed material to add to verbal information, particularly information related to safety.

Some individuals may need additional specialized instruction. Those with a profound hearing impairment combined with severe communication impairment may need instruction from someone skilled in signing. Individuals with multiple disabilities, such as someone who is deaf and blind, may need specialized one-on-one instruction.

Visual Impairment

Visual impairment is used to describe people with varying degrees of vision loss, including low vision, legally blind and totally blind. The definition of low vision varies, but generally, low vision is defined as an uncorrectable visual impairment that interferes with people's ability to perform everyday activities. Those who are visually impaired often have some functionally useful sight, such as having 20/70 acuity in the best eye with correction. (A person with 20/70 acuity could see at 20 feet what a sighted person sees at 70 feet.) Legally blind describes people whose central visual acuity does not exceed 20/200 in the better eye with corrective lenses as measured on a Snellen vision chart or whose visual field is less than an angle of 20 degrees. (A person with 20/200 vision could see at 20 feet what a sighted person sees at 200 feet.) Total blindness is the complete absence of vision and light perception.

Most individuals with visual impairment are quite successful in a regular aquatics program. For participants with visual impairment, you can improve learning in the following ways:

- Give most information through hearing and touch.
- Decrease auditory distractions.
- Be sure the area is well lit.
- Minimize glare on the water.
- Give clear verbal directions.
- Speak in a normal voice. It is not necessary to shout.
- Look directly at participants when speaking. Try not to turn away while speaking as they may become disoriented.
- Before the lessons, give participants an orientation to the environment.
- Let participants be directly in front when you demonstrate skills. Having them touch your body while you demonstrate the skill can also aid understanding.
- Let participants keep their faces out of the water in early learning phases so they can hear better and ask questions.
- Let participants wear goggles if pool water is an eye irritant or if they wish to wear contact lenses.
- Let participants wear plastic glasses with plastic lenses in the water. (Do not allow them to dive or jump into the water with glasses on.)

You many need to guide some participants to a particular area of the facility. Following are some tips when guiding participants:

- If participants ask for a guide, touch their forearm with the back of your hand; this lets them know where you are. They should grip your arm just above the elbow. Some participants may simply need to maintain some sort of contact with you (e.g., touching elbows or forearms) rather than gripping you. Let them determine what type of contact works best for them.
- When assisting participants with a guide dog, offer your left arm. The dog is still "on-duty" and acts as a safety officer.
- When assisting participants with a cane, offer your arm on their free side.

SAFETY NOTE

Keep decks free of clutter. Be sure safety lines are in place. Have an auditory signal that means "stop, stand still, danger." Have large-print copies of facility rules available.

Some individuals with impaired vision may need specialized instruction. Those with severe visual impairments may need instruction from someone skilled in mobility training. People with multiple disabilities may need specialized one-on-one instruction.

Tactile Impairment

If individuals have a tactile impairment, its severity will determine how successful they will be in a regular aquatics program. An example of tactile sensitivity represents an inability to discriminate and infer the form of stimuli applied to the skin. You can improve learning in these ways:

- Control the temperature of shower water. People who do not have feeling in the arms or legs can burn themselves without knowing it.
- Check legs and feet for abrasions. Plan activities to avoid scraping feet and legs. People might not feel pain, and as a result, not notice abrasions and cuts.
- If participants lack feeling in their legs, let them wear socks or water shoes to minimize abrasions from underwater surfaces.

Developmental Disabilities

Developmental disabilities encompass conditions affecting intellectual, social and physical development. Developmental disabilities refer to conditions that appear before a person reaches 22 years of age. These disabilities may be a result of trauma to the brain or nervous system affecting development. They can also be caused by childhood accidents, exposure to toxins and poisons and certain conditions that develop during pregnancy or infancy. Often, the exact cause is unknown. Individuals with developmental disabilities usually have difficulties with language, social skills, mobility, learning and/or cognitive ability. Some conditions resulting from developmental disabilities are intellectual disabilities, epilepsy and autism. Some developmental disabilities result from genetic disorders, such as Down, Williams or Fragile X syndromes. A wide range of learning disabilities, such as dyslexia and attention deficit hyperactivity disorder (ADHD), are among conditions resulting from developmental disabilities. Other conditions resulting from developmental disabilities are emotional and behavioral disabilities, such as anxiety disorders, severe depression, bipolar disorder, conduct disorder and schizophrenia. See more detailed information on many of these developmental disabilities in Chapter 9 of *Swimming and Water Safety*.

More staff may be needed to supervise the safety of participants or life jackets may need to be worn to ensure the safety of these participants.

Intellectual Disability

Participants with intellectual disabilities may be developmentally delayed and may take longer to learn new skills. Individuals with mild cognitive disability are usually successful in a regular aquatics program with little or no adaptation. Some individuals with moderate cognitive disability, such as varying degrees of intellectual disability, are successful in regular programs, but others may need a more specialized setting. Those who need ongoing assistance with daily living, who are totally dependent and who need consistent supervision are considered to have severe disabilities. These individuals require specialized programming to even enter the water and learn any skills.

For people with an intellectual disability, you can improve learning in the following ways:

- Do not assume that individuals cannot perform a specific skill or cannot participate in class. Always try to include all participants in activities.
- Be sensitive to the extra time it may take to learn information and master skills.
- Speak slowly and clearly when giving directions or instructions. Keep your sentences short.
- Address and treat adults with an intellectual disability as adults.
- Communicate directly with people with an intellectual disability, not through a third person.
- Some people with intellectual disabilities may have speech impairments. If you cannot understand participants, do not be afraid to ask them to repeat themselves.
- Use various ways to practice skills because participants may be sensitive about having to repeat practice. Variety improves learning.
- Break skills down into component parts.
- Use the progressive part and part-whole methods to teach skills. Using the whole method can be very confusing for people with intellectual disabilities.
- Never take mobility aids away from people with disabilities. Allow them to keep their aids, such as crutches, canes and walkers, close at hand.
- Offer assistance if it appears to be needed. If your offer is declined, do not insist. If your offer is accepted, ask how you can best help.

- Evaluate the safety needs of this group and ways to maximize safety through extra supervision and/or use of life jackets.

 **SAFETY NOTE**

Diving is prohibited for participants with atlantoaxial instability, *a condition of unstable vertebrae sometimes found in people with Down syndrome. Ask the participant with Down syndrome and/or the participant's parent or caretaker if atlantoaxial instability is a health condition associated with the participant. Do not permit diving without a medical release from a health care provider that states in writing that cervical X-rays confirm a normal spine.*

Epilepsy

A person who has recurring seizures has a condition known as epilepsy, also known as seizure disorder. Seizures are the result of sudden, abnormal electrical activity in the brain lasting from 30 seconds to 2 minutes. The great majority of seizures do not cause any harm. In children, epilepsy is often the result of a brain disorder, but epilepsy also occurs in adults often following a stroke, brain tumor or head injury.

Anyone with epilepsy is at a higher risk for drowning and must take care when near the water. No one should ever swim alone, but this is especially true for people with epilepsy. However, most people with epilepsy can join an aquatics program, as long as it is closely supervised. Additionally, anyone with poorly controlled seizures should wear a Type 1 personal flotation device to help support the head in the event of a seizure. If a seizure occurs while in the water, the person should not return to the water that day. A seizure that occurs in the water is an emergency and should be treated as such.

Unless a person has any other disabilities or health conditions combined with epilepsy, you can teach as you would teach people without disabilities. Be vigilant to the following safety issues when working with people with epilepsy:

- Make sure there is someone present at all times who knows what to do if a person has a seizure, such as the lifeguard or the additional presence of a parent or caretaker.
- Be aware of the characteristics of a seizure so that you can respond quickly and appropriately. Someone having a less serious seizure may suddenly stare off into space for a few seconds and then become fully alert again without muscular contractions. A more serious seizure may have the following characteristics:
  - A peculiar sensation (aura) preceding the seizure lasting a few seconds. The person may hear, see, smell or taste something peculiar or not there, may feel pain or may have a sensation that may be a warning to move to safety.
  - A sudden rigidity of the person's body, sometimes after a high-pitched cry.
  - Loss of consciousness.
  - Uncontrolled muscular movement, during which the person may lose bladder and bowel control. The person may salivate, hold his or her breath and clench the jaw. The heart rate increases.
  - After the seizure, a state of drowsiness and confusion. Then the person gradually regains consciousness and may complain of a headache.
- Inform lifeguards that participants in your class have epilepsy.
- Keep the participant from getting over-tired or too cold while in the water.
- Remind the participant to take seizure medication.
- Do not let the participant's seizure medications get wet. Several medications lose efficacy when exposed to the water.
- Some seizures can be brought on by flashing light. If this applies to anyone with epilepsy in your class, recommend that he or she wear polarized sunglasses to reduce the flicker effect of sunlight on the water and other reflective surfaces.

If participants have a seizure while in the water, help them immediately. A seizure in the water requires quick action. The person may go under water without warning or a call for help. The person who is seizing or has just had a seizure may not be breathing or may try to breathe even though underwater. Both conditions can cause life-threatening problems.

If someone has a seizure in the water, support the person to keep the head and face above the water so that he or she can breathe. Call the lifeguard for help and make sure that emergency medical services (EMS) personnel are called.

SAFETY NOTE

Participants who have seizures and who are not under medical control need close supervision, should wear a Type 1 personal flotation device and should probably swim only in an adapted program with specially trained personnel.

Autism

Autism, also called autistic spectrum disorder, is usually first diagnosed in early childhood. The exact cause of autism is unknown although the prevalence of autism is on the rise. According to Centers for Disease Control and Prevention 2007 figures, 1 out of every 150 8-year-olds in the United States has autism. Autism frequently occurs with other conditions, such as seizures, attention deficit hyperactivity disorder, sleep disorders and depression or a cognitive impairment. Individuals with autism may have difficulty with fine or gross motor skills and sensory perception.

Autism affects how a person communicates, interacts with others socially and participates in many activities. In social interactions, some individuals with autism may not make eye contact or be able to appreciate others' perspective. These social impairments may lead people with autism to make statements or interact with others in ways outside of what is considered typical social behavior. Communication impairments associated with autism often result in slower processing of information and delayed, atypical or nonexistent speech.

Many people with autism may engage in ritualized or repetitive behavior and may not adjust well to changes in routine or environment. Some people with autism react fearfully to new situations, while others have very little fear, which may lead them into dangerous situations. In an aquatics environment this means that some people with autism may need significantly more time to adjust to being around water, while others need vigilant supervision because they may be unable to fully appreciate the dangers associated with water.

It is important to recognize that autism is a spectrum of disorders. Each person with autism is unique and may have different needs for participation in aquatics. People who are lower functioning may have many more apparent needs than others who are higher functioning. Sometimes the individual needs of higher functioning people with autism are overlooked because they do not possess the social and/or communication skills to express their needs. Individuals who are very low functioning may require specialized aquatics instruction.

For people with autism, you can improve learning in the following ways:

- Maintain routines.
- Give warnings of upcoming changes in activities or schedule.
- Use visuals to give directions, if possible, and try to pair with verbal instructions.
- Verbal messages should be short and clear.
- Respect each individual's functional needs.

Learning Disability

Individuals with learning disabilities have problems that affect the brain's ability to receive, process, analyze or store information. These problems can make it difficult for participants to learn as quickly as those who do not have learning disabilities. There are many kinds of learning disabilities, such as attention deficit disorder (ADD), ADHD, dyslexia and more. Most people affected by learning disabilities have more than one type. Certain kinds of learning disabilities can interfere with participants' ability to concentrate or focus and cause their minds to wander. (Do not confuse learning disabilities with intellectual disabilities.) Information processing is the brain's ability to integrate information received through the senses and to direct motor activity. Characteristics, such as hyperactivity, distractibility and emotional instability, may interfere with participants' ability to understand, follow directions and learn motor skills.

For people with learning disabilities, you can improve learning in the following ways:

- Minimize distractions.
- Try to keep the same general format and organization for each lesson.
- Provide structure for skill learning and practice.
- Be ready to change activities frequently because participants' attention spans may be short.
- Use music and songs as tools to signal the beginning and end of a lesson and to signal a transition from one activity to another.
- Teach participants to verbalize actions before practicing skills.
- Stage and divide practice into smaller chunks with frequent breaks.
- Use inconspicuous methods, such as a physical cue, to tell participants when you feel they are tuning you out.
- Use multisensory strategies when giving directions and presenting skills.
- Emphasize common elements between skills already learned and new skills you are introducing.
- Have clear expectations for participants' behavior. Keep the rules simple and be ready to redirect participants' behaviors in positive ways. Enforce policies uniformly and consistently.

Emotional or Behavioral Disability

Individuals with an emotional or behavior disturbance may have difficulty relating to the aquatic environment. Many terms are used to describe emotional or behavioral disorders. Currently, participants with such disorders are categorized as having emotional disturbance, which is defined under the Individuals with Disabilities Education Act as–

- A condition exhibiting one or more of the following characteristics over a long period of time and to a marked degree that adversely affects a child's educational performance:
  - An inability to learn that cannot be explained by intellectual, sensory or health factors.
  - An inability to build or maintain satisfactory interpersonal relationships with peers and teachers.
  - Inappropriate types of behavior or feelings under normal circumstances.
  - A general pervasive mood of unhappiness or depression.
  - A tendency to develop physical symptoms or fears associated with personal or school problems." [Code of Federal Regulations, Title 34, Section 300.7(c)(4)(ii)]

For participants with emotional or behavior disturbances, you can improve learning in the following ways:

- Be sure you clearly state and discuss the rules.
- Be sure parents or caregivers understand the rules as well.
- Be sure participants and their parents clearly understand the consequences for inappropriate behaviors and displays of emotion.
- Consistently enforce all rules and safety procedures.
- Praise appropriate behavior.
- Plan all parts of the lesson to prevent unoccupied time.

SAFETY NOTE

Do not hesitate to use time-out procedures or to stop the class for the day if participants cannot control their behavior.

Most individuals with emotional and behavioral disabilities can be successful in regular programs. However, if they do not progress in learning aquatic skills, if their behavior jeopardizes the safety of other participants or peers or if instruction of the whole class is inhibited, they may need a more specialized adapted aquatics program.

Mobility Impairment

Mobility impairment refers to the large number of health conditions affecting people's mobility. Some of the health conditions that cause mobility impairment include amputation, paralysis, cerebral palsy and stroke. There are varying degrees of limitation caused by mobility impairments. Here are some examples:

- Motor function. Motor function refers to the brain's ability to direct both reflexive and voluntary movements. The brain and nervous system control the muscular and skeletal systems. Impairment in any of these systems can result in decreased physical capability.
- Loss of motor function. Complete loss of use of a body part can result from congenital or traumatic amputation. Prosthesis, such as an artificial limb, may be used for land activities. Often people who use prostheses can function quite well on land. However, most prostheses cannot be worn in the water. As a result, entering and exiting the water may pose some difficulties.
- Impairment of motor function. Motor function also can be temporarily impaired because of illness or trauma, a permanent but stable condition or a progressively degenerative condition, such as muscular dystrophy or amyotrophic lateral sclerosis, also called Lou Gehrig's disease. Other temporary conditions that impair motor function include recovery from orthopedic surgery, broken bones and muscle strains and sprains. For such people, aquatics can play an important part in rehabilitation.

When participants with motor impairment are in water, increased buoyancy can make mobility easier than on land. Participants with limited movement are more comfortable and more mobile in the water than anywhere else. Many disabilities are less obvious when the body is in water. People with degenerative conditions can still function in water long after motor function on land is severely diminished.

For people who have mobility impairment, you can improve learning aquatic skills in the following ways:

- Be sure participants can independently access the aquatic area.
- At first, teach the strokes without modifying them.
- Concentrate on what participants are able to do well and improve swimming abilities using their strengths.
- Emphasize stroke pull along the midline of the body to decrease body roll for participants with balance problems.
- Avoid activities that involve dragging body parts on the deck or underwater surfaces. Abrasion injuries can result.
- Encourage participants to use their full range of motion in all joints.
- Use a hands-on approach to move participants' limbs through desired motor patterns. Be careful not to force any movement against joint resistance.
- Avoid letting participants get chilled to decrease the risk of cramping or circulation problems.
- Stop the activity when participants become tired. This is particularly important for people with a degenerative condition.
- Offer assistance to participants if it appears to be needed. Assist only if your offer is accepted and ask how you can best help.
- When speaking for more than a few minutes with people in wheelchairs, consider kneeling or sitting down so they do not have to look up at you.
- Do not lean on an occupied wheelchair for support.
- Slippery and uneven surfaces may pose problems for some people walking with assistive devices. If a wheelchair is available, offer it to them. If not, offer assistance or show them an easier route.

SAFETY NOTE

Avoid activities that can cause skin abrasions. If participants have lower back instability (such as paralysis or spina bifida), prohibit diving and any other activity that could twist the spine.

People who walk unaided and have good communication and breathing skills should have little difficulty in a regular aquatics program. Using a wheelchair or crutches and braces on land does not mean they cannot succeed in a regular program. However, the more body parts affected by disability, the more likely it is that participants may need specialized instruction. People limited in all four extremities (quadriplegia), need specialized, one-on-one instruction to be successful or receive rehabilitative benefit.

Cerebral Palsy

Cerebral palsy is a group of disorders affecting balance and posture that develop in childhood. Cerebral palsy results from damage to the parts of the brain that are responsible for muscle control. People with cerebral palsy have a difficult time controlling the movements of their bodies and many develop serious muscular damage due to spasticity or stiffness in the muscles later in life. The limitations caused by cerebral palsy range from mild to severe. One person with cerebral palsy may walk unassisted while another may lack ability to control most body movements. Many individuals with cerebral palsy have no cognitive impairment, but are often assumed to because of impaired speech. Some children with cerebral palsy may also have intellectual disabilities, learning disabilities, epilepsy and/or hearing or vision impairment. A person with cerebral palsy might have any of the following characteristics:

- Limited range of movement in affected arms and legs (or limbs).
- Limited control over voluntary movement of affected limbs or joints
- Random or involuntary movements
- Absence of normal muscle tone or an overabundance of muscle tone
- Abnormal muscle reflex patterns
- Impaired speech
- Possible seizures

People with cerebral palsy whose symptoms are mild can participate successfully in aquatics programs. Swimming is very good for increasing and maintaining range of motion in joints and muscle flexibility. The water also gives people with cerebral palsy a safe environment for physical activity. The increased buoyancy of water and the warmth of a heated pool also relieve body stiffness and stress. Specialized aquatics instruction may be needed for persons with cerebral palsy whose impairment is more severe.

For people with cerebral palsy, you can improve learning in the following ways:

- Be sure participants can independently access the aquatic area.
- At first, teach the strokes without modifying them.
- Concentrate on what participants are able do well and improve swimming abilities using their strengths.
- Emphasize stroke pull along the midline of the body to decrease body roll for participants with balance problems.
- Avoid activities that involve dragging body parts on the deck or underwater surfaces. Abrasion injuries can result.
- Encourage participants to use their full range of motion in all joints.
- Use a hands-on approach to move participants' limbs through desired motor patterns. Be careful not to force any movement against joint resistance.
- Avoid letting participants get chilled to decrease the risk of cramping or circulation problems.
- Stop the activity when participants become tired. This is particularly important for people with a degenerative condition.
- Offer assistance to participants if it appears to be needed. Assist only if your offer is accepted and ask how you can best help.
- Evaluate the participants' balance, their tendency to tip over and their ability to recover to a standing position. Determine ways to ensure safety by considering extra supervision and/or use of life jackets.

Kinesthetic Impairment

Kinesthetic awareness refers to the sense that detects bodily position, weight or movement of the muscles, tendons and joints. An example of kinesthetic sensitivity is the ability to determine (or remember) the position of the arm, or the trajectory of arm movements, without using vision. For people with a kinesthetic impairment, you can improve learning in the following ways:

- Be aware that participants will have problems orienting the body in water because they cannot feel where body parts are. If flotation or buoyancy is a problem, try adding weights to the ankles to reduce the effect of buoyancy.
- Use your hands to manipulate participants' arms and legs through the desired skill.

SAFETY NOTE

Encourage adult participants to help each other by teaching them support positions and how to help people recover from a float or glide.

Other Physical Conditions

Several medical conditions demand special attention in aquatic programs. Individuals with these conditions should consult their health care provider before joining any aquatics program. See Chapter 9 in *Swimming and Water Safety* for more on these types of conditions.

SAFETY NOTE

Do not let participants become chilled or fatigued. Let participants' comfort guide their participation.

Modifications

If participants are not successful learning skills, you may need to change the skills. The following sections discuss several ways to do this. As a general rule, modify a skill only as much as needed to help participants succeed.

Modifying Skills

Not all participants will perform skills exactly the same way. Individuals have their own center of buoyancy, percentage of body fat and muscle mass, lung capacity, range of joint motion, strength, coordination, height and weight. No two bodies float or move identically in water. It is up to you to help participants develop the most efficient stroke possible.

Having people with disabilities in class does not mean you automatically modify skills or strokes. Give people with disabilities the same instruction you give all other participants.

Make modifications only after the initial teaching of a skill. Once you see how participants perform skills, you can provide coaching, make corrections and try modifications. Do not be too quick to decide that something is too hard for participants with disabilities. Give them time to practice and offer positive and corrective feedback on how to improve their skill. Then make changes to improve performance.

Some participants with disabilities find certain skills impossible. People who are completely paralyzed will never be able to do a kick. Those with only one arm must pull close to the midline of the body to move forward in a straight line.

Some participants with disabilities find certain skills difficult. Participants with loss of some motor function may have problems balancing on one side for the sidestroke. The elementary backstroke might not be comfortable for people with a visual impairment because they would be gliding headfirst with no way of telling where they are. Difficult skills may take much longer to learn. Use verbal cues as needed for safety. With time and patience, most participants can meet the course requirements.

When considering modification of a skill or stroke–

- Let participants try skills or strokes several times before you consider modifying them. They will get the feel for the activity, and you can identify particular problem areas. Participants might have solutions as well.
- Change only one part of a skill at a time. Making too many changes at one time may be confusing.
- Let participants try several alternatives. Swimming on each side in the sidestroke, for example, may help identify which side is more efficient.
- Discuss modifications with participants. They know best how their bodies feel and move.
- Do not make assumptions about what is or is not possible for participants. Try everything.
- Allow for practice time before deciding something does not work. Learning new skills takes more time if an old habit must be corrected.

Other Modifications

Use the following guidelines to help ensure participants' success:

- Give additional instruction time. Extra practice, more feedback and individual attention often increase learning. Scheduling practice time outside of lessons and/or arranging for additional instruction may improve learning.

- Adjust the instructor-to-participant ratio. With more severe disabilities or a greater number of individuals who need more attention, additional instructors may be needed. This might include assistant instructors or therapists (Certified Therapeutic Recreation Specialists). Those who have had experience or training with individuals with disabilities can give the most support.
- Change class placement. Some class groupings are more conducive to learning than others are. It is more difficult to mainstream people with a disability into a large class, a class with several participants with behavior problems, a class of participants with a higher or lower skill level and/or a class in which people with a disability are not accepted by peers. Try to find an appropriate class setting.
- Change instructors. Some Water Safety instructors have had additional training in adapted aquatics. Other instructors have had more experience in teaching classes with mainstreamed participants. Some instructors let their own fears, insecurities or inexperience interfere with their teaching. Sometimes participants and instructors are simply not compatible. For any of these reasons, it is acceptable to change instructors. Consider allowing less experienced instructors to co-instruct with more experienced instructors.

Exploring Alternative Programs

If placement in a typical aquatics program does not seem to be working, you have several alternatives. You should explore these alternatives to find an appropriate solution to the problem. Simply removing participants from the course is not an appropriate solution. People should be excluded only on the basis of medical advice or when there are no alternatives to an exceptionally bad situation.

The following are signs that the program placement is not appropriate:

- Participants express unhappiness, frustration and/or anger toward self or others.
- Participants are not making progress in learning skills, even with extra time, help, practice and skill modification.
- Participants are in conflict with other participants in class.
- Participants are frequently absent.
- Participants have frequent illnesses and/or injuries during the course.
- There is a large gap between participants' functional ability and that of the rest of the class.
- Participants request frequent trips to the bathroom.

You might find it useful to consult with others about how to make aquatics more successful for all your participants. Seeking advice from Water Safety instructors trained to teach aquatics to individuals with disabilities can be very helpful. Physical therapists, recreation therapists, special education teachers, and other Water Safety instructors who have individuals with disabilities in their courses are excellent resources. Parents and caregivers also can give valuable information. Individuals with disabilities know themselves best and often can give you insight. Your local Red Cross chapter may provide or help you locate specialized training.

No matter what class placement is made, remember that placement can always be changed. Placement should be flexible allowing individuals with disabilities access to the aquatic programs most appropriate to their needs at the time. As needs change, placement should change.

Part D:

The Courses

CHAPTER

7

Parent and Child Aquatics

American Red Cross Parent and Child Aquatics familiarizes young children (from ages 6 months to about 3 years) to the water and prepares them to learn to swim in the American Red Cross Preschool Aquatics or Learn-to-Swim courses. It is not designed to teach children to become good swimmers or to survive in the water on their own. Parent and Child Aquatics gives parents safety information and teaches techniques to help orient their children to the water. It also provides direction regarding how to supervise water activities in a responsible manner. These courses are a bonding experience that will fill instructors, parents and children with wonderful lifelong memories.

This chapter provides the information you need to conduct the Parent and Child Aquatics levels. General administrative notes are covered first, followed by the outlines for the levels and descriptions of the required skills listed. The descriptions include suggested learning progressions and teaching tips for the required skills.

Administrative Notes

Prerequisites

There are no skill prerequisites for Parent and Child Aquatics. Children must be at least 6 months old to enroll. A parent is required to accompany each child in the water and participate in the classes. Parent and Child Aquatics introduces infants and young children to aquatics in two levels. All participants begin in Level 1. Once infants or young children are able to comfortably perform the skills in Level 1, they progress to Level 2. Level 2 builds on the skills learned in Level 1.

If a child completes Parent and Child Aquatics Level 1 and is nearly 4 years old or older, he or she may be ready to enroll in Preschool Aquatics Level 1. If a child completes Parent and Child Aquatics Level 2, is nearly 4 years old or older and can demonstrate the exit skills assessment of Preschool Aquatics Level 1, he or she may be ready to enroll in Preschool Aquatics Level 2.

INSTRUCTOR'S NOTE

Parents, guardians, childcare providers, grandparents, other adults and older siblings may participate with the child in the Parent and Child Aquatics courses. For the sake of simplicity, however, the term "parent" is used throughout.

Course Length

There is no minimum or maximum course length. Generally, Parent and Child Aquatics works well in sessions of 7 to 10 lessons, with each lasting no more than 30 minutes, and meeting at least twice a week.

Class Size

It is recommended that Parent and Child Aquatics classes maintain an instructor-to-parent and child ratio of at least one instructor to no more than 10 pairs. If any participants have special needs, there may be a need for co-instructors. Please work with the child's parents to determine what will work best in that circumstance.

Facility

It is recommended that Parent and Child Aquatics courses be taught only in well-maintained swimming pools.

To make your program more successful, whenever possible, the facility for the Parent and Child Aquatics classes should have–

- Dry, comfortable changing tables.
- Sanitary crawling areas.
- Adequate garbage disposal, especially for soiled diapers.
- Working showers, with warm water and soap available.
- Adequate air circulation and warm air temperatures.
- Secured pool entrances, especially when classes are not in session.
- A storage space for instructional aids and toys.

Temperature

Infants and young children are more susceptible to hypothermia than older children, even at relatively warm temperatures. Take the following measures to keep infants and young children from getting chilled:

- Maintain a water temperature of at least 83° F (28.3° C), which is more comfortable for young children.
- Keep the air temperature at least 2° F above water temperature. If the water and air temperature are cooler, the lessons will need to be shortened.
- Ask parents to keep a dry towel available to wrap around their child when exiting the water.

Depth

Most of the activities in Parent and Child Aquatics require parents to hold and provide support to their children. During most of the lesson, the water should be deep enough for parents to comfortably be in a position to keep their shoulders and their children at the surface of the water, and be able to walk forward and backward.

Infants and young children can also learn a great deal when actively exploring the aquatic environment under their own power. During some parts of the lesson, if possible, allow opportunities for independent exploration for children who can walk. If the water throughout the facility is too deep for these children, seek ways to reduce the depth. Ways to achieve this include the following:

- Use a facility with a gradually sloping shallow area and/or graduated steps so that a small child can stand alone in waist-deep or chest-deep water.
- Use teaching platforms on which children can stand safely.

Parents should continue to remain within arm's reach of their children while allowing them to explore without support. Direct parental supervision is necessary at all times during Parent and Child Aquatics lessons.

Noise and Distractions

Because infants and young children may be easily distracted, you should seek to control the sights and sounds in the environment. Consider the following suggestions:

- Limit loud, distorted sounds as much as possible.
- Hold the class in an isolated area of the pool to limit distractions from other patrons who are moving about and shouting or crying.
- Encourage participants to talk in normal voices and not shout over the noise.
- Store unused toys and equipment out of sight.
- If possible, take any child who is over-stimulated to a quieter area of the pool to calm down and adjust to the environment.

References

This chapter outlines the completion goals and descriptions for each skill in each level. The following additional materials are available as references:

- *Swimming and Water Safety* manual
- *Water Safety Instructor's CD-ROM*
- *Longfellow's WHALE Tales K–6 Educational Packet*
- *Teaching Swimming and Water Safety* DVD
- *Longfellow's WHALE Tales* DVD

Support Materials

The *Water Safety Instructor's CD-ROM* contains tools and resources to help you inform parents about the knowledge and skills they are learning in the Parent and Child Aquatics levels. These tools also help inform parents about the continuation of their children's experience of learning to swim with information about Preschool Aquatics and Learn-to-Swim.

Newsletters to Parents

A newsletter for each level of Parent and Child Aquatics provides you with a tool to let parents know what they are learning at each stage. Each newsletter highlights new skills that will be introduced and provides water safety messages. It also encourages parents to sign up their children for the next level, giving them a glimpse into what skills are to come. There also is a designated area on the newsletters that can be personalized with facility information.

Achievement Cards

Achievement cards for each level allow you to provide a progress report to parents. This tool gives you the opportunity to let parents know what skills their children have achieved and what skills still need work. There also is a designated area on the achievement cards that can be personalized with facility information.

Certificates

Two options are available for acknowledging participation in Parent and Child Aquatics. A certificate for each level is available on the *Water Safety Instructor's CD-ROM.* As an alternative, participants may be issued an *American Red Cross Swimming and Water Safety Certificate* indicating Parent and Child Aquatics Levels 1 or 2.

Safety Considerations

Parent and Child classes are unique because participants come in pairs. There can be up to 10 pairs, or 20 people, in one class. If the class is disorganized, safety may be compromised. Refer to **Chapter 3** for different patterns of class organization. Adjust the patterns to the characteristics of Parent and Child Aquatics classes. Following are some important safety considerations to remember:

- Maintain a safety-first mindset.
- Do not let children hyperventilate or have breath-holding contests. Limit children to a single inhalation whenever you ask them to hold their breath or submerge.
- Always be clear and concise when giving directions to avoid collisions. Make sure parents understand where you want them to go and the direction you want them to move.
- Have the parents spread out and maintain good spacing to avoid collisions with other parents.
- Move in wide circle or line patterns. The movement can be together or staggered depending on the activity, size of the pool, size of the class and the comfort level of participants.
- Be sure that parents maintain constant supervision, both on the deck and in the water by staying within arm's reach.
- Maintain appropriate eye contact as much as possible.
- Know when enough is enough.

It is recommended that young children who are still in diapers be required to wear swim diapers or cloth diapers covered by tight-fitting rubber pants. Diapers or swim pants may hold in some feces; however, they are not leak-proof and can still contaminate the pool water. Inform parents that they must change their children's diapers often and make frequent trips to the toilet.

Entering the Water

Before participants enter the water, be sure to point out the characteristics of the pool and the limits of the teaching area, such as water depth, construction design (steps, ladders and ramps) and water temperature. These characteristics and limits will influence the comfort level of the children and the confidence level of the parents.

Some children need to be introduced to the water slowly. Advise parents to take their time and not force children to progress faster than they are comfortable. It may be necessary to repeat each water adjustment skill several times at the start of several lessons until children are used to getting wet.

Practice entry skills without submersion until children are ready. Infants and young children should enter the water only on the parent's cue. The parents must keep a careful grip on their child to prevent him or her from slipping, falling backward or fully submerging.

Submersions

All submersions must be voluntary on the part of children. You and the parents should watch closely and try to avoid letting children swallow water or get water up the nose. Do not let children submerge more than 3 times per lesson in the initial learning phases of skills at this level. Any crying, sputtering or coughing indicates that the child was not ready or properly prepared to submerge. Teach the parents how to prepare their child for submersion and how to avoid letting water enter the child's mouth and nose. Crying may indicate that the child is still in the initial learning phase and may not be ready to try submersion. Advise parents that not all children are ready to submerge at any given time. This is a developmental issue, and parents should not worry if their child is "behind" others in the class. Caution parents never to force children to perform a skill; this only delays their readiness to try additional skills.

Breath-control skills help children prepare for and perform full submersion. Children should be able to demonstrate breath control on cue by performing skills, such as blowing bubbles and breath-holding, when submerging the mouth, nose, eyes and when fully submerged.

Exiting the Water

When children exit the water, advise parents to always maintain supervision and be in a position to assist their child if he or she starts to slip on the steps or stairs. Also, be sure that the children are not able to run away from their parents, as they may slip, fall and hurt themselves.

Teaching Young Children

Teaching aquatic skills to young children requires an extra dose of patience and additional teaching skills. The following sections give essential information for orienting children to the water and preparing them for entry into Red Cross Preschool Aquatics or Learn-to-Swim.

Despite the similarities between young children, each one is unique. All children have individual qualities and characteristics that make them different. Children learn new motor skills at different ages and at different rates, and they have different preferences for activities. Children are affected by their family member's, especially their parents', comfort in and around the water. Parents who are fearful of the water or who have different cultural or social attitudes toward swimming may affect their child's success.

Children also differ in their learning styles. Some children want to be shown how to do something, while others want to hear how to do it. Then there are those children who do better discovering things on their own, with some guidance. Younger children are less likely to respond to complex verbal explanations. Most young children will imitate adults. Therefore, it is crucial that accurate demonstrations of skills are given and repeated. If too much time is spent talking about how to do something, minds will wander and the children will not learn the skills as quickly. Be aware of each child's and parent's differences when planning presentations of skills for classes.

Since Parent and Child Aquatics requires a parent to participate in the water with each child, you are more of a facilitator of parent-child interaction than an instructor of the child. Your job is to guide, instruct and provide positive, corrective feedback to help parents as their children explore the aquatic world. You and the parent should keep some important things in mind when in the water with a child.

- Maintain appropriate eye contact as much as possible.
- Demonstrate basic skills accurately and often.
- Praise effort regardless of the level of success.
- Never force children to perform a skill; this only delays their readiness to try additional skills. Allow children to progress at their own pace through the skills.
- When teaching skills that require breath control, such as fully submerging the child or having the child swim or float on the front with the face in the water, tell the parent to always take a breath with the child and exaggerate loudly when inhaling.
- Make sure the child is calm and happy before entering and leaving the pool.

Learning and Development in Children

Infants and young children undergo rapid and remarkable changes, especially between birth and age 5. During this time, children's' abilities to think, feel, move and play all change dramatically. Because children are so different from adults, it is important to understand the learning and developmental stages and changes and how they affect children's readiness for aquatic activities.

The learning process is one way parents and instructors see how young children grow. Learning involves changes in observable behavior that results from practice and experience. Parents or instructors can control some of the factors that influence young children's learning in the home or teaching environment. As an instructor, you influence the learning process by setting goals, encouraging practice and providing feedback and motivation. However, you must focus on the children's learning rather than on your teaching. Observe what movements come naturally for children and use teaching methods that help the children develop swimming abilities based on their natural abilities. Keep the basic objectives of breath control, relaxing and body position in mind as you help parents understand what their children are doing as it relates to propelling themselves through the water.

Instruction is only one of many influences on learning in young children. Proper practice is essential for learning motor skills. Young children usually benefit most from short practice segments, with frequent rest periods throughout the lesson. A distributed practice schedule with frequent rest periods is beneficial because it–

- Minimizes fatigue.
- Gives children time to absorb what they are learning.
- Helps children stay motivated and interested in the activity.
- Keeps learning fun when playing games that achieve the learning objectives between practices.

Applying these principles in your Parent and Child Aquatics courses means that your classes should meet more often for shorter periods of time. For example, five 20-minute lessons per week may help young children learn better than two 30-minute lessons. Other factors that influence learning are explained in **Chapters 2 and 5**.

Fearful Children

To understand fearful children, it helps to understand their learning and development processes. One way to reduce fear is to be consistent in your lessons. If you start, end and organize each lesson the same way, children become familiar with the routine and may participate more easily. To reduce the impact of learned fears, plan carefully and give a lot of positive reinforcement. Tell parents not to show fear as the child may perceive and adopt that fearful behavior. Children enjoy the water more when they can learn at their own pace, experience success, practice repeatedly and receive praise for their efforts. For more information about understanding and working with fearful children, see **Chapter 5**.

The Parent and Child Aquatics Course Outlines

The foundation of Red Cross Parent and Child Aquatics is a set of basic skills that prepares infants and young children to become comfortable in the water so they are willing and ready to learn to swim. These basic skills include adjusting to the water environment, showing comfort while maintaining a front or back position in the water and demonstrating breath control (i.e., blowing bubbles or voluntarily fully submerging under water).

Not every level includes skills in all categories, nor is it necessary to introduce the skills in the order of categories in the preceding list because young children do not learn skills in a single straight progression. When helping children acquire skills at more advanced levels, you may need to let them practice the skills at lower levels until they are more proficient and comfortable. It is very important, however, to integrate water safety skills in each lesson of each level, so parents learn what they can do to be safe in, on and around the water. Refer to the sample block plans and sample lesson plans on the *Water Safety Instructor's CD-ROM* for examples of how to organize the presentation of these skills.

Skills to Be Taught to Parents

Starting each lesson with a parent orientation gives you the opportunity to describe the goals of the session and what parents can expect. Remember that Parent and Child Aquatics is as much about providing parents with information and techniques to create safer aquatic experiences for their children as it is about orienting young children to the water. Ensure that parents learn and practice the following skills throughout the lessons:

- How to properly supervise children and maintain safe behavior in and around the water.
- How to enter and exit the water. Establish– and strictly enforce–a rule that a child must get adult permission before entering any body of water.
- How to use holding and support techniques and when to use them.

- How to determine their child's readiness to try basic skills.
- Proper submersion techniques (supported and unsupported).
- The importance of cues and how to use them.
- How to help children learn and practice skills appropriate for their ages, current developmental level and ability.
- How to play and the importance of playing as a way to learn.
- How to select, properly fit and use U.S. Coast Guard-approved life jackets.
- Basic water safety information and rescue skills, such as reaching and throwing assists.

Skills to Be Taught to Infants and Young Children

Level 1 and Level 2 skills and activities are highlighted in the following outlines and then detailed in the pages immediately following. These skills should be repeated throughout the lessons. It is helpful to organize each lesson in a similar manner to create a familiar environment for children.

You will notice the term "explore" is used frequently in the level outlines. The intent is for children to experiment and to try different approaches to accomplishing skills, building on what comes naturally. At this point, specific performance criteria are not important. What is important in Parent and Child Aquatics is that children become comfortable in the water and acquire a foundation for learning how to swim. As children attempt new skills, praise them for even the slightest accomplishments.

Terms Used in the *Water Safety Instructor's Manual*

The following terms are used to explain the completion requirements at each level.

- Explore—to try various ways to perform skills. May or may not be done with support, but always with close supervision.
- Support—can be given by a parent or instructor or with a flotation device.
- Assistance—is provided by the parent or instructor. The participant performs a skill unsupported, but may begin and end the skill with support.
- Demonstrate—the participant performs a skill.
- Independently—to demonstrate without support or assistance, but still with close supervision.
- Discuss—primarily related to water safety topics. Information can be presented by the instructor using push, pull and balance techniques. For more information on push, pull and balance techniques, see **Chapter 5** of Fundamentals of Instructor Training.

Level 1

The goals of Level 1 are to provide experiences and activities for children to–

- Learn to ask for permission before entering the water.
- Learn how to enter and exit the water in a safe manner.
- Feel comfortable in the water.
- Explore submerging to the mouth, nose, eyes and completely.
- Explore buoyancy on the front and back position.
- Change body position in the water.
- Learn how to play safely.
- Experience wearing a U.S. Coast Guard-approved life jacket.

Level 2

Level 2 builds upon the skills learned in Level 1. The goals of Level 2 are to provide experiences and activities for children to–

- Establish expectation for adult supervision.
- Learn more ways to enter and exit the water in a safe manner.
- Explore submerging in a rhythmic pattern.
- Glide on the front and back with assistance.
- Perform combined stroke on front and back with assistance.
- Change body position in the water.
- Experience wearing a U.S. Coast Guard-approved life jacket in the water.

Parent and Child Aquatics Level 1

Level 1 introduces basic skills to parents and children. Parents are taught to safely work with their child in the water, including how to appropriately support and hold their child in the water and how to prepare and encourage their child to participate fully and try the skills. Children are introduced to basic skills that lay a foundation to help them learn to swim. Several water safety topics also are introduced that are directed to parents.

INSTRUCTOR'S NOTE

The skills in the outline are not in a teaching order. Refer to the sample block plan and lesson plan for examples of how to organize the skills.

Parent and Child Aquatics Level 1 Outline

Recommended Equipment

- Pool toys, such as floating rubber animals
- U.S. Coast Guard-approved life jackets of appropriate sizes for parents and children
- Flotation devices, such as foam noodles, kickboards or barbells

Skills	Completion Goals	References
Holding and Support Techniques		
Face-to-face positions		
■ Chin support	Demonstrate (parent)	WSIM, page 46
■ Shoulder support	Demonstrate (parent)	WSIM, page 46
Back-to-chest postition		
■ Cuddle	Demonstrate (parent)	WSIM, page 47
Side-to-side position		
■ Hip straddle	Demonstrate (parent)	WSIM, page 49
Working with the Child		
Cueing	Demonstrate (parent)	WSIM, page 124
Water Adjustment, Entry and Exit		
Getting Wet		
■ Getting wet with toys	Explore	WSIM, page 124
■ Getting wet kicking	Explore	WSIM, page 124
Water Entry		
■ Lifting in	Demonstrate (parent)	WSIM, page 125
■ Walking in	Demonstrate (parent)	WSIM, page 125

Skills	Completion Goals	References
Water Adjustment, Entry and Exit *(continued)*		
Exploring the Pool		
■ Out-of-water exploration	Explore	WSIM, page 126
■ In-water exploration	Explore, with support	WSIM, page 126
Water Exit		
■ Lifting out	Demonstrate (parent)	WSIM, page 126
■ Walking out	Demonstrate (parent)	WSIM, page 126
Breath Control		
Blowing bubbles on the surface	Explore, with support	WSIM, page 126
Blowing bubbles with mouth and nose submerged	Explore, with support	WSIM, page 127
Underwater exploration	Explore, with support	WSIM, page 127
Submerging mouth, nose and eyes	Explore, with support or independently	WSIM, page 127
Buoyancy on Front		
Front float	Explore, with support	WSIM, page 128
Front glide	Explore, with support	WSIM, page 128
Buoyancy on Back		
Back float	Explore, with support	WSIM, page 129
Back glide	Explore, with support	WSIM, page 129
Changing Direction		
Roll from front to back	Explore, with support	WSIM, page 129
Roll from back to front	Explore, with support	WSIM, page 130
Swim on Front		
Passing from instructor to parent	Explore, with support	WSIM, page 130
Leg action	Explore, with support	WSIM, page 130
Swim on Back		
Leg action	Explore, with support	WSIM, page 132
Water Safety		
The importance of wearing a life jacket	Discuss (parent) and Demonstrate (parent and child)	SWS, page 18; WSIM, page 62
How to call for help and the importance of knowing first aid and CPR	Discuss (parent) and Demonstrate (parent and child)	SWS, pages 45 & 48; WSIM, page 64
Basic water safety rules	Discuss (parent)	SWS, pages 12 & 16; WSIM, page 65
General water safety around the home	Discuss (parent)	SWS, pages 25 & 32; WSIM, page 66
Recreational water illnesses	Discuss (parent)	SWS, page 15; WSIM, page 67
Sun safety	Discuss (parent)	SWS, page 15; WSIM, page 68

Parent and Child Aquatics Level 1 Skills

Holding and Support Techniques

Holding and support techniques are described and illustrated in **Chapter 3**, pages 44–53.

TEACHING TIP

When supporting children during swimming activities, parents should always move so that their child gets used to feeling the sensation of moving in the appropriate direction.

Working with the Child

Cueing

Cueing is used to prepare children for upcoming skills. Parents should be taught to use cue words, such as "ready, set, go" or "1, 2, 3," as each skill is learned and repeated anytime the skill is practiced. Children should be taught to enter the water only with permission from the parent and when cued to do so. Cue the children the same way each time. When preparing children for a skill–

1. Explain and/or demonstrate the expectation. Say, "we're going to blow bubbles" or "show me how you blow bubbles," then blow bubbles.
2. Say the cue words. Say, "ready, set, go" or "1, 2, 3." Be consistent with the cadence each time. If it is a breath-control skill, follow the cue words with an exaggerated breath to encourage the child to do the same.
3. Have the child perform the skill.
4. Always praise the child for even the slightest effort or accomplishment.

Water Adjustment, Entry and Exit

Getting Wet

Getting Wet with Toys

Sitting next to the child at the edge of the pool and providing support as needed–

1. The parent and child dip toys, washcloths, sprinkling cans or cupped hands into the pool and sprinkle water onto each other's legs, arms and trunk.
2. The parent dips a hand into the pool and sprinkles water onto the child's head and face.

TEACHING TIPS

- *Make it fun by singing a familiar song, but change the words to match the actions, such as "this is the way we wash our…" Also, always have at least two alternate activities ready, just in case the primary activity does not fully engage participants.*
- *Make use of the child's imagination and have the child create different types of rain patterns while pouring water, such as making it rain softly, like a sprinkle, or hard, like in a thunderstorm.*

Getting Wet Kicking

1. The parent sits next to the child at the edge of the pool, providing support as needed.
2. The parent kicks the water while sitting on the side of the pool and encourages the child to imitate the behavior.

INSTRUCTOR'S NOTES

- *Some children need to go through this process at the start of several lessons until they are used to the water temperature and getting wet. Advise parents to take their time and not to force a child to get in the water before he or she is used to it.*
- *Some children may not be able to reach the water with their legs from the side of the pool. If this is the case, skip this activity.*

TEACHING TIP

Make use of the child's imagination and have the child create waves of differing heights by kicking softer and harder.

Water Entry

SAFETY NOTE

A child should enter the water only on the parent's cue. The parent must keep a careful grip on the child to prevent him or her from slipping, falling backward or submerging the head.

Lifting In

1. Either the parent or instructor maintains contact with the child while the parent enters the water in one of the following ways:
   - Using the ladder
   - From a sitting position on the deck
   - Rolling over onto his or her stomach and sliding into the water
2. The parent stands in water in front of the child holding the child under the armpits (**Fig. 7-1**).
3. The parent cues the child and then lifts the child into the water to chin level then holds the child in the hip straddle position.

Fig. 7-1

Walking In

1. The parent holds the child using the hip straddle and enters the pool using steps or a ramp.

2. The parent walks or bends down to a depth that is appropriate for the child and the skill to be learned. The parent talks calmly or sings to the child as they enter the pool.

INSTRUCTOR'S NOTE

Remind parents to practice entry skills without fully submerging until the child is ready.

Exploring the Pool

Out-of-Water Exploration

- The parent and child walk around the deck area (before getting wet) to familiarize the child with the pool area.
- The child observes different depths and parts of the pool, such as steps and ladders, with close parental supervision.

In-Water Exploration—With Support

- The parent uses a holding position that is comfortable for the child, such as a face-to-face or side-to-side position.
- The parent and child travel around the teaching area. The parent talks calmly or sings to the child as they travel.

INSTRUCTOR'S NOTE

Instructor's Note: Have the parent keep the child's shoulders in the water as much as possible. This will help keep the child from getting chilled.

Water Exit

Lifting Out

1. The parent cues the child, then lifts the child from the pool and sits him or her on the deck next to the ladder.
2. The instructor maintains contact with the child while the parent exits the water in one of the following ways:
   - Using the ladder
   - Lifting him- or herself onto the deck

Walking Out

The parent holds the child using the hip straddle position and exits the pool using steps or a ramp.

Breath Control

Blowing Bubbles on the Surface—With Support

1. The parent holds the child in a face-to-face position. The child's face should be chin level to the surface of the water.
2. Making direct eye contact with the child, the parent cues the child then blows bubbles. The parent encourages the child to imitate the behavior.

TEACHING TIPS

- *Have the parent place a light object, such as a colorful toy or small ball, in front of the child. Encourage the child to move the object along the surface of the water by blowing it.*
- *If the child is having trouble understanding what you are trying to teach, try the following:*
  1. *Take a breath, hold it for about 1 second then blow gently on the child's cheek. Then take a breath, hold it for about 1 second then exhale on to the object or in the water (blow bubbles).*
  2. *Repeat this pattern several times until the child understands.*

Blowing Bubbles with Mouth and Nose Submerged—With Support

1. The parent holds the child in a face-to-face or side-to-side position.
2. The parent blows bubbles with the mouth submerged, then encourages the child to imitate the behavior.
3. The parent blows bubbles with the mouth and nose submerged, then encourages the child to imitate the behavior.

SAFETY NOTE

Parents should keep children from swallowing water and take care to avoid fully submerging children.

TEACHING TIP

Have parents blow bubbles slowly and gently and hum when exhaling, as an example to the child. The air moves out through the nose when humming and prevents water from entering the nose.

Underwater Exploration—With Support

1. The parent holds the child in a face-to-face or side-to-side position.
2. The parent submerges an object, such as a toy.
3. The parent submerges the mouth, nose and eyes looking toward the toy, and then encourages the child to imitate the behavior and look for the toy.

TEACHING TIP

Put different color objects on the bottom of the pool. Encourage the child to look at a particular colored object.

Submerging Mouth, Nose and Eyes—With Support

When the parent and child are ready to try submerging, teach the parent the following steps:

1. The parent holds the child using the shoulder support and moves backwards slowly so that the child is gliding forward on the front.
2. The parent makes eye contact with the child and makes sure that the child is focused and ready.
3. The parent says the cue words, inhales loudly, holds a breath, submerges the face then exhales in the water. Repeat 2 or 3 times to provide an example to the child.

4. The parent tells the child it is his or her turn to try.
5. The parent cues the child then gently pulls the child closer to his or her body along the surface of the water while inhaling loudly, then holds a breath.
6. As the child draws near, the parent gives the child a quick gentle blow in the face about a half second before the child submerges. This will make most children flinch and hold their breath.
7. The parent slightly loosens the grip, but keeps the hands on the child, and allows the child to submerge to the eyes or just below the surface of the water for about 2 seconds.
8. Then the parent brings the child up gently and provides encouragement and praise.

INSTRUCTOR'S NOTE

Remind the parents to keep the child's shoulders in the water after the submersion. Do not let children submerge more than 3 times per lesson until they are able to submerge without crying, sputtering or coughing. These signals indicate the child may not be ready to submerge. Warn parents never to force a child to do a skill; this only delays his or her readiness and willingness to try additional skills.

Buoyancy on Front

When supporting children, parents should hold the children gently. This allows the children to experience their own buoyancy as much as possible.

Front Float—With Support

1. The parent holds the child in a face-to-face position. The child's face should be close enough to almost touch the water, but should not be in the water.
2. The parent walks backward slowly just enough to allow the child's legs to float up to the surface. The parent talks calmly or hums while supporting the child.

INSTRUCTOR'S NOTE

If the child is relaxed, the legs will float up to the surface. If the child is not relaxed, the child will try to stand and rest the feet on the parent's legs or torso.

Front Glide—With Support

1. The parent holds the child in a face-to-face position. The child's face may be in or out of the water.
2. The parent travels backward and talks calmly or sings to the child as they move around the teaching area (**Fig. 7-2**).

Fig. 7-2

TEACHING TIP

The parent should take an exaggerated breath then blow bubbles, putting the face in the water. It is not necessary to tell the child to do the same. Eventually the child will likely try to imitate. Be sure that the child does not take repeated exaggerated breaths.

Buoyancy on Back

When supporting children, parents should hold the children gently. This allows the children to experience their own buoyancy as much as possible.

TEACHING TIP

Allow participants to practice for what length of time they are comfortable. If practicing for only 2 seconds is preferred then start with 2 seconds and build on that time.

Back Float—With Support

1. The parent holds the child in the cuddle or the hip support on back position. The child's ears may be in or out of the water.
2. The parent talks calmly or sings to the child as they stand or move slowly around the teaching area.

TEACHING TIP

Have the parent ask the child to look back for the parent's eyes while performing the back float.

Back Glide—With Support

1. The parent holds the child in the hip support on back or back support position. The child's ears may be in or out of the water.
2. The parent moves backward gliding the child on his or her back.

Changing Direction

Roll from Front to Back—With Support

1. The parent holds the child in a support position on the front (**Fig. 7-3, A**). The parent should move to generate some momentum.
2. The parent cues the child, then rotates him or her onto the back with the child's ears in or out of the water (**Fig. 7-3, B**).
3. Parent moves his or her hands to hold the child in a support position on the back (**Fig. 7-3, C**).

Fig. 7-3, A

Fig. 7-3, B

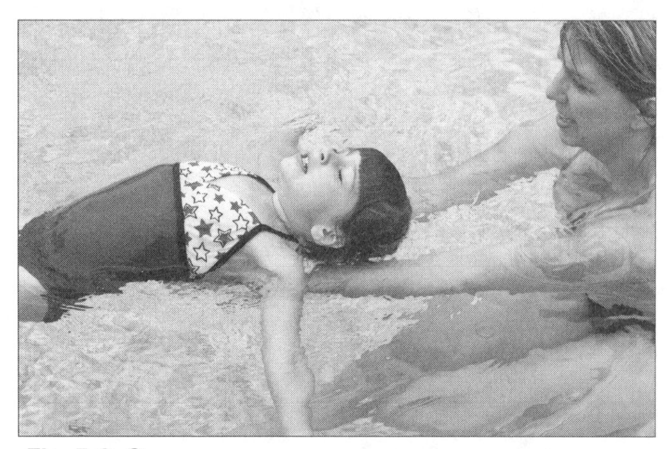

Fig. 7-3, C

Roll from Back to Front—With Support

1. The parent holds the child in a support position on the back (**Fig. 7-4, A**). The parent should move to generate some momentum.
2. The parent cues the child, then rotates him or her onto the stomach with the child's face out of the water (**Fig. 7-4, B**).
3. The parent moves his or her hands to hold the child in a support position on the front (**Fig. 7-4, C**).

Swim on Front

When practicing these skills, talk, sing, laugh, play and have fun. It is important for the participants to enjoy the aquatic experience without fear. It is equally important for children to avoid swallowing and breathing in water. Therefore, the sooner that breath control is introduced and learned, the better the child will perform without fear and the happier the child will feel.

Passing from Instructor to Parent—With Support

1. Hold the child in the side support position with the child's head out of water. Move forward to gain momentum (**Fig. 7-5, A**).
2. Cue the child, then gently glide and release the child to his or her parent's arms (**Fig. 7-5, B**). The pass should be smooth and gentle with the child staying at the same level in the water.
3. Do not lose contact with the child. Be sure the parent has made contact before you let go.
4. The parent gains control of the child in the shoulder support position, pulls the child to the the chest and gives a hug and praise (**Fig. 7-5, C**).

Leg Action—With Support

1. The parent holds the child in the hug position and moves backwards.
2. The parent moves the legs in a way that is natural and comfortable for the child, either in an alternating (such as a flutter kick) or a simultaneous (such as a dolphin kick or breaststroke kick) action.
3. As the child is able to kick on his or her own, the parent moves into a face-to-face or side support position. The child's face may be in or out of the water.

INSTRUCTOR'S NOTE

Tell the parent to watch for the child's natural leg movement and, if needed, move back to the hug position to help move the child's legs. Then move back to the shoulder or hip support position to try again.

TEACHING TIP

Tell the parent to place his or her hands under the child's knees and thumbs on the calf to move the legs, keeping them just under the surface of the water. Keep the child's legs in close together and move them up and down in the flutter kicking motion, or bend the knees forward, move them apart slightly and then straight together, similar to a breaststroke kick motion. Initially, the child will choose a motion that he or she feels comfortable performing. The idea is to get the legs to move any direction. Specific kicks will be taught as the child develops.

Fig. 7-4, A

Fig. 7-5, A

Fig. 7-4, B

Fig. 7-5, B

Fig. 7-4, C

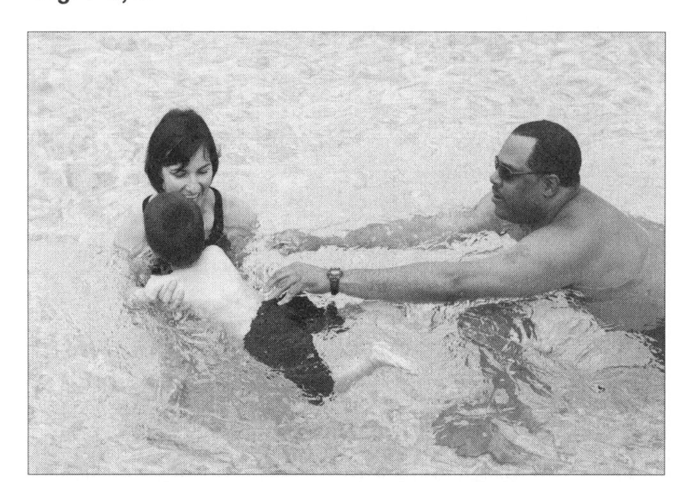

Fig. 7-5, C

Fig. 7-6

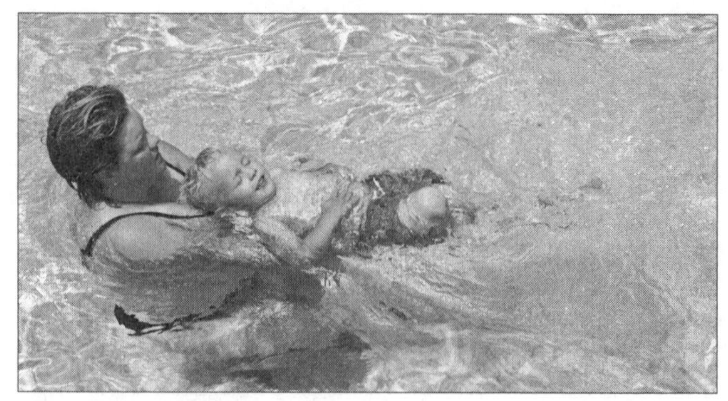

Fig. 7-7

4. The parent walks backward and cues the child to move the legs (**Fig. 7-6**). The parent talks calmly or sings to the child as they move around the teaching area.

Swim on Back

When practicing these skills, talk, sing, laugh, play and have fun. It is important for the participants to enjoy the aquatic experience without fear.

Leg Action—With Support

1. The parent holds the child in the hip support on back position. Have the parent adjust the child so that his or her head rests on the parent's shoulder.
2. The parent moves backward gliding the child on his or her back while moving the legs in the direction that is natural and comfortable for the child.
3. The parent moves the child to the hip support on back position with the child's head in front of the parent's chest.
4. The parent moves backward gliding the child on his or her back and cues the child to kick the legs (**Fig. 7-7**).

TEACHING TIPS

- *Have the parent assist the child with moving the legs by placing the hands under the knees and the thumbs on the shins. Keep the child's feet just under the surface of the water.*
- *Suggest to the parent to have the child place his or her hands on the stomach or hold a small flotation device or toy on the stomach until the child is comfortable with the arms relaxed to the side.*

Water Safety

The concept of water safety should be central to every part of an aquatics program. The following water safety topics are required for Parent and Child Aquatics Level 1:

- The importance of wearing a life jacket
- How to call for help and the importance of knowing first aid and CPR
- Basic water safety rules
- General water safety around the home
- Recreational water illnesses
- Sun safety

Wrap up each class session by emphasizing the safety component of the skills they learned.

Add topics as necessary so that you integrate water safety into each lesson. When selecting additional topics, think about current events in or special needs of your local area or region. Refer to **Chapter 4** for details on these topics and for additional topics.

Parent and Child Aquatics Level 2

Level 2 builds on the skills introduced in Level 1. Participants improve on these skills and learn more advanced skills in Level 2.

INSTRUCTOR'S NOTE

The skills in the outline are not in a teaching order. Refer to the sample block plan and lesson plan for examples of how to organize the skills.

Parent and Child Aquatics Level 2 Outline

Recommended Equipment

- Toys, such as floating rubber animals and weighted diving objects
- U.S. Coast Guard-approved life jackets of appropriate sizes for parents and children
- Flotation devices, such as foam noodles, kickboards or barbells
- Reaching equipment

Skills	Completion Goals	References
Holding and Support Techniques		
Face-to-face positions		
■ Hip support on front	Demonstrate	WSIM, page 46
Back-to-chest postition		
■ Hip support on back	Demonstrate	WSIM, page 47
■ Back support	Demonstrate	WSIM, page 47
■ Arm stroke	Demonstrate	WSIM, page 48
Side-to-side position		
Shoulder support	Demonstrate	WSIM, page 49
Water Adjustment, Entry and Exit		
Water Entry		
■ Seated position	Demonstrate, with assistance	WSIM, page 135
■ Seated position—rolling over and sliding in	Demonstrate, with assistance	WSIM, page 135
■ Stepping or jumping in	Demonstrate, with assistance	WSIM, page 135
■ Using a ladder	Demonstrate	WSIM, page 136
■ Using stairs	Demonstrate	WSIM, page 136
Exploring the Pool	Explore, independently, in shallow water	WSIM, page 136
Water Exit		
■ Using side of pool	Demonstrate, with assistance	WSIM, page 137
■ Using a ladder	Demonstrate	WSIM, page 137

Skills	Completion Goals	References
Breath Control		
Underwater exploration		
■ Opening eyes and retrieving objects below the surface	Explore, with support, in shallow water	WSIM, page 137
■ Opening eyes and retrieving submerged objects	Explore, with assistance, in shallow water	WSIM, page 137
Bobbing	Explore, independently	WSIM, page 138
Buoyancy on Front		
Front float	Demonstrate, with assistance	WSIM, page 138
Front glide	Demonstrate, with support or assistance	WSIM, page 138
Front glide to the wall	Demonstrate, with assistance	WSIM, page 139
Buoyancy on Back		
Back float	Demonstrate, with support or assistance	WSIM, page 140
Back glide	Demonstrate, with support or assistance	WSIM, page 140
Changing Direction		
Roll from front to back	Demonstrate, with assistance	WSIM, page 141
Roll from back to front	Demonstrate, with assistance	WSIM, page 141
Swim on Front		
Passing between adults	Demonstrate, with assistance	WSIM, page 141
Drafting with breathing	Demonstrate, with assistance	WSIM, page 142
Leg action—alternating or simultaneous movements	Demonstrate, with assistance	WSIM, page 142
Arm action—alternating or simultaneous movements	Demonstrate, with support or assistance	WSIM, page 143
Combined arm and leg actions on front with breathing	Explore, with assistance	WSIM, page 144
Swim on Back		
Leg action—alternating or simultaneous movements	Demonstrate, with assistance	WSIM, page 145
Arm action—alternating or simultaneous movements	Demonstrate, with support or assistance	WSIM, page 145
Combined arm and leg actions on back	Explore, with support or assistance	WSIM, page 145
Water Safety		
Wearing a life jacket in the water	Discuss (parent) and Demonstrate (child)	SWS, page 18; WSIM, page 62
Reaching assists	Discuss/demonstrate (parent)	SWS, page 55; WSIM, page 69
Basic water safety rules review	Discuss (parent)	SWS, pages 12 & 16; WSIM, page 66
Safety at the beach and at the waterpark	Discuss (parent)	SWS, page 20; WSIM, page 71
Water toys and their limitations	Discuss (parent)	SWS, page 16; WSIM, page 72

Parent and Child Aquatics Level 2 Skills

Holding and Support Techniques

Holding and support techniques are described and illustrated in **Chapter 3**, pages 44–53.

Water Adjustment, Entry and Exit

Water Entry

Seated Position—With Assistance

1. The child sits on the edge of the pool, with the parent standing in the water facing the child.
2. The parent grasps the child's hands, wrists, forearms or armpits.
3. The parent cues the child to push off the pool edge then lifts the child into the water.
4. The parent returns the child who is strong and coordinated enough to the side of the pool, and places the child's hands on the edge of the pool wall.

TEACHING TIP

When supporting children during swimming activities, parents should always move so that their child gets used to feeling the sensation of moving in the appropriate direction.

Seated Position—Rolling Over and Sliding In—With Assistance

The parent sits next to the child at the edge of the pool.

The parent rolls over onto his or her stomach, slides into the pool then holds on to the wall.

The parent encourages the child to imitate the behavior (**Fig. 7-8**).

Stepping or Jumping In—With Assistance

1. The parent stands in the water. The child stands with the feet at the edge of the pool. The parent stands to the side of the child.
2. The parent grasps one of the child's hands and cues the child to step or jump straight out into the water (**Fig. 7-9**).
3. As the child steps or jumps in, the parent allows the child to submerge.

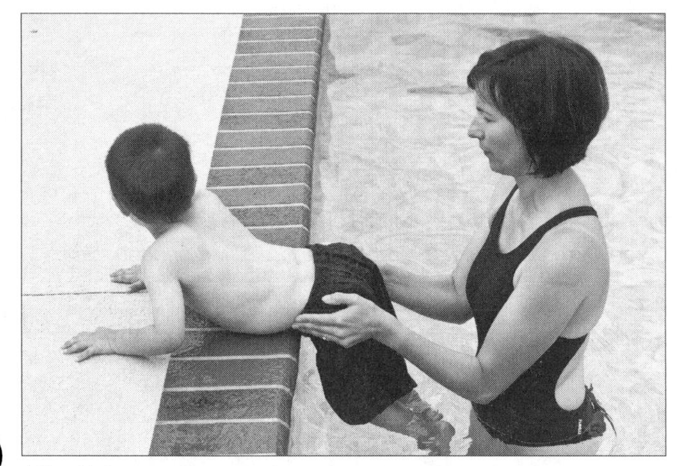

Fig. 7-8

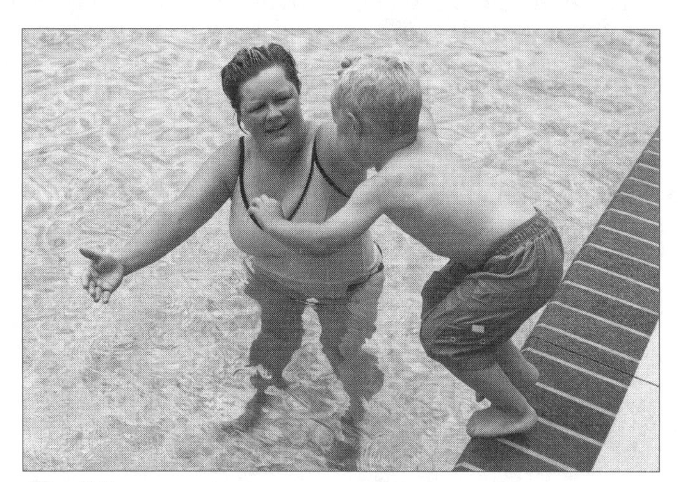

Fig. 7-9

4. The parent assists the child to the surface using the shoulder support then helps the child return to the side of the pool.

INSTRUCTOR'S NOTE

While cueing the child to step or jump straight out, the parent should take an exaggerated breath to encourage the child to hold his or her breath.

SAFETY NOTES

- *This skill should only be taught after the child is comfortable fully submerging.*
- *The child should jump straight out from the wall without turning. The parent may assist by holding the child's hand(s) but should not let the child jump directly into the parent's arms. Do not try to catch the child in mid-air or allow the child to jump directly into the parent's arms.*

Using a Ladder—Independently

1. The child stands next to the ladder.
2. The parent holds the railing and walks backward down the ladder then encourages the child to imitate the behavior.
3. The parent stands at the bottom of the ladder to ensure the child's safety.

Using Stairs—Independently

1. The child stands next to the stairs.
2. The parent holds the railing, walks down the stairs then encourages the child to imitate the behavior.
3. The parent stands at the bottom of the stairs to ensure the child's safety.

Exploring the Pool—Independently

See Level 1, Exploring the Pool, on page 126.

Variation for Level 2:

- Have the child travel by moving the feet along the bottom at shallow depths (e.g., 1 to 3 feet, if available) while using the pool wall for support.
- Parent stands in the water remaining within arm's reach of the child.

INSTRUCTOR'S NOTE

Point out the limits of the teaching area. These limits will depend on the age, height and comfort level of the children; height and confidence level of the parents; and the characteristics of the pool. If the child is not strong or coordinated enough, skip this step.

Water Exit

Using Side of Pool—With Assistance

1. The child grasps the edge of the pool wall.
2. The child pulls up to the elbows.
3. The child pulls up to the stomach and leans forward.
4. The child puts one leg up on the deck.
5. The child safely stands up or sits down on the pool deck.

INSTRUCTOR'S NOTE

Help the child as little as possible, but provide enough assistance for the child to be successful.

Using a Ladder—Independently

1. The child is near the ladder with the parent within arm's reach.
2. The instructor demonstrates how to exit the pool by using the ladder.
3. The parent stands behind the child as he or she exits the pool. The parent encourages and praises the child for imitating the instructor's behavior.

SAFETY NOTE

Watch for children slipping on the steps or stairs or running away from their parents.

Breath Control

Underwater Exploration

Opening Eyes and Retrieving Objects Below the Surface—With Support

1. The parent holds the child in the hip straddle position then stoops down so the child's face is at chin level with the surface of the water.
2. The parent submerges an object, such as a toy, to a depth that allows the child to get his or her face wet while grabbing for the toy.
3. The parent encourages the child to grab for the toy.

Opening Eyes and Retrieving Submerged Objects—With Assistance

1. The child stands in chest-deep water with the parent at his or her side. If the child cannot stand, hold the child using the shoulder support on the side.
2. The parent or instructor submerges an object to a depth that requires the child to get his or her face wet while grabbing for the toy.
3. The child attempts to pick up the object while submerging.

TEACHING TIP

Put different color objects on the bottom of the pool. Instruct the child to pick up a particular colored object.

Bobbing—Independently

This drill can be practiced with children who are old enough to understand and follow directions. Practice by bobbing to the mouth, then the nose, then the eyes and finally the entire head.

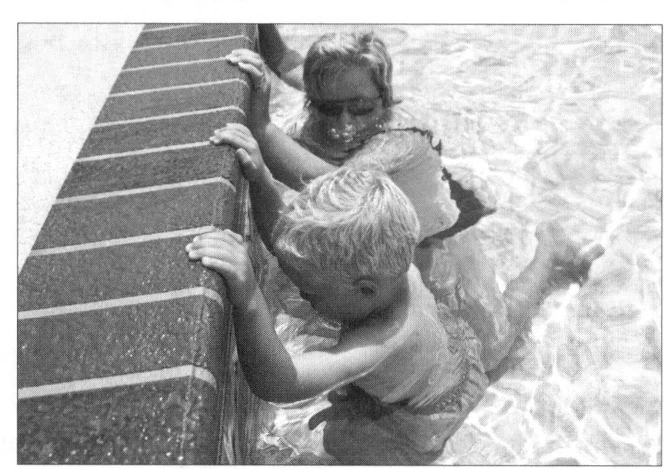

Fig. 7-10

1. The child holds onto the edge of the pool wall. The parent stands in the water within arm's reach of the child (**Fig. 7-10**).
2. On the parent's cue, the child takes a breath; submerges mouth, nose and eyes; and blows bubbles.
3. The child returns to the surface, takes a breath and submerges again.
4. The child repeats this action and bobs rhythmically, 1 breath about every 2 or 3 seconds. Start with 2 bobs and build on the number of bobs.

Buoyancy on Front

Front Float—With Assistance

1. The parent holds the child in the hip support on front or shoulder support position. The child's face may be in or out of the water.
2. The parent walks backward just enough to let the legs float up.
3. The parent makes eye contact with the child, cues the child and briefly releases support so that the child moves forward slightly, free-floating between the parent's outstretched arms with the face in the water.
4. The parent resumes support by grasping the child's shoulders or armpits.

SAFETY NOTE

Because the parent will be releasing the support, introduce these skills only after children are comfortable submerging their face in the water.

Front Glide—With Support or Assistance

With Support

1. The parent holds the child in a face-to-face position.
2. The parent positions a flotation device (barbell or foam noodle) under the child's armpits so it supports the child.

3. The parent maintains a secure hold on the flotation device and walks backward.
4. The parent cues the child then releases the flotation device allowing the child to glide using the flotation device between the parent's outstretched arms.
5. The parent resumes support by grasping the flotation device and/or child's shoulders or armpits.

With Assistance

1. The parent holds the child in a face-to-face position and moves backwards to generate some momentum. The child extends the arms to the front.
2. The parent makes eye contact with the child and makes sure that the child is focused and ready, cues the child then gently pulls the child closer on the surface.
3. The parent releases support for about 2 seconds while continuing to move backwards so that the child moves forward, gliding freely between the parent's outstretched arms.
4. The parent resumes support by grasping the child's shoulders or armpits.

Fig. 7-11, A

Fig. 7-11, B

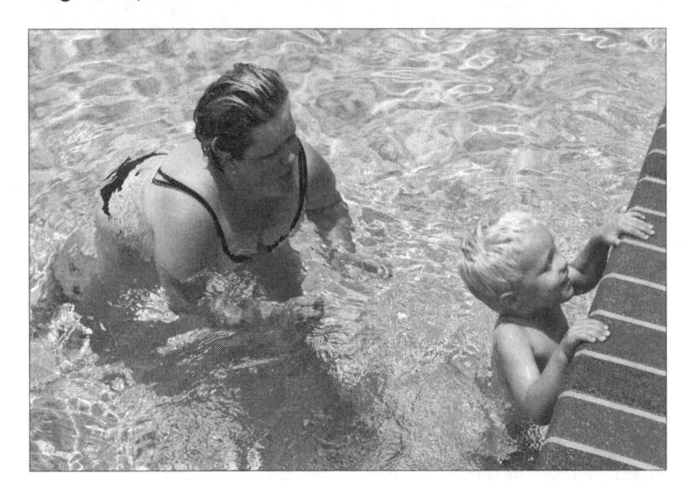

Fig. 7-11, C

Front Glide to the Wall—With Assistance

Children need to know how to get to the wall and hold on for safety. Practice this activity with children who are strong and coordinated enough to hold on to the wall unassisted and glide unassisted. If the child cannot glide unassisted, the parent should not release support.

1. The parent holds the child in the shoulder support position on the side (**Fig. 7-11, A**). The parent and child stand in the water facing the pool wall, about 2 to 3 body lengths from the pool wall. The parent should be in a position to see the child's face.
2. The parent cues the child then moves the child forward on the surface to gain momentum.
3. The parent gently releases the child and allows him or her to glide unassisted to the pool wall (**Fig. 7-11, B**).
4. The parent secures the child's hand to the edge of the pool wall (**Fig. 7-11, C**).

SAFETY NOTES

- *Be sure children are able to hold onto the wall for a few seconds at a time unassisted before practicing this skill.*
- *You and the parent should watch for the child swallowing water or getting water up the nose. Do not use this skill with a child who cries, chokes or shows discomfort.*

TEACHING TIP

If the child needs assistance on the approach to the wall, put one hand in the middle of the child's back and gently push the child toward the wall. Once the child reaches the wall, remove your hand. Allow the child to submerge naturally. Most children will instinctively reach up and grab the wall. If the parent helps with two hands, the child will likely continue to depend on the parent for help. Using the one hand, the parent helps the child make it to the wall without the child knowing that he or she is being helped. If the child does not reach up to grab the wall after submerging, help by gently bringing him or her up and securing the hands to the wall.

Buoyancy on Back

Back Float—With Support or Assistance

With Support

1. The parent holds the child in the hip support on back or back support position.
2. The parent places a flotation device on the child's torso and tells the child to grasp the device.
3. The parent walks backward with the child just enough to allow the legs to float up.
4. The parent cues the child and briefly releases support so that the child floats using the flotation device between the parent's outstretched arms.
5. The parent resumes support by placing his or her hands underneath the child's back or hips.

With Assistance

1. The parent holds the child in the hip support on back or back support position. The child relaxes the arms to the side.
2. The parent walks backward with the child just enough to allow the legs to float up (**Fig. 7-12**).
3. The parent cues the child and briefly releases support so that the child floats freely between the parent's outstretched arms.
4. The parent resumes support by placing his or her hands underneath the child's back or hips.

Fig. 7-12

Back Glide—With Support or Assistance

With Support

1. The parent holds the child in the hip support on back or back support position.
2. The parent places a flotation device on the child's torso and tells the child to grasp it so it supports the child.
3. The parent cues the child, walks backward and glides the child on his or her back.

With Assistance

1. The parent holds the child in the hip support on back or back support position. The child relaxes the arms to the side or places the hands on the stomach.
2. The parent walks backward with the child. When the parent and child gain momentum, the parent cues the child and briefly releases support so that the child glides freely between the parent's outstretched arms. When releasing support, remove the hand from under the back. When the child becomes comfortable and kicks while on the back, remove the hand from under the head for a few moments at a time.
3. The parent resumes support by placing his or her hands underneath the child's back.

INSTRUCTOR'S NOTE

Vary this skill by having the child hold onto the side of the pool, place his or her feet against wall, then release the wall and gently glide backward with the parent supporting the head and back.

Changing Direction

Roll from Front to Back—With Assistance

1. The parent places the child in a face-to-face position.
2. The parent gains forward momentum to move the child into a front glide, then cues the child by tapping the back of the child's head.
3. The parent grasps the child's same wrist (e.g., right hand to right wrist, left hand to left wrist) and pulls the wrist under. This causes the shoulder to dip, helping to turn the child over onto his or her back.
4. As the child turns, the parent supports the back of the child's head. At the end of the turn, the child should be in a back float with the parent's support.

Roll from Back to Front—With Assistance

1. The parent holds the child in the hip support on back or back support position. The child relaxes the arms to the side.
2. The parent walks backward with the child into a back glide then reaches across the child's body to grasp the child's wrist. The parent's other hand supports the back of the head.
3. The parent cues the child and pulls the child's arm across the body to assist with the roll. At the end of the turn, the child should be in a front float with the parent's support.

Swim on Front

Passing Between Adults—With Assistance

When the child becomes comfortable with his or her face in the water, the instructor can pass the child to the parent.

1. The instructor and parent stand about 6 feet apart. The instructor holds the child in a shoulder support on side position and leans forward to make eye contact.
2. Cue the child then push the child toward the parent in a gliding motion on the surface of the water for about 2 feet, then let go.
3. Let the child glide and kick unassisted for about 2 seconds.
4. The parent catches the child and helps him or her up with a light touch using the shoulder support.

Drafting with Breathing—With Assistance

Introduce this skill only after the children are comfortable holding a breath with the face in the water for at least 2 to 4 seconds at a time. While practicing this skill, the parent releases the child and continues to move backwards, creating a current between the parent and child. The child will remain close to the parent.

INSTRUCTOR'S NOTE

Children should be unsupported with their faces in the water for no more than 2 to 4 seconds.

SAFETY NOTE

Teach parents to watch for bubbles as a sign that the child needs a breath. The parent should immediately lift the child so the face clears the water to ensure he or she does not inhale while still under water. Do not use drafting with a child who cries, chokes or shows discomfort.

When the child is comfortable with drafting, have the parent practice drafting and breathing with the child.

Fig. 7-13

1. The parent holds the child in the shoulder support or hip support on front position.
2. The parent drafts the child with the face in the water for about 3 seconds (**Fig. 7-13**).
3. The parent regains support under the child's shoulder or chest and cues the child to breathe.
4. The parent drafts the child again for about 2 or 3 seconds.
5. Repeat steps 2 and 3 again if the child is comfortable and happy.
6. The parent resumes support by grasping the child's shoulders or armpits and then gives a hug and praise.

INSTRUCTOR'S NOTE

As the child gets comfortable, encourage the child to kick and pull with the arms. The parent must maintain eye contact and pay very close attention to know when the child is ready to put the face in the water and draft. Any sputtering, coughing or crying indicates the child is not ready for this skill. Warn parents never to force a child to do a skill; this only delays his or her readiness to try additional skills.

Leg Action—Alternating or Simultaneous Movements—With Assistance

Add leg action to the gliding skills previously described. Whether using a flotation device (**Fig. 7-14**) or assistance from the parent (**Fig. 7-15**), have parents cue and encourage the child to move the legs in a way that is natural and comfortable for the child, either in an alternating (such as a rudimentary flutter kick) or a simultaneous (such as a rudimentary dolphin kick or breaststroke kick) action.

Fig. 7-14

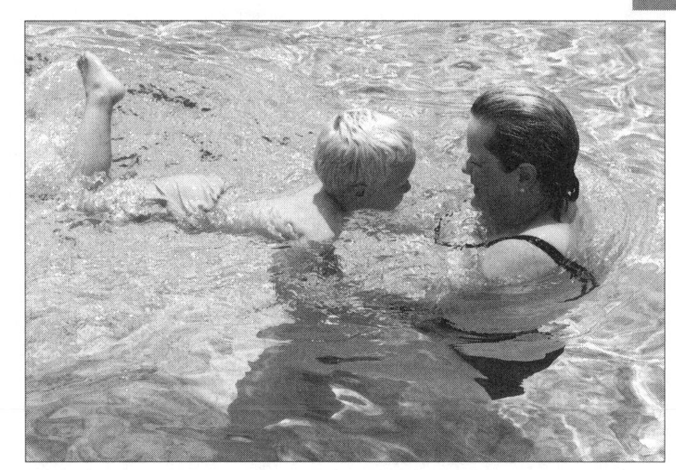

Fig. 7-15

Arm Action—Alternating or Simultaneous Movements—With Support or Assistance

Add arm action to the gliding skills previously described. Have parents encourage the child to move the arms in a way that is natural and comfortable for the child, either in an alternating (such as a rudimentary front crawl) or a simultaneous (such as a rudimentary butterfly or breaststroke) action.

With Support—Stationary

1. The parent holds the child in the arm stroke position.
2. The parent encourages the child to try different alternating or simultaneous arm movements (rudimentary front crawl, butterfly or breaststroke arm action) with underwater recovery. The parent helps guide the child's arm movements.

With Support

1. The parent holds the child in a side support position. The child's face may be in or out of the water.
2. The parent walks forward with the child while the child moves the arms using an alternating or simultaneous arm movement (**Fig. 7-16**).

INSTRUCTOR'S NOTE

The child may use a flotation device, such as a barbell or foam noodle, for support. The parent must remain within arm's reach of the child whenever a flotation device is used.

With Assistance

1. The parent holds the child in the hip support on front or shoulder support position.
2. The parent walks backward with the child. When the parent and child gain momentum, the parent cues the child and briefly releases support so that the child moves forward, moving his or her arms between the parent's outstretched arms.
3. The parent resumes support by grasping the child's shoulders or hips.

Fig. 7-16

Fig. 7-17

Combined Arm and Leg Actions on Front—With Support

With Support

1. The parent holds the child in the shoulder support on the side position. The child's face may be in or out of the water.
2. The parent walks forward and cues the child to combine any type of arm and leg movement and blow bubbles (**Fig. 7-17**).

With Assistance

1. The parent and child stand in the water facing the pool wall about 2 to 3 body lengths from the pool wall. The parent holds the child in the shoulder support on the side position. The child's face may be in or out of the water.
2. The parent moves forward to gain momentum, cues the child, then gently glides and passes the child to the pool wall while the child performs any type of arm and leg movement and blows bubbles.
3. The parent secures child's hand to the edge of the pool wall.

Combined Arm and Leg Actions on Front with Breathing—With Assistance

1. The parent holds the child in a face-to-face position.
2. The parent prepares the child to do a front glide with the face in the water.
3. The parent drafts the child and encourages the child to combine any type of arm and leg movement.
4. The parent cues the child to take breaths every few strokes. The parent places his or her hands under the child's chest and lifts the child to raise the face out of the water for a breath. This is necessary until the child is strong enough to lift the head unassisted.
5. The parent resumes support.

SAFETY NOTE

Watch for bubbles as a sign that the child needs a breath. The parent should immediately lift the child so the face clears the water to ensure he or she does not inhale while still under water.

Swim on Back

Leg Action—Alternating or Simultaneous Movements—With Assistance

Add leg action to the gliding skills previously described. Whether using a flotation device or assistance from the parent (**Fig. 7-18**), have parents cue and encourage the child to move the legs in a way that is natural and comfortable for the child, either in an alternating (such as a rudimentary flutter kick) or a simultaneous (such as a rudimentary breaststroke kick) action.

Arm Action—Alternating or Simultaneous Movements—With Support or Assistance

Add arm action to the gliding skills previously described. Have parents encourage the child to move the arms in a way that is natural and comfortable for the child, either in an alternating (such as rudimentary back crawl) or a simultaneous (such as finning or rudimentary elementary backstroke) action.

With Support

1. The parent places the child in the hip support on back or back support position.
2. The parent cues the child to move his or her arms in an alternating or simultaneous movement.
3. The parent assists the child to a standing position or back to the pool wall.

TEACHING TIP

Starting from the hip support on back position with the child's head on the parent's shoulder, have the parent move his or her arms to a position on the outside of the child's arms. Have the parent grasp the top of the child's hand and wrist then guide the arms in an alternating or simultaneous movement.

With Assistance

1. The parent places the child in the hip support on back or back support position.
2. The parent walks backward with the child. When the parent and child gain momentum, the parent cues the child and briefly releases support so that the child moves between the parent's outstretched arms.
3. The parent resumes support by placing his or her hands underneath the child's back.

Combined Arm and Leg Actions on Back—With Support or Assistance

With Support

1. The parent places the child in the hip support on back or back support position.
2. The parent walks backward with the child and cues the child to combine any type of arm and leg movement (**Fig. 7-19**).

Fig. 7-18

Fig. 7-19

With Assistance

1. The parent places the child in the hip support on back or back support position.
2. The parent walks backward with the child. When the parent and child gain momentum, the parent cues the child and briefly releases support so that the child moves forward, moving his or her arms and legs between the parent's outstretched arms.
3. The parent resumes support by placing his or her hands underneath the child's back.

Water Safety

The concept of water safety should be central to every part of an aquatics program. The following Water Safety topics are required for Parent and Child Aquatics Level 2:

- The importance of wearing a life jacket
- Reaching assists
- Basic water safety rules review
- Safety at the beach and the waterpark
- Water toys and their limitations

Wrap up each class session by emphasizing the safety component of the skills they learned.

Add topics as necessary so that you integrate water safety into each lesson. When selecting additional topics, think about current events in or special needs of your local area or region. Refer to **Chapter 4** for details on these topics and for additional topics.

CHAPTER

8

Preschool Aquatics

American Red Cross Preschool Aquatics, consisting of three levels, is an integral part of the overall Red Cross instructional aquatic and water safety program. The primary objective of Preschool Aquatics is to promote the developmentally appropriate learning of fundamental water safety and aquatic skills by young children about 4 and 5 years of age. Skills are grouped into aquatic and water safety categories in the following way:

- Water Entry and Exit
- Breath Control and Submerging
- Buoyancy
- Changing Direction and Position
- Treading
- Swim on Front and Back
- Water Safety

This chapter provides the information you need to conduct the Preschool Aquatics levels. General administrative notes are covered first, followed by outlines for the levels and descriptions of the required skills listed. The descriptions include suggested learning progressions and teaching tips for the required skills.

Administrative Notes

Prerequisites

The recommended ages for children in Preschool Aquatics is about 4 and 5 years old. Participation should not be determined by age alone. When determining if Preschool Aquatics is appropriate for a child, consider their developmental readiness, maturity and experience in the water. For some preschool children, Parent and Child Aquatics still may be appropriate, while a few may be able to go directly into Learn-to-Swim.

There are no skill prerequisites for Preschool Level 1. For Preschool Levels 2 and 3, children must be able to demonstrate the exit skills assessments of the previous level. Integrate an evaluation of all children prior to the start of a session or during the first lesson, regardless of level, to determine an appropriate starting point for each child.

Upon completion of Preschool Aquatics, children may enroll in Red Cross Learn-to-Swim. A child who completes Preschool Aquatics Levels 1 or 2 and is 6 years old may enroll in the next level of Preschool Aquatics or move on to Learn-to-Swim Level 2. A child who completes Preschool Aquatics Level 3 may enroll in Learn-to-Swim Level 3.

Course Length

No level has a minimum or maximum length. In general, typical sessions consist of 8 to 10 lessons of about 30 minutes each.

Class Size

Class sizes may range from one-on-one instruction to the Red Cross recommendation of at least 1 instructor for every 6 children in a Preschool Aquatics class. Close supervision is necessary to make practice effective and keep the members of the class safe. To increase safety and instructional quality, consider having fewer children per instructor based on such factors as having a class of children who are showing fear and anxiety, children who may need special attention or teaching in water that is relatively deep for children.

Using co-instructors is an effective way to increase the amount of individual attention each child receives. While Water Safety instructor aides may assist in classes, only certified Water Safety instructors should be co-instructors.

Facility

It is recommended that Preschool Aquatics classes be taught only in well-maintained swimming pools. If conducting classes at open bodies of water, such as lakes, consider that they are more likely to carry harmful organisms and are subject to wide variations in temperature, clarity and weather conditions. Always check with facility management to ensure that open bodies of water have been checked for safety.

Optimal conditions at the facility can make your program more successful. When possible, a facility for Preschool Aquatic classes should have–

- Adequate air circulation and sufficiently warm air temperatures.
- Secured pool entrances when classes are not in session.
- A storage space for instructional equipment and toys.
- Working showers, with warm water and soap available.

Temperature

Young children are more susceptible to hypothermia than older children, even at relatively warm temperatures. Take the following measures to keep young children from getting chilled:

- Typically, water temperature that is at least 83° F (28.3° C) is more comfortable for young children.

- Keep the air temperature at least 2° F above water temperature.
- If you cannot control water and air temperatures, keep the lessons short.
- Keep dry towels available for children when exiting the water especially if the air temperature and humidity are low.

Depth

Many young children learn best when actively exploring the aquatic environment under their own power and control. When the water is too deep for children to stand safely and comfortably, seek ways to reduce the depth. Course requirements are based on the assumption that the facility has water shallow enough for children to stand independently. Ways to achieve this include–

- Using a facility with a gradually sloping shallow area and/or graduated steps so that a child of average size can stand alone in waist-deep and chest-deep water.
- Using teaching platforms on which children can stand safely.

When the depth cannot be controlled, for many activities you must support children, one at a time while other children remain on the side. Allow children to hold the wall or use flotation devices between individual practices of skills, if necessary. Practicing activities as a group may not be possible initially. Making children sit and take turns is not an optimal learning strategy so other techniques are preferable. Safety always should be the first priority, however.

Noise and Distractions

You must control sights and sounds in the environment because young children are easily distracted. Consider the following suggestions:

- Limit loud, distorted sounds as much as possible.
- Hold the class in an isolated area of the pool to limit distractions from other patrons who are moving about and shouting or crying.
- Encourage children to talk in normal voices and not shout over the noise.
- Store unused toys and equipment out of sight.
- Ask another available instructor, instructor aide or parent, if available, to take any child who is over-stimulated to a quieter area of the pool to calm down and adjust to the environment. If no one else is available to help, be creative and find a way to calm that child down without compromising the safety of the other participants.

Course Requirements

For each of the three Preschool Aquatics levels, there are completion requirements given in the outlines in this chapter. Refer to the sidebar in **Chapter 7** for definitions of the terms used to explain the completion requirements at each level. As your class proceeds, use the skills checklist on the *Water Safety Instructor's CD-ROM* to chart children's progress as they satisfy the requirements. To receive a certificate for a given level, children must meet the requirements for the level. This includes demonstrating the completion requirement for all of the skills listed on the outlines, as well as performing the exit skills assessments.

To help children prepare for the exit skills assessments, start to combine skills as they begin achieving success with the skills individually. For example, once they are able to step into the water repeatedly, front glide for a couple body lengths and recover to a vertical position, have them put the skills together.

An important objective of using developmentally appropriate practice is to customize safety and swimming skills to match an individual swimmer's capabilities. You may be flexible in applying performance standards, but the child must be able to meet the objectives of the exit skills assessment to receive a certificate for the course level. Additionally, extenuating circumstances, such as the limitations of someone with a disability or other health condition, may keep a child from meeting the performance standards. For example, a child may be unable to move a joint in a particular way, but can still move through the water in a modified way. Base your judgment in such cases on whether the child performs the skill as close to the standard as his or her condition allows. As you learned in Fundamentals of Instructor Training, you teach to the standard and test to the objective.

Resources

The pages that follow outline the required skills for each level, including completion requirements and descriptions for each skill and exit skills assessments for each level. The following additional materials are available as references:

- *Swimming and Water Safety* manual
- *Water Safety Instructor's CD-ROM*
- *Longfellow's WHALE Tales K–6 Educational Packet*
- *Teaching Swimming and Water Safety* DVD
- *Swimming and Diving Skills* DVD
- *Longfellow's WHALE Tales* DVD

Support Materials

Keeping children and their parents informed of progress is one of the most important things you can do to ensure optimal learning and customer satisfaction in your classes. The *Water Safety Instructor's CD-ROM* contains tools and resources to help you communicate with children and their parents as they progress through the Preschool Aquatics levels.

Raffy Learns to Swim and Waddles in the Deep

Two booklets are an integral part of American Red Cross Preschool Aquatics. *Raffy Learns to Swim* is designed to support Preschool Aquatics Levels 1 and 2 and Learn-to-Swim Level 1, and *Waddles in the Deep* is designed to support Preschool Aquatics Level 3 and Learn-to-Swim Levels 2 and 3. These booklets provide a way for you to communicate with parents. Refer to **Chapter 4** for booklet details.

Newsletters to Parents

A newsletter for each level of Preschool Aquatics provides you with a tool to let parents and children know what they are learning at each stage. Each newsletter highlights new skills that will be introduced and provides water safety messages. It encourages parents to sign their children up for the next level, giving them a glimpse into what skills come in the next level. The newsletter contains a designated area that can be personalized with facility information.

Achievement Cards

Achievement cards for each level provide you with a progress report for children who do not meet the completion requirements. This tool gives you the opportunity to let children and their parents know what skills they have achieved and what skills still need work. There is a designated area that can be personalized with facility information.

Certificates

Children who meet the requirements for a level are eligible to receive a certificate for their achievement. A full-color certificate for each level is available on the *Water Safety Instructor's CD-ROM.* As an alternative, children may be issued an *American Red Cross Swimming and Water Safety Certificate* indicating Preschool Aquatics Levels 1, 2 or 3.

Safety Considerations

Safety-first should be your attitude and primary focus during each and every lesson. Follow these safe practices when working with preschool-age children:

- Teach children to ask for permission to enter the water.
- Teach children to know who is supervising them.
- Discourage children from swallowing water.
- Remind children to try to use the toilet before coming into the pool.
- Make sure children shower before entering the pool.
- When working with one child at a time–
  - Do not turn your back to the rest of the class.
  - Stay within quick reach of the rest of the class.
  - Work efficiently and try to give equal time to each child. If absolutely necessary to

guarantee safety, have the other children sit on the side while waiting their turn, but realize that this is a poor teaching technique that limits active practice time.

- Do not let children hyperventilate or have breath-holding contests. Limit children to a single inhalation whenever you ask them to hold their breath or submerge.

At the beginning of a course at each level, tell parents and children what to expect. Be sure to explain the goal to children in very simple terms. Before children enter the water the first time, show them the area in which they will be swimming. Explain the safety rules for your facility and quiz them on what each rule means to be sure they understand. Explain the objectives of the class–to feel comfortable in the water, to learn to swim independently or to improve swimming skills and to remain safe in and around the water. Stress the importance of following your directions, trying new things and lots of practice. Do not promise that they will learn to swim right away, but explain that it will take time.

Teaching Preschool Children

Teaching aquatic skills to preschool children requires patience. The following sections give essential information for evaluating young children's aquatic readiness, orienting children to the water and preparing them for entry into Red Cross Learn-to-Swim.

Despite the general similarities among children of similar ages, each one is unique. All children have individual qualities and characteristics that make them different from other children who are the same age. Children learn motor skills, such as swimming, at different ages. They learn at different rates, and they have different preferences for activities.

Children also differ in their learning styles. Some children want to be shown how to do something, while others prefer to listen to and follow directions. Many children do better discovering things on their own, with some guidance. Do not spend too much time on one learning style, as children who learn in other ways will not learn as quickly. Ideally, try to incorporate teaching that involves all learning styles. Be aware of such differences when planning presentations of skills for the class. At this age, children want to please and be like their friends, are more likely to agree to rules and begin to show more independence. Keep the following in mind when in the water with a child:

- Maintain appropriate eye contact.
- Observe how children perform skills so you can provide appropriate feedback.
- Demonstrate skills but do not expect children to copy them exactly.
- Praise attempts regardless of the level of success.
- Depending on a child's success, increase or decrease the difficulty of tasks to allow them to be successful more often than not. Know when enough is enough.
- Make sure children are calm and happy before entering and leaving the water.
- Remember that the skills and requirements are not cast in stone, but need to be modified to meet the needs of individual children.

Whether you use direct teaching strategies (i.e., explain, demonstrate and try, task setting, reciprocal practice) or indirect teaching strategies (i.e., active exploration, guided discovery, using task cards for active exploration and guided discovery), the descriptions of the skills are presented in a step-by-step approach that can be adjusted to match the chosen teaching style.

In Preschool Aquatics, especially in Level 1, you use many of the techniques that are used by parents in Parent and Child Aquatics, including cueing, as skills are practiced. See Parent and Child Aquatics **Chapter 7** for more detail on cueing. You also use many of the holding and support techniques that are described in **Chapter 3**.

Learning and Development in Children

During the preschool years, children's abilities to think, feel, move and play all change dramatically. Because young children are different from adults and even older children, it is important to understand these complex learning and developmental changes and how to evaluate children's readiness for aquatic activities.

The learning process is one way parents and instructors see how children grow. Learning involves changes in observable behavior that results from practice or experience. The instructor can control the factors that influence young children's learning in the teaching environment. As an instructor, you direct the learning process by setting goals, encouraging appropriate and sufficient practice and providing feedback and motivation. The critical factor is that you must focus on children's learning rather than on your teaching. Instruction is only one of many influences on learning for children.

Sufficient practice is essential for learning motor skills. Children at this age still need to mix practice with fun and frequent rest periods. Play games that allow children to achieve learning objectives while providing sufficient amounts of goal-oriented practice. Playing the right kinds of learning games helps children practice and improve their skills to–

- Minimize fatigue.
- Improve the depth of learning.
- Stay motivated and interested in the activities.

Applying these principles in your Preschool Aquatics courses means that your classes normally should meet more often for shorter periods. Other factors that influence learning are explained in **Chapters 2 and 5**.

Tips for Working with Preschoolers

- Keep activities short. Unless the activity is very engaging, preschoolers may pay attention for only a few minutes before they need a new activity to keep them interested. Take cues from children. If they seem bored, disinterested or tired of the activity, switch to another approach or skill that is more fun and interesting to them.
- Make learning fun and creative. Preschoolers like to sing songs, use silly words and play simple games. Keep the learning activity fun by incorporating rhymes, songs and games.
- Integrate pretend play into learning. Children this age are interested in playing pretend and may even have imaginary friends. Encourage pretend play in the lessons by creating games where children act as mythical characters, animals or superheroes.
- Use games to get children's attention. Games, such as Follow the Leader or Simon Says, are designed to get children to mimic your movements or try different skills they might not try otherwise. Games engage children in learning through fun and play.
- Move around a lot. Preschoolers are full of energy. They do not want to sit around. While they may stay in their own space, they may not sit or stand still.
- If you must work with one child at a time, work quickly and effectively with each one. Encourage them to watch their classmates so that they stay engaged in the activity. Avoid making children sit or stand in lines unless their safety is an issue.
- Explain the buddy system and pair off children. Emphasize that this system may help children learn from one another and provide added safety.
- Consider first letting children show you how they perform the various skills as you introduce them. This is a good way to ease the fear of the unknown (the first days of swim class or the first attempt at trying a new skill) in some beginners. You can evaluate what they already know, what they are willing to try and determine a good pace for introducing the skills.
- Encourage children to explore different movements in the water. Observe what comes naturally to them and build on their strengths. As the session progresses, provide a wide variety of experiences to achieve the skills of the level. If you approach your task with creativity and enthusiasm, learning to swim will be fun, safe and rewarding for everyone.

Fearful Children

Fearful children present challenges that all Water Safety instructors must learn how to deal with. Children may experience different levels of fear.

You will get better at helping children overcome fear of learning to swim with experience.

Children enjoy the water more when they can take their own time, experience success, practice repeatedly and receive praise for their efforts. For more information about understanding and working with fearful children, see **Chapter 5**.

Readiness

Throughout the preschool years, young children continue to develop more advanced physical, language and cognitive skills. They are more likely to agree to rules and begin to show more independence. Importantly, they may begin to understand the risks associated with water better than they did when they were younger. The scope and depth of these cognitive skills gradually improves with age.

The fitness levels of young children vary widely, just as do other segments of the population. Generally, they have less body fat than older children (making them more prone to chilling) and they are not as strong or have as much endurance as older children.

Children acquire different skills gradually. The way that they perform a skill, such as leg kicking or arm pulling, the first few times will look very different from how they will be able to perform the same skill after lots of practice and experience. Just as young children take up to 5 years to learn to walk in an adult-like fashion, they may take at least that much time to begin to acquire more proficient aquatic skills. In the water young children start with awkward ineffective motions. With sufficient practice and time, children will improve their proficiency in aquatic skills. One key is for children and instructors to be patient and give each child sufficient time and practice to acquire skills. For more information about children's readiness, see **Chapter 5**.

Evaluating Readiness

Evaluating children's readiness is necessary to determine what skills to teach, when to teach the skills and how to approach teaching the skills. Consider each child's developmental age, attitude, ability to understand and general coordination levels when preparing your lesson plan. See Chapters 3 and 5 for more details. Each beginner-level skill prepares children for the next more advanced skill. As children become comfortable and confident practicing a skill, introduce the next level of complexity of that skill or the next skill in the learning progression.

The Preschool Aquatics Outlines

Red Cross Preschool Aquatics is designed to give young children a positive, developmentally appropriate aquatic learning experience. Preschool Aquatics Level 1 is designed to orient young preschool children to the aquatic environment and to help them gain basic aquatic skills in each category at the most rudimentary levels. It also helps children develop comfort in, on and around water.

In Preschool Aquatics Levels 2 and 3, children build upon the basic skills to begin learning rudimentary propulsive swimming movements on both the front and back. Appropriate personal safety and rescue skills are included to help children meet safety goals. Preschool Aquatics Level 2 helps children gain greater independence in the skills and develop more comfort in and around water. Preschool Aquatics Level 3 helps children start to gain basic swimming propulsive skills to be comfortable in and around water.

It is not necessary to introduce the skills in the order they appear on the level outlines because young children do not learn skills in a single straight progression. When helping children acquire skills at more advanced levels, you may need to let them practice the skills at lower levels until they are more proficient and comfortable. It is very important, however, to integrate water safety skills in each lesson of each level so children learn what they can do to be safe in and around the water. Refer to the sample block plans and sample lesson plans on the *Water Safety Instructor's CD-ROM* for examples of how to organize the presentation of these skills.

Preschool Aquatics Level 1

In Level 1, you teach the most elementary aquatic skills, which children continue to build on as they progress through the Preschool Aquatics and Learn-to-Swim levels. At this first level, children start developing good attitudes and safe practices around the water.

INSTRUCTOR'S NOTE

The skills in the outline are not in a teaching order. Refer to the sample block plan and lesson plan for examples of how to organize the skills.

Preschool Aquatics Level 1 Outline

Equipment

- Submersion items (such as diving rings and eggs)
- U.S. Coast Guard-approved life jackets (correct sizes for children)
- Flotation devices, such as foam noodles, barbells and kickboards

Skills	Completion Requirements	References
Water Entry and Exit		
Enter water using ladder, steps or side	Demonstrate, independently	WSIM, page 156
Exit water using ladder, steps or side	Demonstrate, independently	WSIM, page 156
Breath Control and Submerging		
Blowing bubbles through mouth and nose	Demonstrate, at least 3 seconds	WSIM, page 157
Submerging mouth, nose and eyes	Demonstrate	WSIM, page 157
Opening eyes under water and retrieving submerged objects	Demonstrate, at least 2 times, in shallow water	WSIM, page 158
Buoyancy on Front		
Front glide	Demonstrate, with support, at least 2 body lengths	WSIM, page 158
Recover from a front glide to a vertical position	Demonstrate, with support	WSIM, page 159
Buoyancy on Back		
Back glide	Demonstrate, with support, at least 2 body lengths	WSIM, page 159
Back float	Demonstrate, with support, at least 3 seconds	WSIM, page 160
Recover from a back float to a vertical position	Demonstrate, with support	WSIM, page 160
Changing Direction and Position		
Roll from front to back	Demonstrate, with support	WSIM, page 160
Roll from back to front	Demonstrate, with support	WSIM, page 160

Skills	Completion Requirements	References
Treading		
Arm and hand actions	Explore, in chest-deep water	SWS, page 85 WSIM, page 161
Swim on Front		
Alternating leg action	Demonstrate, with support, at least 2 body lengths	WSIM, page 161
Simultaneous leg action	Demonstrate, with support, at least 2 body lengths	WSIM, page 161
Alternating arm action	Demonstrate, with support, at least 2 body lengths	WSIM, page 162
Simultaneous arm action	Demonstrate, with support, at least 2 body lengths	WSIM, page 162
Combined arm and leg actions on front	Demonstrate, with support, at least 2 body lengths	WSIM, page 162
Swimg on Back		
Alternating leg action	Demonstrate, with support, at least 2 body lengths	WSIM, page 162
Simultaneous leg action	Demonstrate, with support, at least 2 body lengths	WSIM, page 163
Alternating arm action	Demonstrate, with support, at least 2 body lengths	WSIM, page 163
Simultaneous arm action	Demonstrate, with support, at least 2 body lengths	WSIM, page 163
Combined arm and leg actions on back	Demonstrate, with support, at least 2 body lengths	WSIM, page 163
Water Safety		
Staying safe around aquatic environments	Discuss	SWS, pages 12&16; WSIM, page 72
Recognizing the lifeguards	Discuss	
Don't Just Pack It, Wear Your Jacket	Discuss/demonstrate	SWS, 18; WSIM, page 73 WSIM, page 62 LWT
Recognizing an emergency	Discuss	SWS, page 44; WSIM, page 74
How to call for help	Demonstrate	SWS, page 45; WSIM, page 63
Too Much Sun Is No Fun	Discuss/demonstrate	SWS, page 13; WSIM, page 68 LWT

Exit Skills Assessment

All Preschool Aquatics Level 1 skills can be performed with support.

1. Enter independently, using either the ladder, steps or side, travel at least 5 yards, submerge to mouth and blow bubbles for at least 3 seconds then safely exit the water. (Children can walk, move along the gutter or "swim.")
2. While in shallow water, glide on front at least 2 body lengths, then roll to back and float on back for 3 seconds then recover to a vertical position.

Preschool Aquatics Level 1 Skills

Water Entry and Exit

Enter Water Using Ladder, Steps or Side—Independently

Teach children how to enter the water safely. It may be necessary for children to adjust to the water temperature before practicing entering skills. See Parent and Child Aquatics in **Chapter 7** for water adjustment techniques. As a group or one at a time, have children enter the water in any of the following ways:

- Using the ladder–children step backward down the ladder (i.e., with their backs to the water and facing the ladder) while holding on to the railings with both hands.
- Using steps–children walk down the steps, facing the water and holding on to a railing, if available.
- From the side–children sit on the side, roll over on to the stomach, slide in feetfirst and hold on to the side with the shoulders in the water.

SAFETY NOTE

Maintain contact with any child who needs help while entering the water when first learning the skill. In the beginning, discourage children splashing for the comfort of less eager classmates.

TEACHING TIP

Once children are in the water, you may need to start with some adjustment activities, such as walking through waist-deep or chest-deep water while holding onto the wall or your hand for support. As confidence builds, they may try walking by themselves away from the wall or holding onto the gutter and moving along the pool wall by sliding their hands ("spidering" or "monkey walking"). If using a pool that is too deep for children to stand, you may help children one at a time adjust to the water by holding a child in a support position and giving him or her a short and fun ride. Never turn your back on the rest of the class.

Exit Water Using Ladder, Steps or Side—Independently

As a group or one at a time, have children exit the water in any of the following ways:

- Using the ladder–children walk up the ladder with their back to the water, facing the ladder and holding on to the railings with the hands.
- Using steps–children walk up the steps, facing the side and holding on to a railing if available.
- From the side–children pull themselves up to the elbows, then to the stomach, then put one leg up on the side, continue to climb out of the water then stand or sit on the deck safely.

SAFETY NOTE

Maintain contact with any child who needs help getting out of the water when first learning the skill. Be alert to other children reentering the pool.

Breath Control and Submerging

Children should learn breath-control skills from the beginning. With patience, practice and repetition, children can learn the basic skills of breath control, which makes it easier to relax and learn more advanced skills.

Blowing Bubbles Through Mouth and Nose

Practice blowing bubbles from any stationary position as a group. If necessary, hold children one at time using the hip straddle or a face-to-face position.

Have children–

1. Take a breath and hold it for 1 or 2 seconds.
2. Put the mouth in the water and blow slowly.
3. Repeat steps 1 and 2 until comfortable.
4. Next, take a breath and hold it for 1 or 2 seconds.
5. Put the mouth and nose in the water and blow slowly.

TEACHING TIPS

Techniques for encouraging children to blow bubbles through their mouth and nose include the following:

- *First, have them blow with their faces out of the water. Pretend that your index finger is a candle they can blow out. Continue by asking if the child can still blow out the "magic candle" when it is under water. It will only blow out if they forcefully blow bubbles. Rapidly moving the hand and tucking the index finger inside your closed hand simulates the candle going out.*
- *Tell them that blowing bubbles through the nose is like blowing the nose. Explain that this keeps water from going in the nose.*
- *Have them hum and the air will blow through the nose keeping the water out of the nose.*

Submerging Mouth, Nose and Eyes

Many aquatic skills require swimmers to briefly hold the breath and submerge the face. The ability to hold the breath for short periods of time is an important part of breath control and an important safety skill. If necessary, children may practice submerging first with support from you, an aide or a partner and then practice without support. The eyes may be open or closed at first.

Have children–

1. Stand in chest-deep water. Less confident children can face the wall and hold onto it.
2. Take a breath and hold it.
3. Squat to submerge the mouth. Exhale through the mouth then stand up.
4. Next, take another breath and hold it.
5. Squat to submerge the mouth and nose. Exhale through the mouth and nose then stand up.
6. Next, take another breath and hold it.
7. Squat to submerge the mouth, nose and eyes. Exhale through the mouth and nose then stand up.
8. Gently exhale through the mouth and nose and return to the surface.

TEACHING TIP

Start practicing submerging for 1 or 2 seconds and gradually build to about 5 seconds.

SAFETY NOTE

Do not let children hyperventilate or have breath-holding contests. Limit children to a single inhalation whenever you ask them to hold their breath or submerge.

Opening Eyes and Retrieving Submerged Objects

After children are comfortable holding their breath and submerging the face, practice submerging with the eyes open. If the child cannot stand in the water, refer to Parent and Child Aquatics, Level 2, page 137.

- Standing in shallow water, hold objects just below the surface.
- Have children take a breath then submerge the face and take the object from your hand.
- Gradually increase the depth by holding an object about 2–3 feet under water and having them take turns retrieving the object from your hand.

TEACHING TIPS

- *If the water depth is shallow enough, children can work in pairs taking turns submerging and recovering objects for each other without direct control by the instructor.*
- *Integrate some simple submersion games, such as "underwater tea party," "ring-around-the-rosy" and "talk to the fish." Children are capable of designing their own submersion and recovery games that encourage opening the eyes under water.*
- *Hold different color objects and instruct children to pick up a particular colored object.*

Buoyancy on Front

Front Glide—With Support

1. Stand next to the child who is facing the wall about 3 feet from the wall.
2. Have the child extend the arms forward while you get ready to support the child using the shoulder support on the side position.
3. Cue the child to take a breath, lean forward, put the face in the water and push off the bottom. As the child pushes off the bottom, provide support as necessary to get the child into a horizontal position then help him or her glide to the wall.

INSTRUCTOR'S NOTES

- *If the water is too deep for children to stand, begin with the shoulder support on the side position.*
- *Some children may not be able to perform a front glide with the face in the water at first.*

TEACHING TIPS

- *Start by having children stand up straight in the water or on the deck to learn the streamlined position. Tell them to hold their arms straight up over the ears with one hand on top of the other. Have them put their legs together. Tell them "With your head down, legs together and toes pointed, you are in the streamlined position for gliding." Make sure the arms are over the ears and not in front of the face.*
- *You can also hold children in the hip support on front position. Have them extend their arms and legs and glide them through the water. Encourage them to take a breath and put their face in the water. When the face is down you may loosen your support.*
- *Children may practice the glide using a flotation device for support.*

Recover from a Front Glide to a Vertical Position—With Support

While holding the child in the shoulder support on the side position in the front glide, move with the child from the horizontal to vertical position helping the child to recover. To recover to a vertical position have the child–

1. Breathe out slowly.
2. Lift the head and press down with the arms.
3. Pull the knees under the body toward the chest.
4. Place the feet on the bottom then stand up.

Buoyancy on Back

Back Glide—With Support

1. Have the child hold the wall, bend the knees and put the balls of the feet on the wall.
2. Have the child relax and put the head back, ears in or out of the water, and look up.
3. Use the hip support on back or the back support position, then cue the child to push gently off the wall.
4. Have the child raise the hips so the stomach is up and the arms to the side.
5. Have the child keep the legs straight with the feet slightly under the surface and glide on the back.

INSTRUCTOR'S NOTE

Pushing off from the wall can be used when performing the back glide and the combined arm and leg actions on back.

TEACHING TIPS

- *Start by having children stand up straight in the water or on the deck to learn the streamlined position. Tell them to hold their arms straight up over the ears with one hand on top of the other. Have them put their legs together. Tell them "With your head back, legs together and toes pointed, you are in the streamlined position for gliding." Make sure the arms are over the ears.*
- *Children may practice the glide using a flotation device for support.*

Back Float—With Support

In shallow water–

1. Have the child submerge to the neck.
2. Have the child hold the arms over head and slightly out to the side.
3. Using the hip support on back or back support position, have the child lay the head back until the ears are in the water and look straight up.
4. Have the child raise the body gently at the hips and push the chest and stomach toward the surface.
5. Have the child keep the legs relaxed, knees slightly bent and feet slightly beneath the surface.
6. Help the child float in this position as long as possible or at least 3 seconds.

INSTRUCTOR'S NOTES

- *As children experience buoyancy, gradually decrease support by removing the hand from under the back, keeping the other hand under the head.*
- *If the water is too deep for children to stand, have children start from the wall and follow the steps for the back glide to move into a back float.*

TEACHING TIP

Start by having children stand up straight in the water or on the deck. Tell them to hold their arms up with the elbows bent and the hands to the side about a foot away from the head. Have them arch the back and look up with the head back. Tell them "With your head back and ears in the water, you are in the position for floating on the back." Remind them to keep their feet under water and relax as much as possible.

Recover from a Back Float to a Vertical Position—With Support

While holding the child in the hip support on back or back support position in the back float, move with the child from the horizontal to vertical position helping the child to recover. To recover to a vertical position have the child–

1. Take a breath, tuck the chin toward the chest and bring the knees forward by bending at the hips.
2. Sweep the arms back and down, then forward in a circular motion.
3. Exhale then stand up.

Changing Direction and Position

The ability to change direction and position are important skills for personal safety and self-rescue. Both abilities involve controlling balance of the body in the water.

Roll from Front to Back—With Support

1. Hold the child in a support position on the front. Move backward to generate some momentum.
2. Cue the child, then rotate him or her onto the back with the child's ears in or out of the water.
3. Move your hands to hold the child in a support position on the back.

Roll from Back to Front—With Support

1. Hold the child in a support position on the back. Move backward to generate some momentum.
2. Cue the child, then rotate him or her onto the stomach with the child's face out of the water.
3. Move your hands to hold the child in a support position on the front.

Treading

Arm and Hand Actions

Children stand in chest-deep water and practice moving the arms in a smooth continuous motion just below the surface of the water. Encourage children to periodically lift the feet off the bottom.

Swim on Front

Children learn the basics of alternating and simultaneous leg and arm movements on front to provide a foundation for learning the front crawl, breaststroke and butterfly in the future. Rather than trying to teach any specific stroke qualities now, guide them in exploring how they can use their arms and legs to help them move through the water. These initial attempts likely will not look like later kicks or arm actions, but the important element is that children are exploring how their arms and legs work in the water. For example, there is no need initially for arm pulls to recover over the water because children are just experimenting with the pulling or propulsive phase of arm actions.

Following are some suggestions for helping children practice arm and leg movements separately and then as part of a combined stroke:

- While sitting on the edge of the pool, ask children to show you different ways they can kick their legs or pull their arms. Encourage them to try both alternating ("one at a time") and simultaneous ("at the same time") movements.
- While bracketing on the wall, ask children to place their face in or out of the water then kick their legs. You can ask them to show you how they can kick making their legs go up and down (alternating as a rudimentary flutter kick or simultaneous as a rudimentary dolphin kick) or out and in (in a circle like a rudimentary breaststroke kick).
- While holding them at the surface of the water, ask children to show you how they can stroke with their arms one at a time and then at the same time. They can practice with their faces in or out of the water. They can also practice arm and leg actions at the same time with your support.
- While using flotation devices, such as foam noodles, barbells or kickboards extended in front, ask children to show you different ways they can kick to move through the water. Using foam noodles or barbells held under the arm pits, ask children show you how they can pull the water with their arms and kick their legs.

Alternating Leg Action—With Support

First attempts at alternating up and down leg action on the front may resemble either a bicycling action or a rudimentary flutter kick with bent knees.

Guide children so that they kick with the–

- Legs close together and mostly straight just under the surface.
- Knees, ankles and feet relaxed. Make some, but not too much, splash with the feet.

Simultaneous Leg Action—With Support

Simultaneous leg action on the front may resemble a rudimentary breaststroke or dolphin kicks. In these kicks, both legs move at the same time and in the same way in the water. Use one or both of the methods described below to guide the child's leg action.

Guide children in a simultaneous out and in motion to–

- Separate and spread the legs, knees and ankles out.
- Squeeze the legs and feet together quickly.

You can also guide children in a simultaneous up and down motion with the–

- Legs extended and close together just under the surface.
- Knees, ankles and feet relaxed.
- Hips moving up and down.

Alternating Arm Action—With Support

Guide children to move their arms in a continuous alternating motion to–

- Move the arms forward, palms down and fingers together but relaxed (not cupped), one at a time under the water.
- Sweep each arm down and pull the water back toward the feet.
- Recover the arms under water with hands in position to glide forward again.

Simultaneous Arm Action—With Support

Guide children to–

- Move both arms forward at the same time with palms facing down and fingers together but relaxed.
- Sweep both arms out and down to pull the water back toward the feet at the same time.
- Recover both arms under water with hands in position to glide forward again.

Combined Arm and Leg Actions on Front—With Support

Have children pull with the arms and kick with the legs on front as described in this section. Encourage them to use the alternating arm motion with the alternating kick or a simultaneous arm motion with the simultaneous kick.

Swim on Back

Children learn the basics of alternating and simultaneous leg and arm motions on back to provide a foundation for learning the elementary backstroke and the back crawl in the future. Rather than trying to teach the specific stroke patterns now, you should guide them to explore using their arms and legs to travel through the water on their backs in a comfortable manner.

Following are some suggestions for having children practice arm and leg motions separately and then as part of the combined stroke:

- While sitting on the edge of the pool, ask children to show you how they can kick their legs or stroke their arms.
- While holding them at the surface of the water, ask children to show you how they can stroke with their arms one at a time and then at the same time. They can practice arm and leg action at the same time with your support. See **Chapter 3** to learn the support and holding positions that are appropriate for certain skills.
- While using flotation devices, such as foam noodles, barbells or kickboards held across the stomach or extended overhead, ask children to show you how they can kick their legs.

Alternating Leg Action—With Support

Alternating up and down leg action on the back may resemble a bicycling action, or a rudimentary flutter kick with bent knees.

Guide children so that they kick in a continuous up and down motion with the–

- Legs and knees close together and just under the surface with some splash.
- Knees, ankles and feet relaxed, but knees can be bent.

TEACHING TIP

Tell children to pretend to kick a ball upward.

Simultaneous Leg Action—With Support

Simultaneous leg action on the back may resemble a rudimentary elementary backstroke or dolphin kick. Both legs move at the same time and in the same way in the water. Use one or both of the methods described below to guide the child's leg action.

Guide children so they kick using a simultaneous out and in motion to–

- Separate and spread the legs, knees and ankles out.
- Squeeze the legs and feet together quickly to make the water swirl.

You can also guide children in a simultaneous up and down motion with the–

- Legs extended and close together just under the surface.
- Knees, ankles and feet relaxed.
- Encourage them to allow the hips to move up and down.

Alternating Arm Action—With Support

Alternating arm action on the back may resemble a rudimentary back crawl or the arms may simply perform an alternating finning action while staying under the water.

Guide children to–

- Reach back, extending the arms up to the shoulders or over the head one at a time.
- Sweep and push the water back toward the feet one at a time.
- Remind them that when one is pulling, the other arm is coming back up.

Simultaneous Arm Action—With Support

Guide children to–

- Bend the arms and move the hands out from the side and up toward the shoulders.
- Push the water toward the feet in a short sweeping stroke with both hands at the same time.

Combined Arm and Leg Actions on Back—With Support

Have children stroke with the arms and kick with the legs on back as described in this section. Encourage them to use the alternating arm actions with the alternating leg actions or the simultaneous arm actions with the simultaneous leg actions. The arms do not have to recover over the water either in the alternating or simultaneous actions because the purpose is to practice the basic coordination and propulsive actions. If children naturally bring the arms out of the water, that is okay.

Water Safety

The concept of water safety should be central to every part of an aquatics program. The following Water Safety topics are required for Preschool Aquatics Level 1:

- Staying safe around aquatic environments
- Recognizing the lifeguards
- Don't Just Pack It, Wear Your Jacket
- Recognizing an emergency

- How to call for help
- Too Much Sun Is No Fun

Wrap up each class session by emphasizing the safety component of the skills they learned. Add topics as necessary so that you integrate water safety into each lesson. When selecting additional topics, think about current events in or special needs of your local area or region. Refer to **Chapter 4** for details on these topics and for additional topics.

Exit Skills Assessment

When children complete Preschool Aquatics Level 1, they should be comfortable getting in and moving through the water and be willing to put their face in the water. Children should also be able to use arm and leg movements while supported. There are two parts to the exit skills assessment, both can be performed with support.

1. Enter independently, using either the ladder, steps or side, travel at least 5 yards, submerge to mouth and blow bubbles for at least 3 seconds then safely exit the water. (Children can walk, move along the gutter or "swim.")
2. While in shallow water, glide on front at least 2 body lengths, then roll to back and float on back for 3 seconds then recover to a vertical position.

Preschool Aquatics Level 2

The objectives of this level are to build on the basic aquatic skills learned in Level 1 and to give children further success with fundamental aquatic skills performed to a slightly more advanced degree than at Level 1. Most skills in this level are performed with assistance. This level marks the beginning of independent aquatic locomotion skills. Children continue to explore using simultaneous and alternating arm and leg actions on the front and back to gain more proficiency for future strokes. Level 2 also adds to the self-help and basic rescue skills introduced in Level 1.

Preschool Aquatics Level 2 Outline

Equipment

- Submersion items (such as diving rings and eggs)
- U.S. Coast Guard-approved life jackets (correct sizes for children)

Skills	Completion Requirements	References
Water Entry and Exit		
Water Entry ■ Stepping in	Demonstrate, with assistance, in shoulder-deep water	WSIM, page 167
Water Exit ■ Exit water using ladder, steps or side	Demonstrate, independently, in chest-deep water	WSIM, page 167
Breath Control and Submerging		
Bobbing	Demonstrate, with support, at least 3 times	WSIM, page 167
Opening eyes under water and retrieving submerged objects	Demonstrate, independently, at least 2 times, in chest-deep water	WSIM, page 167
Buoyancy on Front		
Front float	Demonstrate, with support and assistance, at least 3 seconds	WSIM, page 168
Front glide	Demonstrate, with assistance, at least 2 body lengths	WSIM, page 168
Recover from a front float or glide to a vertical position	Demonstrate, with assistance, in chest-deep water	WSIM, page 168
Buoyancy on Back		
Back float	Demonstrate, with assistance, at least 5 seconds	WSIM, page 168
Back glide	Demonstrate, with assistance, at least 2 body lengths	WSIM, page 168
Recover from a back float or glide to a vertical position	Demonstrate, with assistance, in chest-deep water	WSIM, page 168

Skills	Completion Requirements	References
Changing Direction and Position		
Roll from front to back	Demonstrate, with assistance	WSIM, page 169
Roll from back to front	Demonstrate, with assistance	WSIM, page 169
Treading		
Using arm and leg actions	Demonstrate, with assistance, at least 5 seconds, in shoulder-deep water	WSIM, page 169
Swim on Front		
Combined arm and leg actions on front	Demonstrate, with assistance, at least 3 body lengths	WSIM, page 169
Swim on Back		
Finning arm action	Demonstrate, with assistance, at least 3 body lengths	WSIM, page 170
Combined arm and leg actions on back	Demonstrate, with assistance, at least 3 body lengths	WSIM, page 170
Water Safety		
Staying safe around aquatic environments	Discuss	SWS, pages 12 & 16; WSIM, page 72
Recognizing the lifeguards	Discuss	SWS, page 18; WSIM, page 73
Don't Just Pack It, Wear Your Jacket	Discuss/demonstrate	SWS, page 18; WSIM, page 62 LWT
Recognizing an emergency	Discuss	SWS, page 44; WSIM, page 74
How to call for help	Discuss/demonstrate	SWS, page 45; WSIM, page 63
Too Much Sun Is No Fun	Discuss	SWS, page 13; WSIM, page 68 LWT

Exit Skills Assessment

All Preschool Aquatics Level 2 skills can be performed with assistance.

1. Glide on front at least 2 body lengths, roll to back, float on back for 5 seconds then recover to a vertical position.
2. Glide on back for at least 2 body lengths, roll to front, float for 5 seconds then recover to a vertical position.
3. Swim using combined arm and leg actions on front for 3 body lengths, roll to back, float for 5 seconds, roll to front then continue swimming on front for 3 body lengths.

Preschool Aquatics Level 2 Skills

Water Entry and Exit

Water Entry

Stepping In—With Assistance

Have children–

1. Stand up at the edge of the pool with the toes curled over the edge.
2. Step out away from the edge and in to the water. You may need to hold some children's hand until they get used to this skill.
3. Move back to the side. Assist children as needed.

SAFETY NOTE

Do not let children step in water less than shoulder deep. Do not try to catch children in midair or stand in front of a child who is stepping in.

Water Exit

Exit Water Using Ladder, Steps or Side—Independently

Refer to Preschool Aquatics, Level 1, page 156. In this level, children should be able to exit repeatedly and easily from chest-deep water independently.

Breath Control and Submerging

Bobbing—With Support

Have children hold the wall for support and–

1. Take a breath and hold it.
2. Submerge the mouth, nose and eyes or fully submerge for 1 or 2 seconds.
3. Blow bubbles slowly and come up.
4. Repeat steps 1–3 several times.

SAFETY NOTE

Do not let children hyperventilate or have breath-holding contests. Limit children to a single inhalation whenever you ask them to hold their breath or submerge.

Opening Eyes Under Water and Retrieving Submerged Objects—Independently

Have children take a breath then fully submerge and pick up an object.

- If standing in shallow water, have children pick up an object from the bottom.
- If in water where children cannot stand, have them hold on to the wall. Hold an object about 2 to 3 feet under the water so that children have to fully submerge to retrieve the object. Have them take turns retrieving the object from your hand. If children let go of the wall, help them get back to the wall as needed.

Buoyancy on Front

Front Float—With Support and Assistance

With Support

1. Hold the child in a face-to-face position. The child's face should be in the water.
2. Walk backward slowly just enough to allow the child's legs to float up to the surface and float for at least 3 seconds.

With Assistance

Children should be able to float on front for at least 3 seconds with assistance as needed.

Front Glide—With Assistance

If the pool is too deep for children to stand but they are comfortable gliding with their faces in the water–

1. Hold children above the waist from behind. Have them put their feet on your legs just above your knees and squat to shoulder depth.
2. Tell them to move into a streamlined position.
3. Have children take a breath and put the face in the water.
4. Then have children push off and glide at least 2 body lengths.

To have children push off from the wall–

1. Have them hold the side of the pool wall with one hand and extend the other arm in front.
2. Place the feet against the pool wall, about hip-width apart.
3. Take a breath and hold it.
4. Let go of the wall and extend the arms into a streamlined position.
5. Push off the wall to begin.

Recover from a Front Float or Glide to a Vertical Position—With Assistance

Refer to Preschool Aquatics, Level 1, page 159. In this level, children should be able to recover from a front glide with assistance as needed.

Buoyancy on Back

Back Float—With Assistance

Refer to Preschool Aquatics, Level 1, page 160. In this level, children should be able to float on back for at least 5 seconds with assistance as needed. Children may need to do slight kicks (breaststroke or scissors kick) and finning motions to help keep the body floating.

Back Glide—With Assistance

Refer to Preschool Aquatics, Level 1, page 159. In this level, children should be able to do the back glide at least 2 body lengths with assistance as needed.

Recover from a Back Float or Glide to a Vertical Position—With Assistance

Refer to Preschool Aquatics, Level 1, page 160. In this level, children should be able to recover from a back float with assistance as needed.

Changing Direction and Position

Roll from Front to Back—With Assistance

1. Place the child in a face-to-face position.
2. Gain forward momentum to move the child into a front glide, then cue the child by tapping the back of the child's head.
3. Grasp the child's same wrist (e.g., right hand to right wrist, left hand to left wrist) and pull the wrist under. This causes the shoulder to dip, helping to turn the child over onto his or her back.
4. As the child turns, support the back of the child's head. At the end of the turn, the child should be in a back float with assistance as needed.

Roll from Back to Front—With Assistance

1. Hold the child in the hip support on back or back support position. The child relaxes the arms to the side.
2. Walk backward with the child into a back glide, then reach across the child's body to grasp the child's wrist. Your other hand supports the back of the child's head.
3. Cue the child and pull his or her arm across the body to assist with the roll. At the end of the turn, the child should be in a front float with assistance as needed.

Treading

Using Arm and Leg Actions—With Assistance

Have children tread water for at least 5 seconds by–

- Standing in shoulder-deep water and moving the arms using slow, continuous motions just below the surface of the water.
- Kicking using any leg action, such as modified breaststroke or scissors kick or rotary kick, that is efficient in holding the head above the surface.

TEACHING TIP

Have children practice initially with flotation support, such as while suspended from a foam noodle or barbell in chest-deep water, until they are comfortable. Encourage children to experiment with arm movements that help them maintain their position. Arm actions can start out large and exaggerated.

Swim on Front

Combined Arm and Leg Actions on Front—With Assistance

Refer to Preschool Aquatics, Level 1, page 162. In this level, children should be able to do combined arm and leg actions on front for. at least 3 body lengths with assistance as needed.

INSTRUCTOR'S NOTE

Pushing off from the wall can be used when performing the combined arm and leg actions on front. See Front Glide in this level for a description.

Swim on Back

Finning Arm Action—With Assistance

Providing assistance as needed, have children–

1. Move into a back float with the head back and arms at the side. The hands are relaxed under the surface of the water with the palms facing the bottom of the pool.
2. Bend the elbows, slowly move the hands out from the side and push the water toward the feet in short strokes. Arm movements may be simultaneous or slightly alternating.

INSTRUCTOR'S NOTE

Finning works well with both alternating and simultaneous kicking.

Combined Arm and Leg Actions on Back—With Assistance

Refer to Preschool Aquatics, Level 1, page 163. In this level, children should be able to do combined arm and leg actions on back for at least 3 body lengths with assistance as needed.

Water Safety

The concept of water safety should be central to every part of an aquatics program. The following Water Safety topics are required for Preschool Aquatics Level 2:

- Staying safe around aquatic environments
- Recognizing the lifeguards
- Don't Just Pack It, Wear Your Jacket
- Recognizing an emergency
- How to call for help
- Too Much Sun Is No Fun

The water safety topics in this level are the same as those in Level 1. They are repeated to ensure that children start to really understand these very important concepts. When you present the topics to children, be sure to vary your approach. For example, rather than just telling children how to recognize the lifeguards, ask them questions to see if they can tell you how to recognize the lifeguards. As another example, when presenting "Too Much Sun is No Fun," restate the main points then make it fun by having them simulate putting sunscreen all over the exposed parts of their bodies.

Wrap up each class session by emphasizing the safety component of the skills they learned. Add topics as necessary so that you integrate water safety into each lesson. When selecting additional topics, think about current events in or special needs of your local area or region. Refer to **Chapter 4** for details on these topics and for additional topics.

Exit Skills Assessment

When children complete Preschool Aquatics Level 2, they should be gaining confidence in the water and should be willing to fully submerge. Children should also be able to use arm and leg movements with assistance as needed. There are three parts to the exit skills assessment, all can be performed with assistance.

1. Glide on front at least 2 body lengths, roll to back, float on back for 5 seconds then recover to a vertical position.
2. Glide on back for at least 2 body lengths, roll to front, float for 5 seconds then recover to a vertical position.
3. Swim using combined arm and leg actions on front for 3 body lengths, roll to back, float for 5 seconds, roll to front then continue swimming on front for 3 body lengths.

Preschool Aquatics Level 3

The objective of Level 3 is to build on the skills learned in Levels 1 and 2 by providing additional guided practice of basic aquatic skills at slightly more proficient performance levels and greater distances and times. Skills in this level are performed independently. You teach children to improve coordination of combined simultaneous arm and leg actions and alternating arm and leg actions. As in all levels, you present additional safety skills and improve comprehension of previous knowledge.

Preschool Aquatics Level 3 Outline

Equipment

U.S. Coast Guard-approved life jackets (correct sizes for children)

Skills	Completion Requirements	References
Water Entry and Exit		
Water Entry ■ Jumping in	Demonstrate, independently, in at least shoulder-deep water	WSIM, page 173
Breath Control and Submerging		
Fully submerging and holding breath	Demonstrate, independently, at least 5 seconds	WSIM, page 173
Bobbing	Demonstrate, independently, at least 5 times, in chest-deep water	SWS, page 78 WSIM, page 173
Buoyancy on Front		
Float in a face-down position ■ Front float ■ Jellyfish float ■ Tuck float	Demonstrate, independently, at least 5 seconds	SWS, page 80 WSIM, page 174
Recover from a front float or glide to a vertical position	Demonstrate, independently	SWS, page 81 WSIM, page 173
Buoyancy on Back		
Back float	Demonstrate, independently, at least 15 seconds	SWS, page 80 WSIM, page 174
Back glide	Demonstrate, independently, at least 2 body lengths	SWS, page 82 WSIM, page 174
Recover from a back float or glide to a vertical position	Demonstrate, independently	SWS, page 80 WSIM, page 174
Changing Direction and Position		
Change direction of travel while swimming on front or back	Demonstrate, independently	WSIM, page 175
Treading		
Arm and leg actions	Demonstrate, independently, at least 15 seconds, in shoulder-deep water	SWS, page 85 WSIM, page 175

Skills	Completion Requirements	References
Swim on Front		
Combined arm and leg actions on front	Demonstrate, independently, at least 5 body lengths	WSIM, page 175
Swim on Back		
Finning arm action	Demonstrate, independently, at least 5 body lengths	WSIM, page 175
Combined arm and leg actions on back	Demonstrate, independently, at least 5 body lengths	WSIM, page 175
Water Safety		
Staying safe around aquatic environments	Discuss	SWS, pages 12 & 16; WSIM, page 72
Don't Just Pack It, Wear Your Jacket	Discuss/demonstrate	SWS, page 18; WSIM, page 62 LWT
Recognizing an emergency	Discuss	SWS, page 44; WSIM, page 74
How to call for help	Discuss/demonstrate	SWS, page 45; WSIM, page 63
Too Much Sun Is No Fun	Discuss	SWS, page 13; WSIM, page 68 LWT
Look Before You Leap	Discuss	SWS, page 52; WSIM, page 75 LWT
Think So You Don't Sink	Discuss	SWS, page 47; WSIM, page 76 LWT
Reach or Throw, Don't Go	Discuss/Demonstrate	SWS, page 70; WSIM, page 70 LWT

Exit Skills Assessment

All Preschool Aquatics Level 3 skills are done independently.

1. Step from side into chest-deep water, move into a front float for 5 seconds, roll to back, float for 5 seconds then return to a vertical position.
2. Move into a back float for 5 seconds, roll to front then recover to a vertical position.
3. Push off and swim using combined arm and leg actions on front for 5 body lengths, roll to back, float for 15 seconds, roll to front then continue swimming for 5 body lengths. (You can assist the child when taking a breath.)

Preschool Aquatics Level 3 Skills

Water Entry

Jumping In—Independently

Have children–

1. Stand up at the edge of the pool where water is at least shoulder deep. Have them curl the toes over the edge of the pool.
2. Jump out away from the edge and in to the water. Help the child back to the side as needed.

SAFETY NOTE

Do not let children jump in water less than shoulder deep. Do not try to catch children in midair or stand in front of them as they jump.

Breath Control and Submerging

Fully Submerging and Holding Breath—Independently

Have children–

- Practice fully submerging for about 5 seconds at a time.
- Exhale (blow bubbles) on the way up.

SAFETY NOTE

Do not let children hyperventilate or have breath-holding contests. Limit children to a single inhalation whenever you ask them to hold their breath or submerge.

Bobbing—Independently

Have children–

1. Stand about 5 feet from the wall then squat and submerge to shoulder depth.
2. Take a breath and hold it.
3. Squat to submerge the head for 1 or 2 seconds.
4. Blow bubbles slowly as they come up, hopping forward toward the wall.
5. Repeat steps 3–4 at least 5 times.

TEACHING TIP

If children are having trouble returning to the surface, have them put their arms in front and push down on the water as they come up.

Buoyancy on Front

Float in a Face-Down Position—Independently

Front Float

Refer to Preschool Aquatics, Level 2, page 168. In this level, children should be able to do the front float for at least 5 seconds independently.

Jellyfish Float

In chest-deep water, have children–

1. Submerge to the neck.
2. Take a deep breath and hold it.
3. Bend forward at the waist and put the head face down in the water.
4. Flex the knees slightly to raise the feet off the bottom. Let the arms and legs hang naturally from the body.
5. Continue holding the breath and relax as much as possible.
6. Allow the back to rise to the surface of the water and float for at least 5 seconds.
7. Drop the feet, exhale slowly and stand up to recover.

Tuck Float

In chest-deep water, have children–

1. Submerge to the neck.
2. Take a breath and hold it.
3. Bend forward at the waist and put the head face down in the water with the chin on the chest.
4. Flex the hips and bring the knees to the chest.
5. Hold on to the legs at mid-calf and allow the body to rise to the surface and float for at least 5 seconds.
6. Exhale slowly, let go of the legs and stand up to recover.

Recover from a Front Float or Glide to a Vertical Position—Independently

Refer to Preschool Aquatics, Level 1, page 159. In this level, children should be able to recover to a vertical position independently.

Buoyancy on Back

Back Float—Independently

Refer to Preschool Aquatics, Level 1, page 161. In this level, children should be able to do the back float for at least 15 seconds independently.

Back Glide—Independently

Refer to Preschool Aquatics, Level 1, page 159. In this level, children should be able to do the back glide for at least 2 body lengths independently.

Recover from a Back Float or Glide to a Vertical Position—Independently

Refer to Preschool Aquatics, Level 1, page 160. In this level, children should be able to recover to a vertical position independently.

Changing Direction and Position

Change Direction of Travel While Swimming on Front or Back—Independently

Being able to change direction while swimming on the front and on the back is an important safety skill. It allows a swimmer to return to safety when pushing off from the wall or to move away from dangerous situations.

Stand about 2 yards from the pool wall in waist- to chest-deep water. Have children—

1. Push off from the wall and swim using combined arm and leg actions on front or back.
2. Continue swimming around you then back to the wall.

Treading

Arm and Leg Actions—Independently

Refer to Preschool Aquatics, Level 2, page 169. In this level, children should be able to tread water using arm and leg actions for at least 15 seconds independently.

Swim on Front

Combined Arm and Leg Actions on Front—Independently

Refer to Preschool Aquatics, Level 1, page 162. In this level, children should be able to perform combined arm and leg actions on front for at least 5 body lengths independently.

At this distance, children will need to take a breath. Encourage children by walking backward in front of them. Every few strokes cue the child to blow bubbles. If necessary during the first few tries, position your hands under the shoulders, briefly lift him or her up to take a breath then allow the child to continue swimming independently.

Swim on Back

Finning Arm Action—Independently

Refer to Preschool Aquatics Level 2, page 170. In this level, children should be able to perform finning arm actions for at least 5 body lengths independently.

Combined Arm and Leg Actions on Back—Independently

Refer to Preschool Aquatics Level 1, page 163. In this level, children should be able to perform combined arm and leg actions on back for at least 5 body lengths independently.

Water Safety

The concept of water safety should be central to every part of an aquatics program. The following Water Safety topics are required for Preschool Aquatics Level 3:

- Staying safe around aquatic environments
- Don't Just Pack It, Wear Your Jacket
- Recognizing an emergency
- How to call for help

- Too Much Sun Is No Fun
- Look Before You Leap
- Think So You Don't Sink
- Reach or Throw, Don't Go

As in Level 2, some of the water safety topics are repeated for reinforcement. Vary your presentation approach to keep it interesting and to test the level of understanding of children. Add topics as necessary so that you integrate water safety into each lesson.

Wrap up each class session by emphasizing the safety component of the skills they learned.

When selecting additional topics, think about current events in or special needs of your local area or region. Refer to **Chapter 4** for details on these topics and for additional topics.

Exit Skills Assessment

When children complete Preschool Aquatics Level 3, they should be increasingly confident in the water. Children are starting to swim independently using arm and leg movements, but may still need assistance when taking a breath. There are three parts to the exit skills assessment, all are performed independently.

1. Step from side into chest-deep water, move into a front float for 5 seconds, roll to back, float for 5 seconds then return to a vertical position.
2. Move into a back float for 5 seconds, roll to front then recover to a vertical position.
3. Push off and swim using combined arm and leg actions on front for 5 body lengths, roll to back, float for 15 seconds, roll to front then continue swimming for 5 body lengths. (You can assist the child when taking a breath.)

CHAPTER 9

Learn-to-Swim

American Red Cross Learn-to-Swim teaches aquatic and personal water safety skills in a logical progression. It consists of six levels. Participants in Level 1 are oriented to the aquatic environment and gain some basic skills in each category. Throughout the levels, participants build on their basic skills to learn various propulsive movements on the front, back and side. As the levels increase, participants learn to refine the different strokes and build endurance. Each level includes exit skills assessments that put together many of the skills learned in the level.

The objectives of the Red Cross Learn-to-Swim courses are to teach people to be safe in, on and around the water and swim well. Skills are categorized in the following way in Levels 1–5:

- Water Entry and Exit
- Breath Control and Submerging
- Buoyancy
- Changing Direction and Position
- Treading
- Swim on Front, Back and Side
- Water Safety

Level 6 focuses on refining strokes and turns and building endurance. Additionally, three "menu" options provide participants the opportunity to learn information and skills for specific aquatic activities, including–

- Personal Water Safety.
- Fundamentals of Diving.
- Fitness Swimmer.

By the end of Level 6, participants have the prerequisite skills and have developed the necessary fitness level for entrance into advanced courses, such as Water Safety Instructor, or other aquatic activities, such as competitive swimming and diving.

This chapter provides the information you need to conduct the Learn-to-Swim levels. General administrative notes are covered first, followed by outlines for the levels and descriptions of the required skills listed. The descriptions include suggested learning progressions and teaching tips for the required skills.

Administrative Notes

The following points apply to all Learn-to-Swim levels.

Prerequisites

The recommended minimum age for entry into Red Cross Learn-to-Swim is about 6 years old. There is no maximum age for any level. There are no skill prerequisites for Learn-to-Swim Level 1. For Levels 2–6, participants must be able to demonstrate the exit skills assessments of the previous level. Instructors should integrate an evaluation of all participants prior to the start of a session or during the first lesson, regardless of level, to determine an appropriate starting point for each participant. Some participants will have some experience with the water and may begin the program at a higher level.

Course Length

There is no minimum or maximum length of time specified. Course sessions are commonly made up of 8 to 10 lessons of 30 to 45 minutes each.

Class Size

Class sizes may range from one-on-one instruction to the Red Cross recommendation of at least one instructor for every 6 to 10 participants in a course. Close supervision is necessary to make practice effective and the class safe. To increase safety and instructional quality, consider having fewer participants per instructor based on such factors as having a class of young children, participants who show fear and anxiety or a class of participants needing special attention. A sufficient number of participants are necessary to successfully meet the objectives in the lesson plans. It is necessary to have enough participants to ensure that all skills can be conducted effectively.

Using co-instructors is an effective way to increase the amount of individual attention each participant receives. While Water Safety instructor aides may assist in classes, only certified Water Safety instructors should be co-instructors.

Facility

It is recommended that Learn-to-Swim classes be taught in well-maintained swimming pools. If conducting classes at open bodies of water, such as lakes, streams and ponds, consider that they are more likely to carry harmful organisms and are subject to wide variations in temperature, clarity and weather conditions. Always check with facility management to ensure open bodies of water have been checked for safety.

Optimal conditions at the facility can make your program more successful. When possible, a facility for Learn-to-Swim classes should have–

- Adequate air circulation and sufficiently warm air temperatures.
- Secured pool entrances when classes are not in session.
- A storage space for instructional equipment and toys.
- Working showers, with warm water and soap available.

Temperature

Younger children and older adults are more susceptible to hypothermia than others, even at relatively warm temperatures. Take the following measures to keep them from getting chilled:

- Maintain a water temperature of at least 83° F (28.3° C).
- Keep the air temperature at least 2° F above water temperature.
- If you cannot control water and air temperature, keep the lessons short.
- Encourage participants to have dry towels available when exiting the water, especially if the air temperature and humidity are low.

Depth

The course requirements are based on the assumption that the facility has water shallow enough for participants to stand and, for some levels, deep enough to learn headfirst entries and diving skills. (The Red Cross recommends a minimum of 9 feet for headfirst entries and diving from poolside and 11 feet, 6 inches for diving from a 1-meter diving board [or deeper if state or local regulations require].) If your facility does not meet these guidelines, you *must not* teach those skills. In such circumstances, headfirst entries are not required for the level. If possible, move the class to another facility with proper depth to teach those skills.

See Safety Note on page 181 for additional information on appropriate depths for headfirst entries and diving.

Course Requirements

For each of the six Learn-to-Swim levels, there are required skills with completion requirements as well as exit skills assessments. Refer to the sidebar in **Chapter 7** for definitions of the terms used to explain the completion requirements at each level. Performance criteria for swimming strokes are provided at each level. As your class proceeds, use the skills checklist on the *Water Safety Instructor's CD-ROM* to chart participants' progress in satisfying the requirements. To be certified at a given level, participants must meet the requirements listed in the level outline, including the individual skills and the exit skills assessments, except for headfirst entries and diving skills if the water is not deep enough.

Detailed descriptions of efficient and effective strokes are provided in the level in which they first appear. Stroke performance charts are provided in each level to describe the performance criteria required for successful completion for that particular level. **Chapter 6** in the *Swimming and Water Safety* manual and the *Swimming and Diving Skills* DVD provide additional detail and images for each stroke.

To help participants prepare for the exit skills assessments, start to combine skills as they begin achieving success with the skills individually. For example, once they are able to step into the water repeatedly, front glide for a couple body lengths and recover to a vertical position, have them put them all together.

You may be flexible in applying performance standards, but the participant must be able to meet the objectives of the exit skills assessment to receive a certificate for the course level. Additionally, extenuating circumstances, such as the limitations of someone with a disability or other health condition, may keep a participant from meeting the performance standards. For example, a participant may be unable to move a joint in a particular way, but can still move through the water in a modified way. Base your judgment in such cases on whether the participant performs the skill as close to the standard as his or her condition allows. As you learned in Fundamentals of Instructor Training, you teach to the standard and test to the objective.

References

This chapter outlines the required skills for each level, including completion requirements and descriptions for each skill and exit skills assessments for each level. The following additional materials are available as references:

- *Swimming and Water Safety* manual
- *Water Safety Instructor's CD-ROM*
- *Longfellow's WHALE Tales K–6 Educational Packet*
- *Teaching Swimming and Water Safety* DVD
- *Swimming and Diving Skills* DVD
- *Longfellow's WHALE Tales* DVD

Support Materials

Keeping participants and the parents of young participants informed of their progress is an important step toward ensuring customer satisfaction in your classes. The *Water Safety Instructor's CD-ROM* contains tools and resources to help you communicate with participants and their parents as they progress through the Learn-to-Swim levels.

Raffy Learns to Swim and Waddles in the Deep

Two booklets are an integral part of the American Red Cross Learn-to-Swim. *Raffy Learns to Swim* is designed to support Preschool Aquatics Levels 1 and 2 and Learn-to-Swim Level 1, and *Waddles in the Deep* is designed to support Preschool Aquatics Level 3 and Learn-to-Swim Levels 2 and 3. These booklets provide a way for you to communicate with parents. Refer to **Chapter 4** for booklet details.

Newsletters to Parents

A newsletter for each level of Learn-to-Swim provides you with a tool to let parents and participants know what they are learning at each stage. Each newsletter informs readers of the new skills being introduced, provides water safety messages and offers suggestions for practicing the skills learned in the lessons outside of class. It also encourages signing up for the next level and gives a glimpse as to what skills are in the next level. There is a designated area that can be personalized with facility information.

Achievement Cards

Achievement cards for each level provide you with a progress report for participants who do not meet the completion requirements. This tool gives you the opportunity to let participants and their parents know what skills they have achieved and what skills still need work. The achievement cards are available in two styles: one for younger audiences and one for more mature customers. There is a designated area that can be personalized with facility information.

Certificates

Participants who meet the requirements for a level are eligible to receive a certificate for their achievement. A full-color certificate for each level is available on the *Water Safety Instructor's CD-ROM.* As an alternative, participants may be issued an *American Red Cross Swimming and Water Safety Certificate* indicating Learn-to-Swim and the level completed.

Applying Techniques for Teaching Learn-to-Swim to Different Ages

For many aquatic facilities, children make up the majority of the learn-to-swim participants. However, many adults are taking the plunge and learning to swim. Because of different levels of maturity, strength and ability, it is usually best that programs be set up so that children, teens and adults are grouped separately.

There are developmental differences among children, teens and adults. The developmental level of participants factors in to how you design and plan lessons. You may need to be flexible and adjust your plans once you meet participants. It is important to consider the developmental level of participants and present your lessons according to their level of understanding and ability. Also, consider differences in maturity, strength, endurance, agility and physical size. For participants at varying ages, you will need to balance the skills and activities that participants can practice together and separately. Refer to **Chapter 5** for additional information on working with different age groups.

Regardless of participants' ages, your initial evaluation and ongoing assessment during sessions will help determine how to implement your lesson plans. Following the concept of the mnemonic COLA–Check, Organize, Lead and Assess–is a good way to accomplish this.

When working with beginners, consider the following helpful tips:

- Explain the buddy system and pair off participants. Emphasize that this system helps participants help each other learn and provides added safety.
- Consider first letting the participants show you how they perform the various skills as you introduce them. You can check what they already know and what they are willing to try, and determine a good pace for introducing skills.
- Encourage participants to explore movement in the water. Observe what comes naturally to them and build on their strengths. As the session progresses, provide a wide variety of experiences to achieve the skills of the level. If you approach your task with creativity and enthusiasm, learning to swim will be fun, safe and rewarding for everyone.

Fearful Participants

People of all ages may experience different levels of fear. You will get better at helping participants overcome fear of learning to swim with experience. See **Chapter 5** for information about fearful participants.

The Learn-to-Swim Outlines

Red Cross Learn-to-Swim is designed to give participants a positive aquatic learning experience. It is not necessary to introduce the skills in the order they appear on the level outlines because participants do not learn skills in a single straight progression. When helping participants acquire skills at more advanced levels, you may need to let them practice the skills at lower levels until they are more proficient and comfortable. Refer to the *Water Safety Instructor's CD-ROM* for resources to aid in making the course more fun and to help participants achieve the requirements for the levels. It is very important to integrate water safety skills in each lesson of each level so participants learn what they can do to be safe in and around the water. Refer to the sample block plans and sample lesson plans on the *Water Safety Instructor's CD-ROM* for examples of how to organize the presentation of these skills.

SAFETY NOTE

Headfirst entries into water less than 9 feet deep should be performed only with proper supervision of a swim coach and in water depths that conform with the rules of the concerned regulating body, such as USA Swimming, the National Collegiate Athletic Association (NCAA), the Amateur Athletic Union (AAU), the National Federation of State High School Associations (NFHS), YMCA of the USA and the international swimming federation (FINA). The swim coach must follow current rules of the regulating body. Higher standards, established by local and state bathing codes, supersede any regulations and recommendations established by competitive organizations.

Learn-to-Swim Level 1—Introduction to Water Skills

The objectives of Level 1 are to learn basic personal water safety information and skills, to help participants feel comfortable in the water and to enjoy the water safely. In Level 1, you teach elementary aquatic skills. At this level, participants start developing positive attitudes, good swimming habits and safe practices in and around the water.

Learn-to-Swim Level 1—Introduction to Water Skills Outline

Equipment

- Submersion items (such as diving rings and eggs)
- U.S. Coast Guard-approved life jackets (correct sizes for participants)
- Flotation devices, such as barbells, foam noodles and kickboards

Skills	Completion Requirements	References
Water Entry and Exit		
Enter water using ladder, steps or side	Demonstrate, independently	WSIM, page 156
Exit water using ladder, steps or side	Demonstrate, independently	WSIM, page 157
Breath Control and Submerging		
Blowing bubbles through mouth and nose	Demonstrate, at least 3 seconds	WSIM, page 184
Bobbing	Demonstrate, with support, at least 3 times	WSIM, page 167
Opening eyes underwater and retrieving submerged objects	Demonstrate, at least 2 times, in shallow water	WSIM, page 158
Buoyancy on Front		
Front glide	Demonstrate, with support, at least 2 body lengths	WSIM, page 158
Recover from a front glide to a vertical position	Demonstrate, with support	WSIM, page 159
Buoyancy on Back		
Back glide	Demonstrate, with support, at least 2 body lengths	WSIM, page 159
Back float	Demonstrate, with assistance, at least 3 seconds	WSIM, page 168
Recover from a back float or glide to a vertical position	Demonstrate, with support	WSIM, page 160
Changing Direction and Position		
Roll from front to back	Demonstrate, with support	WSIM, page 160
Roll from back to front	Demonstrate, with support	WSIM, page 160
Treading		
Arm and hand actions	Explore, in chest-deep water	WSIM, page 161

Skills	Completion Requirements	References
Swim on Front		
Alternating leg action	Demonstrate, with support, at least 2 body lengths	WSIM, page 161
Simultaneous leg action	Demonstrate, with support, at least 2 body lengths	WSIM, page 162
Alternating arm action	Demonstrate, with support, at least 2 body lengths	WSIM, page 162
Simultaneous arm action	Demonstrate, with support, at least 2 body lengths	WSIM, page 162
Combined arm and leg actions on front	Demonstrate, with support, at least 2 body lengths	WSIM, page 162
Swim on Back		
Alternating leg action	Demonstrate, with support, at least 2 body lengths	WSIM, page 162
Simultaneous leg action	Demonstrate, with support, at least 2 body lengths	WSIM, page 163
Alternating arm action	Demonstrate, with support, at least 2 body lengths	WSIM, page 163
Simultaneous arm action	Demonstrate, with support, at least 2 body lengths	WSIM, page 163
Combined arm and leg actions on back	Demonstrate, with support, at least 2 body lengths	WSIM, page 163
Water Safety		
Staying safe around aquatic environments	Discuss	WSIM, page 72 SWS, pages 12 & 16
Recognizing the lifeguards	Discuss	WSIM, page 73
Don't Just Pack It, Wear Your Jacket	Discuss/demonstrate	WSIM, page 62 SWS, page 18 LWT
Recognizing an emergency	Discuss	WSIM, page 74 SWS, page 44
How to call for help	Demonstrate	WSIM, page 63 SWS, page 45
Too Much Sun Is No Fun	Discuss	WSIM, page 68 SWS, page 13 LWT

Exit Skills Assessment

1. Enter independently, using either the ladder, steps or side, travel at least 5 yards, bob 3 times then safely exit the water. (Participants can walk, move along the gutter or "swim.")
2. Glide on front at least 2 body lengths, roll to a back float for 3 seconds and recover to a vertical position. (This part of the assessment can be performed with support.)

Learn-to-Swim Level 1 Skills

Water Entry and Exit

Enter Water Using Ladder, Steps or Side—Independently

Refer to Preschool Aquatics Level 1, page 156.

SAFETY NOTE

Maintain contact with participants who cannot enter or exit the water independently and help them enter or exit one at a time.

Exit Water Using Ladder, Steps or Side—Independently

Refer to Preschool Aquatics Level 1, page 156.

Breath Control and Submerging

Blowing Bubbles Through Mouth and Nose

Refer to Preschool Aquatics Level 1, page 157.

TEACHING TIPS

Techniques for encouraging participants to blow bubbles through their mouth and nose include the following:

- *First, have them take a breath and blow in the air. Pretend that your finger is a candle that they can blow out.*
- *Have participants practice blowing a small ball (Ping-Pong ball) along the surface of the water.*
- *Tell them that blowing bubbles through the nose is like blowing the nose. Explain that this keeps water from going in the nose.*
- *Have them hum and the air will blow through the nose keeping water out of the nose.*

Bobbing—With Support

Refer to Preschool Aquatics Level 2, page 167.

Opening Eyes Underwater and Retrieving Submerged Objects

Refer to Preschool Aquatics Level 1, page 158.

SAFETY NOTE

Do not let participants hyperventilate or have breath-holding contests. Limit participants to a single inhalation whenever you ask them to hold their breath or submerge.

Buoyancy on Front

Front Glide—With Support

Refer to Preschool Aquatics Level 1, page 158.

Recover from a Front Glide to a Vertical Position—With Support

Refer to Preschool Aquatics Level 1, page 159.

Buoyancy on Back

Back Glide—With Support

Refer to Preschool Aquatics Level 1, page 159.

Back Float—With Assistance

Refer to Preschool Aquatics Level 2, page 168. In this level, participants should back float with assistance for at least 3 seconds.

Recover from Back Float or Glide to a Vertical Position—With Support

Refer to Preschool Aquatics Level 1, page 160.

Changing Direction and Position

Roll from Front to Back—With Support

Refer to Preschool Aquatics Level 1, page 160.

Roll from Back to Front—With Support

Refer to Preschool Aquatics Level 1, page 160.

Treading

Arm and Hand Actions

Refer to Preschool Aquatics Level 1, page 161.

Swim on Front

Alternating Leg Action—With Support

Refer to Preschool Aquatics Level 1, page 161.

Simultaneous Leg Action—With Support

Refer to Preschool Aquatics Level 1, page 161.

Alternating Arm Action—With Support

Refer to Preschool Aquatics Level 1, page 162.

Simultaneous Arm Action—With Support

Refer to Preschool Aquatics Level 1, page 162.

Combined Arm and Leg Actions on Front—With Support

Refer to Preschool Aquatics Level 1, page 162. In this level, participants should be able to perform the combined arm and leg actions on front at the level of performance described in stroke performance chart.

Level 1 Stroke Performance Criteria	
Component	**Swim on Front (Combined Stroke Using Any Type of Arm or Leg Action)**
Legs	Alternating or simultaneous kicking motion from a supported position
Arms	Alternating or simultaneous propulsive and recovery actions from a supported position

Swim on Back

Alternating Leg Action—With Support

Refer to Preschool Aquatics Level 1, page 162.

Simultaneous Leg Action—With Support

Refer to Preschool Aquatics Level 1, page 163.

Alternating Arm Action—With Support

Refer to Preschool Aquatics Level 1, page 163.

Simultaneous Arm Action—With Support

Refer to Preschool Aquatics Level 1, page 163.

Combined Arm and Leg Actions on Back—With Support

Refer to Preschool Aquatics Level 1, page 163. In this level, participants should be able to perform the combined arm and leg actions on back at the level of performance described in stroke performance chart.

Level 1 Stroke Performance Criteria	
Component	**Swim on Back (Combined Stroke Using Any Type of Arm or Leg Action)**
Legs	Alternating or simultaneous kicking motion from a supported position
Arms	Alternating or simultaneous propulsive and recovery actions from a supported position

Water Safety

The concept of water safety should be central to every part of an aquatics program. The following water safety topics are required for Learn-to-Swim Level 1:

- Staying safe around aquatic environments
- Recognizing the lifeguards
- Don't Just Pack It, Wear Your Jacket
- Recognizing an emergency

- How to call for help
- Too Much Sun Is No Fun

Wrap up each class session by emphasizing the safety component of the skills they learned.

Add topics as necessary so that you integrate water safety into each lesson. When selecting additional topics, think about current events in or special needs of your local area or region. Refer to **Chapter 4** for details on these topics and for additional topics.

Exit Skills Assessment

When participants complete Learn-to-Swim Level 1, they should be comfortable getting in and moving through the water and be willing to put their faces in the water repeatedly. Participants should also be able to use arm and leg movements while supported. There are two parts to the exit skills assessment.

1. Enter independently, using either the ladder, steps or side, travel at least 5 yards, bob 3 times then safely exit the water. (Participants can walk, move along the gutter or "swim.")
2. Glide on front at least 2 body lengths, roll to a back float for 3 seconds and recover to a vertical position. (This part of the assessment can be performed with support.)

Learn-to-Swim Level 2—Fundamental Aquatic Skills

The objective of Learn-to-Swim Level 2 is to give participants success with fundamental skills. Participants learn to float without support and to recover to a vertical position. This level marks the beginning of true locomotion skills. Participants further develop simultaneous and alternating arm and leg actions on the front and back that lay the foundation for future strokes. As in all levels, you present additional safety skills and improve comprehension of previous knowledge.

Learn-to-Swim Level 2—Fundamental Aquatic Skills Outline

Equipment

- Submersion items (such as diving rings and eggs)
- U.S. Coast Guard-approved life jackets (correct sizes for participants)
- Flotation devices, such as barbells, foam noodles and kickboards

Skills	Completion Requirements	References
Water Entry and Exit		
Enter water by stepping or jumping from the side	Demonstrate, independently, in at least shoulder-deep water	WSIM, page 190
Exit water using ladder, steps or side	Demonstrate, independently, in chest-deep water	WSIM, page 190
Breath Control and Submerging		
Fully submerging and holding breath	Demonstrate, independently, at least 5 seconds	WSIM, page 190
Bobbing	Demonstrate, independently, at least 5 times, in chest-deep water	WSIM, page 190 SWS, page 78
Opening eyes underwater and retrieving submerged objects	Demonstrate, independently, at least 2 times, in chest-deep water	WSIM, page 190
Buoyancy on Front		
Float in a face-down position ■ Front float ■ Jellyfish float ■ Tuck float	Demonstrate, independently, at least 5 seconds	WSIM, page 190 SWS, page 81
Front glide	Demonstrate, independently, at least 2 body legnths	WSIM, page 190 SWS, page 82
Recover from a front float or glide to a vertical position	Demonstrate, independently, in chest-deep water	WSIM, page 190 SWS, page 82
Buoyancy on Back		
Back float	Demonstrate, independently, at least 15 seconds	WSIM, page 191 SWS, page 80
Back glide	Demonstrate, independently, at least 2 body lengths	WSIM, page 191 SWS, page 82
Recover from a back float or glide to a vertical position	Demonstrate, independently	WSIM, page 191 SWS, page 80

Skills	Completion Requirements	References
Changing Direction and Position		
Roll from front to back	Demonstrate, independently	WSIM, page 191 SWS, page 87
Roll from back to front	Demonstrate, independently	WSIM, page 191 SWS, page 87
Change direction of travel while swimming on front or back	Demonstrate, independently	WSIM, page 191
Treading		
Arm and leg actions	Demonstrate, independently, at least 15 seconds, in shoulder-deep water	WSIM, page 191 SWS, page 85
Swim on Front		
Combined arm and leg actions on front	Demonstrate, independently, at least 5 body lengths	WSIM, page 191
Swim on Back		
Finning arm action	Demonstrate, independently, at least 5 body lengths	WSIM, page 192
Combined arm and leg actions on back	Demonstrate, independently, at least 5 body lengths	WSIM, page 192
Water Safety		
Staying safe around aquatic environments	Discuss	WSIM, pages 12 & 16
Don't Just Pack It, Wear Your Jacket	Discuss/demonstrate	WSIM, page 62; SWS, page 18 LWT
Recognizing an emergency	Discuss	WSIM, page 74; SWS, page 44
How to call for help	Discuss/demonstrate	WSIM, page 63; SWS, page 45
Too Much Sun Is No Fun	Discuss	WSIM, page 68; SWS, page 13; LWT
Look Before You Leap	Discuss	WSIM, page 75; SWS, page 28; LWT
Think So You Don't Sink	Discuss	WSIM, page 76; SWS, page 80; LWT
Reach or Throw, Don't Go	Discuss/demonstrate	WSIM, page 70; SWS, page 55; LWT

Exit Skills Assessment

1. Step from side into chest-deep water, move into a front float for 5 seconds, roll to back, float for 5 seconds then return to a vertical position.
2. Move into a back float for 5 seconds, roll to front then recover to a vertical position.
3. Push off and swim using combined arm and leg actions on front for 5 body lengths, roll to back, float for 15 seconds, roll to the front then continue swimming for 5 body lengths. (You can assist the participant when taking a breath.)

Learn-to-Swim Level 2 Skills

Water Entry and Exit

Enter Water by Stepping or Jumping from the Side—Independently

Refer to Preschool Aquatics Levels 2, page 167, Preschool Aquatics Level 3, page 173. Only let participants step in water that is at least shoulder deep.

SAFETY NOTE

Do not let participants step in water less than shoulder deep. Make sure participants step or jump straight out from the side.

Exit Water Using Ladder, Steps or Side—Independently

Refer to Preschool Aquatics Level 1, page 156. In this level, participants should be able to exit the water repeatedly and easily from chest-deep water.

Breath Control and Submerging

Fully Submerging and Holding Breath—Independently

Refer to Preschool Aquatics Level 3, page 173.

SAFETY NOTE

Do not let participants hyperventilate or have breath-holding contests. Limit participants to a single inhalation whenever you ask them to hold their breath or submerge.

Bobbing—Independently

Refer to Preschool Aquatics Level 3, page 173.

Opening Eyes Underwater and Retrieving Submerged Objects—Independently

Refer to Preschool Aquatics Level 2, page 167.

Buoyancy on Front

Float in a Face-Down Position—Independently

Front Float—Independently

Refer to Preschool Aquatics Level 3, page 174.

Jellyfish Float—Independently

Refer to Preschool Aquatics Level 3, page 174.

Tuck Float—Independently

Refer to Preschool Aquatics Level 3, page 174.

Front Glide—Independently

Refer to Preschool Aquatics Level 2, page 168. In this level, participants should be able to do a front glide for 2 body lengths independently.

Recover from a Front Float or Glide to a Vertical Position—Independently

Refer to Preschool Aquatics Level 2, page 168. In this level, participants should be able to recover from a front float or glide to a vertical position independently.

Buoyancy on Back

Back Float—Independently

Refer to Preschool Aquatics Level 1, page 160. In this level, participants should be able to do a back float for at least 15 seconds independently.

Back Glide—Independently

Refer to Preschool Aquatics Level 1, page 159. In this level, participants should be able to do a back glide for 2 body lengths independently.

Recover from a Back Float or Glide to a Vertical Position—Independently

Refer to Preschool Aquatics Level 2, page 168. In this level, participants should be able to recover from a back float or glide to a vertical position independently.

Changing Direction and and Position

Roll from Front to Back—Independently

Refer to Preschool Aquatics Level 2, page 169.

Roll from Back to Front—Independently

Refer to Preschool Aquatics Level 2, page 169.

Change Direction of Travel While Swimming on Front or Back—Independently

Refer to Preschool Aquatics Level 3, page 175.

Treading

Arm and Leg Actions—Independently

Refer to Preschool Aquatics Level 2, page 169. In this level, participants should be able to tread water using arm and leg actions at least 15 seconds independently.

Swim on Front

Combined Arm and Leg Actions on Front—Independently

Refer to Preschool Aquatics Level 1, page 162. In this level, participants should be able to perform combined arm and leg actions on front for at least 5 body lengths independently and at the level of performance described in stroke performance chart.

Level 2 Stroke Performance Criteria

Component	Swim on Front (Combined Arm or Leg Action)
Body position	Trunk and legs may be horizontal to 45 degrees from surface; face in water
Arms—alternating	Alternate propulsive and recovery action; downward or slightly outward motion acceptable; underwater arm recovery acceptable
Arms—simultaneous	Simultaneous propulsive and recovery actions; downward and outward motion acceptable; underwater arm recovery acceptable
Legs—alternating	Alternate kicking action; rudimentary flutter or bicycle action
Legs—simultaneous	Simultaneous kicking action—rudimentary dolphin or breaststroke action

Swim on Back

Finning Arm Action—Independently

Refer to Preschool Aquatics Level 2, page 170. In this level, participants should be able to perform finning arm actions for at least 5 body lengths independently.

Combined Arm and Leg Actions on Back—Independently

Refer to Preschool Aquatics Level 1, page 163. In this level, participants should be able to perform combined arm and leg actions on back for at least 5 body lengths independently and at the level of performance described in stroke performance chart.

Level 2 Stroke Performance Criteria

Component	Swim on Back (Combined Arm or Leg Action)
Body position	Trunk and legs may be horizontal to 45 degrees from surface
Arms—alternating	Alternate propulsive and recovery action; underwater arm recovery acceptable; hand moving downward with minimal backward action acceptable
Arms—simultaneous	Simultaneous propulsive and recovery actions; underwater arm recovery acceptable
Legs—alternating	Alternate kicking action; rudimentary flutter or bicycling action
Legs—simultaneous	Simultaneous kicking action—rudimentary dolphin or elementary backstroke action

Water Safety

The concept of water safety should be central to every part of an aquatics program. The following water safety topics are required for Learn-to-Swim Level 2:

- Staying safe around aquatic environments
- Don't Just Pack It, Wear Your Jacket
- Recognizing an emergency
- How to call for help
- Too Much Sun Is No Fun
- Look Before You Leap
- Think So You Don't Sink
- Reach or Throw, Don't Go

Some of the water safety topics are repeated from Level 1 for reinforcement. Vary your presentation approach to keep it interesting and to test the participants' level of understanding. Add topics as necessary so that you integrate water safety into each lesson. Wrap up each class session by emphasizing the safety component of the skills they learned. When selecting additional topics, think about current events in or special needs of your local area or region. Refer to **Chapter 4** for details on these topics and for additional topics.

Exit Skills Assessment

When participants complete Learn-to-Swim Level 2, they should be increasingly confident in the water. Participants are starting to swim independently using arm and leg movements, but may still need assistance when taking a breath. There are three parts to the exit skills assessment, all are performed independently.

1. Step from side into chest-deep water, move into a front float for 5 seconds, roll to back, float for 5 seconds then return to a vertical position.
2. Move into a back float for 5 seconds, roll to front then recover to a vertical position.
3. Push off and swim using combined arm and leg actions on front for 5 body lengths, roll to back, float for 15 seconds, roll to the front then continue swimming for 5 body lengths. (You can assist the participant when taking a breath.)

Learn-to-Swim Level 3—Stroke Development

The objective of Learn-to-Swim Level 3 is to build on previously learned skills by providing additional guided practice. You teach participants to survival float, swim the front crawl and elementary backstroke. You introduce the scissors and dolphin kicks and build on the fundamentals of treading water. Participants should also learn rules for headfirst entries and begin to learn to enter the water headfirst from a seated position at poolside (if the water is 9 feet deep or deeper). As in all levels, you present additional safety skills and messages.

Learn-to-Swim Level 3—Stroke Development Outline

Equipment

- U.S. Coast Guard-approved life jackets (correct sizes for participants)
- Flotation devices, such as kickboards, foam noodles and pull buoys
- Fins
- Equipment for reaching assists, such as reaching poles and rescue tubes

Skills	Completion Requirements	References
Water Entry		
Enter water by jumping from the side	Demonstrate, into deep water	WSIM, page 196
Headfirst entry from the side in a sitting position*	Demonstrate, in water at least 9-feet deep	WSIM, page 196 SWS, page 126
Headfirst entry from the side in a kneeling position*	Demonstrate, in water at least 9-feet deep	WSIM, page 196 SWS, page 126
Breath Control and Submerging		
Bobbing while moving toward safety	Demonstrate, at least 5 times, in chest-deep water	WSIM, page 196
Rotary breathing	Demonstrate, at least 10 times	WSIM, page 197
Buoyancy on Front		
Survival float	Demonstrate, at least 30 seconds, in deep water	WSIM, page 197 SWS, page 50
Buoyancy on Back		
Back float	Demonstrate, at least 30 seconds, in deep water	WSIM, page 197 SWS, page 80
Changing Direction and Position		
Change from vertical to horizontal position on front	Demonstrate, in deep water	WSIM, page 197
Change from vertical to horizontal position on back	Demonstrate, in deep water	WSIM, page 198

** If water depth is not at least 9 feet, instructors SHOULD NOT teach headfirst entries.*

Skills	Completion Requirements	References
Treading		
Tread water	Demonstrate, 30 seconds, in deep water	WSIM, page 198 SWS, page 85
Swim on Front		
Push off in a streamlined position then begin flutter kicking	Demonstrate, 3–5 body lengths	WSIM, page 199
Push off in a streamlined position then begin dolphin kicking	Demonstrate, 3–5 body lengths	WSIM, page 199
Front crawl	Demonstrate, at least 15 yards	WSIM, page 200 SWS, page 94
Swim on Back		
Elementary backstroke	Demonstrate, at least 15 yards	WSIM, page 202 SWS, page 112
Swim on Side		
Scissors kick	Demonstrate, at least 10 yards	WSIM, page 204 SWS, page 117
Water Safety		
Reach or Throw, Don't Go	Demonstrate	WSIM, page 70 SWS, page 55 LWT
Think Twice Before Going Near Cold Water or Ice	Discuss/demonstrate	WSIM, page 78 SWS, pages 38 & 52 LWT
Look Before You Leap	Demonstrate	WSIM, page 75 SWS, pages 28 & 140 LWT
Exit Skills Assessment **Jump into deep water from the side, swim front crawl for 15 yards, maintain position by treading or floating for 30 seconds and swim elementary backstroke for 15 yards.**		

** If water depth is not at least 9 feet, instructors SHOULD NOT teach headfirst entries.*

Learn-to-Swim Level 3 Skills

Water Entry

Enter Water by Jumping from the Side

One at a time, have participants–

1. Stand at the edge of the pool, hold the arms up and out slightly to the side, curl the toes over the edge, take a breath and jump out from the edge and in the water.
2. Sweep down with the arms and use any kick to return to the surface after entering the water.
3. Level off (to bring the body to the surface in a horizontal position on the front or back) and swim back to the edge of the pool after surfacing.

Headfirst Entry from the Side in a Sitting Position

1. Sit on the pool edge with feet on the edge of the gutter or against the side of the pool.
2. Extend the arms over the head.
3. Focus on a target on the surface that will allow for roughly a 45-degree entry into the water.
4. Lean forward, try to touch the water and push with the legs.
5. Straighten the body and extend both legs upon entering the water.
6. Angle the hands toward the surface of the water to steer the body up.

Headfirst Entry from the Side in a Kneeling Position

1. Kneel on one knee while gripping the pool edge with the toes of the other foot. The toes of the kneeling leg should be in a position to help push from the deck.
2. Extend the arms over the head.
3. Focus on a target on the surface of the water 1–2 feet from the side.
4. Lean forward and try to touch the water. When starting to lose balance, push with the legs.
5. Upon entering the water, straighten the body and extend both legs.
6. Angle the hands toward the surface of the water to steer the body up.

SAFETY NOTE

All headfirst entries must be taught in water at least 9-feet deep. If water depth is not at least 9 feet, instructors SHOULD NOT teach headfirst entries.

Breath Control and Submerging

Bobbing While Moving Toward Safety

Starting away from the wall in water about 1 foot over their heads, have participants practice bobbing back toward the wall. Have participants–

1. Relax and hold the arms out in front.
2. Take a breath and hold it.
3. Bend the knees to submerge.
4. Push off the bottom, or kick up if not at the bottom, and sweep down with the arms to rise to the surface. Position the body at an angle to move forward.
5. Exhale slowly (blow bubbles) right before reaching the surface.

6. Inhale when your mouth clears the surface.
7. Repeat steps 1–6 at least 5 times to the reach the wall.

Rotary Breathing

Rotary breathing is used when swimming the front crawl. Have participants–

1. Turn the head to one side just enough for the mouth to clear the water, but not so far that the body twists.
2. Take a breath.
3. Return the face to the water and exhale slowly.
4. Repeat steps 1–3 in a rhythmic pattern at least 10 times.

TEACHING TIPS

Introduce and practice this skill in a variety of ways:

- *Have participants standing in chest-deep water, bend at the waist, put the face down in the water and practice 10 breaths in a row.*
- *Have participants bracket on the wall and practice 10 breaths in a row while flutter kicking on the front.*
- *While also practicing the flutter kick on the front, have participants use a flotation device and–*
  1. *Exhale and let go of the flotation device with one hand.*
  2. *Roll the body and turn the head to the same side until the mouth clears the water.*
  3. *Keep half of the head in the water and take a breath.*
  4. *Put the face back in the water, grab the flotation device and continue kicking.*

Buoyancy on Front

Survival Float

In this level, participants should be able to survival float for at least 30 seconds. Have participants–

1. Take a breath and hold it, then put the face in the water. Allow the arms and legs to hang freely. Rest in this position for a few seconds.
2. To take another breath, slowly lift the arms to about shoulder height and move the arms forward. Separate the legs, moving one leg forward and one leg back.
3. Exhale slowly into the water (blowing bubbles) then gently press down with the arms while bringing the legs together. This movement lifts the mouth above the water for another breath.
4. Return to the resting position. Repeat these steps to take additional breaths.

Buoyancy on Back

Back Float

Refer to Preschool Aquatics Level 1, page 160. In this level, participants should be able to back float for at least 30 seconds in deep water.

Changing Direction and Position

Change from Vertical to Horizontal Position on Front

Starting from either treading water or after surfacing from jumping into deep water, have participants–

1. Take a breath.
2. Reach forward and pull the water back and kick up (breaststroke or scissors kick).
3. Put the face down, so that the hips rise and the body levels off.
4. Begin swimming.

 **INSTRUCTOR'S NOTE**

It is not always necessary to put the face in the water if the participant is a strong enough swimmer. However, while learning this skill, putting the face in the water makes leveling off easier.

Change from Vertical to Horizontal Position on Back

Starting from either treading water or after surfacing from jumping into deep water, have participants–

1. Kick up (breaststroke or scissors kick), put the head back, arch the back and lean back as if moving into a back float.
2. Extend the arms out and up then push the water toward the feet.
3. Kick again and level off.
4. Begin swimming or floating.

Treading

Tread Water

In this level, participants should be able to tread water for at least 30 seconds in deep water.
Have participants–

1. Stay nearly vertical, with the upper body bent slightly forward at the waist with the legs separated.
2. Make continuous sweeping movements with the forearms and hands just below the surface in front of the body. With the shoulders relaxed and the elbows away from the body, move the forearms out then back in. Rotate the forearms and hands as a single unit so the palms push the water in both directions.
3. Using one of the kicks described below, kick with just enough force to keep the head above water.

With a Modified Scissors Kick

Have participants–

1. Recover by flexing the hips and knees and drawing the heels up.
2. Flex the ankle of the front leg and point the toes of the back foot.
3. Extend the front leg forward and the back leg backward, but not completely straight.
4. At the same time, forcefully press the legs together until they are nearly straight.
5. Repeat steps 1–4 continuously.

With a Modified Breaststroke Kick

Have participants–

1. Recover by flexing the hips and bending the knees so that the legs move up.
2. Flex the ankles, turn the feet out and extend the legs out.
3. Forcefully press the feet and knees down until the legs are nearly extended to about shoulder-width apart. The legs do not come all the way together or straight.
4. Repeat steps 1–3 continuously.

With a Rotary Kick

Have participants–

1. Stay nearly vertical, with the upper body bent slightly forward at the waist, making the same sculling movements with the arms.
2. Keep the back straight and the hips flexed so that the thighs are comfortably forward.

3. Pull up the lower legs so that they are at a nearly 90-degree angle to the thighs and the knees are slightly wider than hip-width apart.
4. Rotate the lower legs at the knees, one leg at a time making large circular movements with the foot and lower leg. One leg moves clockwise and the other counterclockwise.
5. As each foot moves sideways and forward, extend it sharply outward.
6. As one leg kicks, the other leg recovers to kick immediately after the first leg kick. Kick just hard enough to keep the head out of the water.

Swim on Front

TEACHING TIP

Refer to the Water Safety Instructor's CD-ROM *for activities and drills to help participants learn and improve the front crawl.*

When swimming on front, participants should begin in a streamlined position. To achieve a streamlined position in the water, have participants–

1. Extend the arms overhead.
2. Clasp the hands together with the arms against the ears.
3. Extend the legs together with the toes pointed.

SAFETY NOTE

Do not let participants hyperventilate or have breath-holding contests. Limit participants to a single inhalation whenever you ask them to hold their breath or submerge.

Push Off in a Streamlined Position then Begin Flutter Kicking

Have participants–

1. Push off just under the surface of the water in a streamlined position on front. Exhale through the mouth and nose while pushing off.
2. Before losing momentum, start with the legs straight, together and relaxed with the toes pointed. Keep the knees and ankles loose and floppy, and continuously kick up and down.
3. During the downbeat, start with the thigh and follow through with the whole leg and foot.
4. Snap the foot downward as though kicking a ball.
5. During the upbeat, raise the leg straight toward the surface with little or no bend in the knee, until the heel just breaks the surface.
6. Continue kicking for 3–5 body lengths.

Push Off in a Streamlined Position then Begin Dolphin Kicking

1. Push off just under the surface of the water in a streamlined position on front. Exhale through the mouth and nose while pushing off.
2. Before losing momentum, keep the legs together and start the downbeat by bending the knees and extending the legs in a whiplike motion.

3. During the downbeat, bend the knees then extend the legs in a whiplike motion.
4. Extend the legs during the downbeat and straighten the legs on the upbeat until the heels just break the surface. Keep the ankles relaxed.
5. Continue kicking for 3–5 body lengths.

The hips should only rise above and return just below the surface. The kick begins in the upper abdominals, hips and thighs and in a continuous up and down movement.

Front Crawl

In this level, participants should be able to swim the front crawl at least 15 yards at the level of performance described in the stroke performance chart.

TEACHING TIP

One way to teach strokes is to—

1. *Start with body position and the kick.*
2. *Add breathing to the kick.*
3. *Add arms to the kick and breathing.*

Body Position

Have participants–

1. Move into a face-down, streamlined position.
2. Look downward to the bottom of the pool with the neck flat and waterline at the middle of the top of the head.
3. Rotate around the midline of the body throughout the stroke.

Legs

Refer to Push Off in a Streamlined Position then Begin Flutter Kicking on page 199.

Arms

For each arm stroke, have participants–

1. Slide the fingers of one hand into the water first with the palm pitched slightly outward.
2. Allow the hand to enter the water smoothly, keeping the elbow higher than the rest of the arm. The elbow enters the water last.
3. Extend the arm forward in front of the shoulder.
4. Bend the elbow so that the palm and forearm face toward the feet and press backwards.
5. Allow the elbow and hand to move naturally, just outside the shoulders, as the arm travels backward.
6. Continue pressing the palm and forearm directly backwards. The hand follows a path straight backward that traces the side of the body.
7. Keep the elbow slightly wider than the hand so the elbow can remain bent and the palm and forearm facing back.
8. Keep the hand facing back as long as possible and then move upward as the arm extends.
9. Accelerate the hand through the end of the stroke, until the arm reaches full extension.
10. Lift the elbow so that it is the first part of the arm to exit the water.
11. While lifting the elbow, keep the arm relaxed with the forearm hanging down.
12. Swing the arm around the side in a relaxed motion, keeping the hand wider than the elbow.
13. As the hand passes the shoulder, let it lead the rest of the arm until it enters the water.

Breathing and Timing

Participants should learn to breathe during each arm cycle or every 1½ arm cycles. Have participants–

1. Start turning the head toward the recovery arm (the arm that is out of the water) as it exits the water.
2. Look to the side, keeping the face horizontal and the water line at the top of the head. One ear stays in the water.
3. Inhale when body roll is at its maximum and the recovery elbow is high.
4. After inhaling, return the face to the water in a quick motion before the recovery arm reenters the water.
5. Exhale slowly underwater through the mouth and nose between breaths.

Level 3 Front Crawl Stroke Performance Criteria

Body position	Trunk horizontal to 30 degrees from surface; rudimentary body roll; some side-to-side motion of trunk and legs acceptable
Arms	Above-water arm recovery—underwater recovery or arm straight at elbow acceptable; hand enters at or above the level of the head; arm straight at the elbow during power phase acceptable; power phase finishing at hip level acceptable
Legs	Continuous kicking; occasional bicycling action acceptable; legs bent at the hips or knees during downbeat acceptable; feet may break surface of water
Breathing and timing	Face in water and breathes consistently to the side—occasional head lift acceptable; arms and legs show general alternating pattern

Improving Performance of the Front Crawl

Observations	Interventions
Legs and hips too low	Tell participants to lower head position.
Arm recovery and breathing are difficult	Have participants check head position.
Ineffective kick because legs are too rigid	Tell participants to relax and kick as if kicking a ball.
Head lifted up to breathe	Tell participants to exhale underwater then look to the side. One ear stays in water while inhaling.
Feet break the surface too much	Have participants lift head slightly to drop legs. Be sure kick starts from the hip.
Toes "hook" at end of downward beat because ankles are allowed to flex	Have participants keep toes relaxed and floppy. Have them practice with swim fins.
Arms lift out early	Have participants fully extend arms by pushing toward the feet.
Arms sweep wide in recovery	Practice high elbow recovery with relaxed forearm and wrist.
Hands, elbows and arms drag through the water	Have participants lift elbow higher. They may also need more body roll.
Inefficient propulsion because of pulling with straight arms	Stress a high elbow as the arm pulls through. Have participants practice arm pulls with support, such as a pull buoy.
Inefficient stroke because of incorrect breathing	Repeat learning drills for rotary breathing.

Swim on Back

TEACHING TIP

Refer to the Water Safety Instructor's CD-ROM *for activities and drills to help participants learn and improve the elementary backstroke.*

Elementary Backstroke

In this level, participants should be able to swim the elementary backstroke at least 15 yards at the level of performance described in the stroke performance chart.

Body Position

Have participants–

- Move into a horizontal, streamlined position on the back, arms at the sides.
- Keep the head submerged to the ears with the face out of the water.

Legs

Have participants–

1. Start with the legs together and extended with the toes pointed during the glide.
2. From this position, recover the legs by bending and slightly separating the knees then dropping the heels downward to a point under and outside the knees. The knees are spread as hip-width or slightly wider.
3. Keep the thighs in line with the hips–the hips should stay near the surface. Do not drop the hips when dropping the heels.
4. Rotate the knees inward slightly while the ankles flex and the feet turn outward.
5. Finish by pressing the feet backward with a slightly rounded motion, ending with the legs in the glide position. As the feet press backward, they move into a pointed position.

Arms

Have participants–

1. Keep the arms and hands just below the surface throughout the stroke.
2. From the glide position, recover the arms by bending the elbows so the hands (palms facing down or toward the body) slide along the sides to near the armpits.
3. Point the fingers outward from the shoulders so that the palms face back toward the feet.
4. Leading with the fingers, extend the arms out to the sides until the hands are no farther forward than the top of the head.
5. Without pausing, simultaneously press the palms and the insides of both arms in a broad sweeping motion back toward the feet, keeping the arms straight.
6. End this motion with the arms and hands in the glide position.

Breathing and Timing

Have participants–

1. Breathe during each arm stroke. Inhale as the arms recover and exhale as the arms press backward.
2. Start the arm recovery just ahead of the legs.
3. Finish the leg thrust at the same time as the arms.
4. Glide with the body streamlined after the combined propulsion.

Level 3 Elementary Backstroke Stroke Performance Criteria

Body position	Trunk horizontal to 30 degrees from surface; hips may be bent; chin tucked; ears may be out of the water
Arms	Hands may break water surface during recovery; arms extending above or below shoulder level acceptable; power phase finishing at waist level acceptable
Legs	Knees may break the surface of the water during recovery; knees may be wider than hips and ankles; ankles may be bent throughout power phase; occasional scissors kick acceptable; legs may be partially bent at knee at the end of the power phase; legs apart with occasional flutter kick during glide acceptable
Breathing and timing	Occasional breath-holding acceptable; arms and legs move simultaneously; minimal glide with some forward motion acceptable; little or no hesitation before beginning recovery

Improving Performance of the Elementary Backstroke

Observations	Interventions
Body bent downward at the middle; body sitting in the water	Tell participants to tilt head back, look directly overhead and raise the hips toward the surface.
Extreme arch in back during power phase; face may be submerged	Check head position. Stress keeping arms parallel to surface during power phase.
Knees break surface excessively during recovery	Check body position. Participants who are very buoyant should tilt the head forward slightly and round back and shoulders slightly. This lowers hips and legs. The feet should drop down rather than the knees pull up.
Hands reach too far above head	Emphasize sliding hands away from the shoulders in a perpendicular line with the shoulders.
Water washes over face during arm recovery	Check whether participants are tilting head back, lifting the knees or pushing water toward the face with the hands.
Water washes over face during arm pull	Tell participants to tilt chin downward slightly and pull parallel to the surface.
Hands recover from thighs or hips directly into extended position	Emphasize dragging thumbs up sides of body to armpits.
Power phases of arms and legs not together	Emphasize recovery of arms to armpits before legs start the power phase.

Swim on Side

In Level 3, participants learn the kick used in the sidestroke–the scissors kick. Practice on each side. Some people have a dominant side. In this level, participants should be able to perform the scissors kick at least 10 yards at the level of performance described in the stroke performance chart.

TEACHING TIPS

- *Have participants practice the scissors kick on dry-land, bracketing the wall in the water or holding a flotation device with the lead hand.*
- *Refer to the* Water Safety Instructor's CD-ROM *for activities and drills to help participants learn and improve the scissors kick.*

Scissors Kick

Have participants–

1. Lie on the side. Extend the bottom arm and put the head on the shoulder.
2. From the glide position, recover the legs by flexing the hips and knees and drawing the heels slowly toward the buttocks, keeping the knees close together.
3. At the end of the recovery, flex the top ankle and point the toes of the lower foot to prepare for the kick. Move the top leg toward the front of the body and the bottom leg toward the back. When extended, the top leg should be almost straight.
4. Without pausing, kick the top leg straight and press it backwards. At the same time, extend the bottom leg in a motion like kicking a ball until both legs are fully extended and together in the glide position.

Level 3 Sidestroke Performance Criteria

Body position	Body in side-lying position
Arms	Bottom arm extended overhead; top arm against the side
Legs	Perform a rudimentary scissors kick on the side with support
Breathing and timing	Any type of breathing pattern with occasional breath-holding acceptable

Water Safety

The concept of water safety should be central to every part of an aquatics program. The following water safety topics are required for Learn-to-Swim Level 3:

- Reach or Throw, Don't Go
- Think Twice Before Going Near Cold Water or Ice
- Look Before You Leap

As in earlier levels, some of the water safety topics are repeated for reinforcement. In this level, participants are introduced to entering the water in a headfirst position. Rules for headfirst entries are taught in "look before you leap" and should be repeated and built upon to ensure that participants clearly understand where and when it is appropriate to enter the water in a headfirst position. Vary your presentation approach to keep it interesting and to test the participants' level of understanding. Add topics as necessary so that you integrate water safety into each lesson. When selecting additional topics, think about current events in or special needs of your local area or region. Refer to **Chapter 4** for details on these topics and for additional topics. Wrap up each class session by emphasizing the safety component of the skills they learned.

Exit Skills Assessment

When participants complete Learn-to-Swim Level 3, they are starting to show stroke proficiency in the front crawl and elementary backstroke. They demonstrate comfort in deep water and can enter the water headfirst from both sitting and kneeling positions. There is one part to the exit skills assessment–jump into deep water from the side, swim front crawl for 15 yards, maintain position by treading or floating for 30 seconds and swim elementary backstroke for 15 yards.

Learn-to-Swim Level 4—Stroke Improvement

The objectives of Level 4 are to develop participants' confidence in the strokes learned thus far and to improve other aquatic skills. In level 4 participants improve their skills and increase their endurance by swimming familiar strokes (front crawl, elementary backstroke) for greater distances. Participants add the arms to the scissors kick for the sidestroke. Participants also start to learn the back crawl, breaststroke and butterfly and the basics of turning at a wall.

Learn-to-Swim Level 4—Stroke Improvement Outline

Equipment

- U.S. Coast Guard-approved life jackets (correct sizes for participants)
- Flotation devices, such as kickboards and pull buoys
- Equipment for throwing assists, such as ring buoys and throw bags

Skills	Completion Requirements	References
Water Entry		
Headfirst entry from the side in a compact position*	Demonstrate, in water at least 9-feet deep	WSIM, page 208 SWS, page 126
Headfirst entry from the side in a stride position*	Demonstrate, in water at least 9-feet deep	WSIM, page 208 SWS, page 127
Breath Control and Submerging		
Swim underwater	Demonstrate, 3–5 body lengths	WSIM, page 208 SWS, page 91
Feetfirst surface dive	Demonstrate, submerging completely	WSIM, page 209 SWS, page 89
Buoyancy on Front		
Survival swimming	Demonstrate, at least 30 seconds, in deep water	WSIM, page 209 SWS, page 50
Changing Direction and Position		
Front crawl open turn	Demonstrate	WSIM, page 209 SWS, page 132
Backstroke open turn	Demonstrate	WSIM, page 210 SWS, page 133
Treading		
Tread water using 2 different kicks (modified scissors, modified breaststroke or rotary)	Demonstrate, at least 2 minutes	WSIM, page 210 SWS, page 85

** If water depth is not at least 9 feet, instructors SHOULD NOT teach headfirst entries.*

Skills	Completion Requirements	References
Swim on Front		
Front crawl	Demonstrate, at least 25 yards	WSIM, page 210 SWS, page 94
Breaststroke	Demonstrate, at least 15 yards	WSIM, page 211 SWS, page 103
Butterfly	Demonstrate, at least 15 yards	WSIM, page 213 SWS, page 106
Swim on Back		
Push off in a streamlined position and begin flutter kicking	Demonstrate, 3–5 body lengths	WSIM, page 215 SWS, page 88
Push off in a streamlined position and begin dolphin kicking	Demonstrate, 3–5 body lengths	WSIM, page 215 SWS, page 88
Elementary backstroke	Demonstrate, at least 25 yards	WSIM, page 216 SWS, page 112
Back crawl	Demonstrate, at least 15 yards	WSIM, page 216 SWS, page 100
Swim on Side		
Sidestroke	Demonstrate, at least 15 yards	WSIM, page 218 SWS, page 115
Water Safety		
Reach or Throw, Don't Go 1. Reaching assist 2. Throwing assist	Discuss/demonstrate	WSIM, page 70 SWS, page 55 LWT
Recreational water illnesses	Discuss	WSIM, page 67 SWS, page 15
Think So You Don't Sink	Discuss/demonstrate	WSIM, page 76 SWS, pages 47 & 80 LWT
Look Before You Leap	Discuss	WSIM, page 75 SWS, pages 28 & 140 LWT
Exit Skills Assessment 1. Perform a feetfirst entry into deep water, swim front crawl for 25 yards, change direction and position as necessary and swim elementary backstroke for 25 yards. 2. Swim breaststroke for 15 yards, change direction and position as necessary and swim back crawl for 15 yards.		

** If water depth is not at least 9 feet, instructors SHOULD NOT teach headfirst entries.*

Learn-to-Swim Level 4 Skills

Water Entry

Headfirst Entry from the Side in a Compact Position

Have participants–

1. Put one foot forward and one back, with the toes of the leading foot gripping the edge of the pool.
2. Starting from the kneeling position, lift up so that both knees are flexed and off the deck in order to remain close to the water.
3. Extend the arms above the head.
4. Focus on a target that will allow for roughly a 45-degree entry into the water.
5. Bend forward and try to touch the surface of the water with the hands.
6. Push off toward the water. Bring the legs together upon entering the water.
7. Angle the hands toward the surface of the water to steer the body up.

Headfirst Entry from the Side in a Stride Position

Have participants–

1. Stand upright with one leg forward and one leg back, with the toes of the leading foot gripping the edge of the pool.
2. Extend the arms above the head.
3. Focus on a target that will allow for roughly a 45-degree entry into the water. Bend the legs only slightly while bending at the waist toward the water.
4. Try to touch the surface of the water, and lift the back leg until it is in line with the torso. The forward leg should stay as straight as possible.
5. Angle the hands toward the surface of the water to steer the body up.

SAFETY NOTE

All headfirst entries must be taught in water at least 9-feet deep. If water depth is not at least 9 feet, instructors SHOULD NOT teach headfirst entries

Breath Control and Submerging

Swim Underwater

Have participants practice swimming underwater for 3–5 body lengths using the breaststroke or a dolphin kick. When using the breaststroke, start with the arms in front, sweep them wide and back towards the feet and recover to the front. When using the dolphin kick, the arms may be in front or to the side. To build momentum, start with the arms in front and sweep them wide and back towards the feet.

SAFETY NOTE

Do not let participants hyperventilate or have breath-holding contests. Limit participants to a single inhalation whenever you ask them to hold their breath or submerge.

Feetfirst Surface Dive

Have participants–

1. Start by treading water and maintaining a vertical position.
2. Press down forcefully with both hands and kick. Move the hands at the same time and bring them to the sides of the thighs while simultaneously performing a strong scissors or breaststroke kick.
3. Take a breath, at the top of this rise.
4. Keep the body vertical and in a streamlined position as it starts moving downward.
5. Turn the palms outward then sweep the hands upward for more downward propulsion, once downward motion slows. This sweeping action should occur completely underwater.
6. Tuck the body and roll into a horizontal position when the desired depth is achieved.
7. Extend the arms and legs and swim underwater.

Buoyancy on Front

Survival Swimming

In this level, participants must be able to survival swim for at least 1 minute in deep water.
Have participants–

1. Take a breath, bend forward at the waist and bring the hands up alongside the head.
2. Separate the legs into the stride position and extend the arms forward then bring the legs together again and propel diagonally toward the surface.
3. Sweep the arms out and back to the thighs and glide near and almost parallel to the surface.
4. Bend the legs and draw them toward the torso and bring the hands up alongside the head once again when a breath is needed.
5. Extend the arms forward and separate the legs in the stride position once again. Tilt the head back and prepare to breathe out, as in survival floating.
6. Repeat steps 1–5.

INSTRUCTOR'S NOTE

A person who is not very buoyant will likely need to perform these movements slightly faster to prevent sinking before taking a breath.

Changing Direction and Position

TEACHING TIP

Refer to the Water Safety Instructor's CD-ROM *for tips on progressions for teaching the front crawl and back crawl open turns.*

Front Crawl Open Turn

Have participants–

1. When approaching the wall, extend the leading arm until it touches the wall.
2. Bend the elbow of the leading arm and drop the shoulder slightly while rotating the body to move the body toward the wall.
3. Tuck the body at the hips and knees; turn and spin away from the leading hand; swing the feet against the wall, one foot above the other (if the right hand is the leading hand, the right foot will be on top); and extend the other arm toward the opposite end of the pool.
4. During the spin, lift the face out of the water and take a breath.
5. Return the face to the water as the leading hand recovers over the surface.
6. Extend both arms in front as the legs push off. Keep the body in a streamlined position on one side.
7. Rotate in the glide until face-down.
8. Before losing momentum, start flutter kicking to rise to the surface and resume the arm stroke.

Backstroke Open Turn

Have participants–

1. At one stroke short of touching the wall, start to rotate to the front by turning the head and looking toward the pulling arm.
2. Take one more arm pull while completing the rotation onto the stomach. Extend the arm until it touches the wall.
3. Bend the elbow of the leading arm and drop the shoulder slightly while rotating the body to move the body toward the wall.
4. Tuck the body at the hips and knees; turn and spin away from the leading hand; swing the feet against the wall, one foot above the other (if the right hand is the leading hand, the right foot will be on top); and extend the other arm toward the opposite end of the pool.
5. During the spin, lift the face out of the water and take a breath.
6. Return the face to the water as the leading hand recovers over the surface.
7. Extend both arms as the legs push off. Keep the body in a streamlined position on the back.
8. Before losing momentum, start kicking to rise to the surface and resume the armstroke.

Treading

Refer to Learn-to-Swim Level 3, page 198. In this level, participants should be able to tread water using two of the following three different kicks–modified scissors, modified breaststroke or rotary kick–for at least 2 minutes.

Swim on Front

TEACHING TIP

Refer to the Water Safety Instructor's CD-ROM *for activities and drills to help participants learn and improve the front crawl, breaststroke and butterfly.*

Front Crawl

Refer to Learn-to-Swim Level 3, page 200. In this level, participants should be able to swim the front crawl at least 25 yards at the level of performance described in the stroke performance chart.

Level 4 Front Crawl Stroke Performance Criteria

Body position	Body horizontal to 15 degrees from surface; performs body roll; occasional side-to-side motion of trunk and legs acceptable
Arms	Above-water recovery with arm bent at elbow—arm straight at elbow acceptable; hands enter above the level of the head, fingertips first shoulder-width apart; arm extends fully after entry; arm bent at elbow during power phase; power phase finishes beyond the hip
Legs	Continuous kicking that starts from the hips; ankles and knees extended but not rigid; feet remain below the surface—moderate splash acceptable
Breathing and timing	Face in water; breathing to the side; exhale under water on each breath; arms alternate—slight hesitation during breathing acceptable

Breaststroke

In this level, participants should be able to swim the breaststroke at least 15 yards at the level of performance described in the stroke performance chart.

Body Position

Have participants–

1. Move into a face-down, horizontal streamlined position.
2. Extend the arms to the front with the palms face-down and below the surface.
3. Keep the back straight.

Legs

Have participants–

1. Recover by bringing the heels toward the buttocks as much as possible without upsetting body position and allowing the knees to drop toward the bottom of the pool.
2. As the legs recover, gradually separate the knees and heels until the knees are about hip-width apart and the feet are outside the knees. Keep the heels just under the surface.
3. At the end of the recovery, flex the ankles and rotate the feet so that the toes point outward.
4. With a continuous pushing action, forcefully press the feet and knees backward until the legs are extended, toes pointed and the feet and ankles touch, and then hold the legs in a straight line.

Arms

Have participants–

1. Turn the palms outward about 45 degrees to the surface of the water while in a glide position.
2. Slightly bend the arms and press the palms outward until the hands are spread wider than the shoulders.
3. Bend the elbows and sweep the hands downward and inward.
4. Allow the hands to pass under the elbows with the forearms in a nearly vertical position.
5. Sweep the hands inward and upward until the hands are in front of the chest. The hands should be pitched slightly upward and almost touching each other.
6. Continue to bend the elbows while squeezing them to the side of the body.
7. Sweep the hands together in front of the chest then squeeze the elbows close together and push forward with the elbows so that the hands start moving forward.
8. Continue to extend the arms forward while rotating the wrists until the palms are facing down and below the surface at full extension in the glide position.

Breathing and Timing

Participants should breathe during each arm stroke. Have participants–

1. From the glide position, start the power phase with the arms.
2. As the arms and hands start to pull backward, the head and upper body lift naturally for a breath.
3. Take a breath and start to bend the legs to prepare for the kick near the end of the power phase.
4. Without pause, start to recover the arms and drive forward into the water with the upper body.
5. Start the power phase of the kick by pressing backward with the feet as soon as the arms reach full extension, just before the head lowers into position between the arms. The upper body and arms will be in the glide position just before the kick ends.
6. Exhale in a slow, steady manner, mostly through the mouth, in the glide position until just before the next breath.

Level 4 Breaststroke Stroke Performance Criteria

Body position	Trunk horizontal to 30 degrees from surface during glide
Arms	Hands may begin catch wider than shoulder width; arm bend at elbow increases as hand moves toward waist—hands may be level or slightly deeper than elbows; hands may sweep beyond the shoulder, but not beyond waist
Legs	Legs bend at the knees bringing heels toward buttocks; knees may be wider than hips and ankles; heels may break surface of water; ankles may bend throughout power phase; occasional scissors kick acceptable; legs may be partially bent at the knees at the end of the power phase; occasional flutter kick during glide position acceptable
Breathing and timing	Rudimentary form of pull, breathe, kick, glide sequence; minimal glide with some forward motion acceptable

Improving Performance of the Breaststroke

Observations	Interventions
Ineffective kick	Have participants keep ankles flexed and feet rotated outward. They push around and back until the feet touch.
Scissors kick action	Emphasize a narrow kick to avoid scissors action.
Knees and thighs drawn too far under hips	Have participants practice with breaststroke kick with a front glide or using a kickboard.
Propulsion of kick is outward instead of to the rear	Stress pressing feet around and back, not out. Emphasize a semicircular, pushing motion. Wall exercise: gently hold inside of feet during propulsion to add resistance and have the participant feel direction of power. Do this very gently to avoid injury to knees.
Heels move outside knees	Stress proper alignment: knees in line with the hips and heels wider than the knees.
Elbows drop too soon during power phase	Have participants keep elbows high until hands align with them at the end of the down sweep.
Arms pull all the way to the thigh	Have participants shorten the pull and end downward and outward sweep when hands are under the elbows with forearms vertical.
Faulty timing	Have participants practice sequence from glide: pull and breathe, kick and glide.
Ineffective glide while learning	Have participants glide until momentum is almost lost.

Butterfly

In this level, participants should be able to swim the butterfly at least 15 yards at the level of performance described in the stroke performance chart.

Body Position

Have participants move into a face-down, streamlined position.

Legs

Have participants–

1. Begin the kick in the upper abdominals, hips and thighs in a continuous movement with the legs together.
2. Bend the knees to start the downbeat then extend the legs in a whiplike motion.
3. Straighten the legs on the upbeat until the heels just break the surface.
4. The hips rise above and return just below the surface.

Arms

Have participants–

1. Start with the arms extended in front of the shoulders.
2. Simultaneously bend the elbows so that the palms and forearms start facing the feet. Keep the elbows high with the hands directly below and fingertips pointing down and slightly outward.
3. Continue pressing backward toward the feet with the palms and forearms. The hands move from the wide position at the end of the catch to a point at the waist that is just inside the width of the body.
4. Extend the arms toward the feet which causes the arms to come closer to the body.
5. Accelerate the arms and continue pressing the hands back past the hips.
6. Recover by swinging the arms out of the water and wide to the sides with little or no bend in the elbows, making sure to lead this motion with the hands.
7. Move the arms just above the surface to enter the water in front of the shoulders. Keep the wrists relaxed and the thumbs down.
8. The hands enter the water with the thumbs facing down and the elbows remaining slightly flexed in front of or slightly outside of the shoulders.
9. After the entry, extend the elbows to prepare for the next arm stroke.

Breathing and Timing

Have participants–

1. During the arm recovery, bend the knees to prepare for the first kick.
2. As the hands enter the water, press downward with the chin and the chest and extend the legs for the downbeat of the first kick. The upper body angles slightly downward at this point, and appears to bend or "pivot" at the waist.
3. Let the upper body rise toward the surface while bending the knees to prepare for the second kick.
4. Complete the downbeat of the second kick at the finish of pull and just prior to the hands exiting the water.
5. Exhale fully during the underwater pull as the body is rising up.
6. Inhale just as the arms exit the water.
7. Thrust the chin forward (not upward) just as the face clears the water.

Level 4 Butterfly Stroke Performance Criteria

Body position	Trunk may be horizontal to 30 degrees from the surface; face in water
Arms	Above-water arm recovery—arms may contact the water; hands may enter wider than the shoulders; arms may be straight at the elbow during the recovery and catch actions; palms face backwards throughout pull; power phase finishing at waist acceptable; arms may be bent at elbow during finish
Legs	Legs may be partially extended at the knee during the downbeat; minimal movement of the hip during the downbeat acceptable; legs may bend at the knees during upbeat—feet may break the surface; some flutter action acceptable
Breathing and timing	Arms pull and recover with minimal leg kick; arms may hesitate at side before recovery

Improving Performance in the Butterfly

Observations	Interventions
Weak arm propulsion, hands enter water too wide or narrow	Emphasize extending arms forward on entry. Keep elbows up and palms facing backward. Conduct arm-strengthening drills.
Hands "slip" by entering water too flat	Emphasize firm wrists, hands and fingers; hands angled down and out and thumbs rotated down.
Loss of propulsion because of dropped elbows	Stress keeping elbows higher than hands but lower than shoulders. Make sure participants are not lifting the body up excessively during the early part of the arm pull, which may force them to push down on the water instead of back.
Loss of propulsion because of pushing arms too wide during backward press under body	Emphasize bending elbows and pressing arms backward with hands coming close together under the body.
Body bobs because arm action stops at point of entry	Emphasize extending the arms forward and having a good kick when the hands enter. Make sure the chin and chest press forward. Make sure that the hands do not dive downward.
Ineffective kick because knees are not fully extended during downbeat	Have participants press feet down and use knees to snap lower legs to full extension. Conduct underwater dolphin kick drills.
Not enough breathing time because of narrow kick	Check coordination of breathing and arm pull. Have participants increase the size of the kick until it is about 2 feet from top to bottom. Make sure the knees are bending enough to set up the kick.
Difficulty in getting arms out and around during recovery	Emphasize accelerating hands through finish and into recovery. Emphasize second kick. Be sure swimmer is not lifting upper body too high out of the water on breath.

Swim on Back

TEACHING TIP

Refer to the Water Safety Instructor's CD-ROM *for activities and drills to help participants learn and improve the elementary backstroke and back crawl.*

When swimming on back, participants should begin in a streamlined position. To achieve a streamlined position in the water, have participants–

- Extend the arms overhead.
- Clasp the hands together with the arms against the ears.
- Extend the legs together with the toes pointed.

Push Off in a Streamlined Position then Begin Flutter Kicking

Have participants–

1. Push off just under the surface of the water in a streamlined position on back. Exhale through the mouth and nose while pushing off.
2. Before losing momentum, start with the legs straight, together and relaxed with the toes pointed. Keep the knees and ankles loose and floppy, and continuously kick up and down.
3. During the upbeat, start with the thigh and follow through with the whole leg and foot.
4. Snap the foot upward as though kicking a ball.
5. During the downbeat, lower the leg straight down with little or no bend in the knee, about 12 to 18 inches.
6. Continue kicking for 3–5 body lengths.

Push Off in a Streamlined Position then Begin Dolphin Kicking

1. Push off just under the surface of the water in a streamlined position on back. Exhale through the mouth and nose while pushing off.
2. Before losing momentum, keep the legs together and start the upbeat by bending the knees and extending the legs in a whiplike motion.
3. During the upbeat, bend the knees then extend the legs upward until the toes reach the surface in a whiplike motion.
4. Extend the legs during the upbeat and straighten the legs on the downbeat. Keep the ankles relaxed.
5. Continue kicking for 3–5 body lengths.

The kick begins in the upper abdominals, hips and thighs and in a continuous up and down movement.

Elementary Backstroke

Refer to Learn-to-Swim Level 3, page 202. In this level, participants should be able to swim the elementary backstroke at least 25 yards at the level of performance described in the stroke performance chart.

Level 4 Elementary Backstroke Stroke Performance Criteria	
Body position	Body horizontal to 15 degrees from surface; trunk and legs are aligned; slight chin tuck, ears near or below the surface
Arms	Hands remain under the surface and recover near or at the side of the body; arms may extend at or be above shoulder level; arms nearly straight at elbow at beginning of catch; arms partially bent at elbow during extension—wrists may be bent; power phase ends at the level of the hips
Legs	Knees remain below the surface of the water; knees and hips aligned; knees may be wider than ankles; heels drop by bending knees; ankles rotate outward with toes wider than the heel of the foot; lower legs move symmetrically in a circular pattern as knees return to a fully extended position; legs together, toes pointed with minimal movement
Breathing and timing	Relaxed rhythmic breathing pattern; arms and legs begin recovery at same time; some glide occurs at end of power phase

Back Crawl

In this level, participants should be able to swim the back crawl at least 15 yards at the level of performance described in the stroke performance chart.

Body Position

Have participants–

1. Move into a horizontal, streamlined position on the back.
2. Have the waterline run from the middle of the top of the head to the tip of the chin with the ears under water.

Legs

Have participants–

1. Hold the legs straight, together and relaxed. Keep the knees and ankles loose and floppy, and kick up and down.
2. Start the upbeat by bending the knee and whipping the foot upward until the leg is straight and the toes reach the surface, like kicking a ball.
3. Keep the leg nearly straight in the downbeat.
4. At the end of the downward motion, bend the knee and start the upward kick.

Arms

Have participants–

1. With the arm straight, place one hand in the water above the head, just outside the shoulder, little finger first. Keep the palm facing out, the wrist bent slightly and the hands relaxed with fingers straight.
2. Reach downward 8 to 12 inches at an angle then bend the elbow so that the palm and forearm are facing toward the feet and fingertips are pointing to the side of the pool.
3. Keep the arm to the side of the body and the hand and forearm horizontal following a straight path pushing water toward the feet with the fingertips pointing to the side. Accelerate toward the feet with the wrist extended and the palm pitched slightly downward.

4. End with the arm straight and the hand below the thigh.
5. Relax the wrist and lift the arm straight up with the thumb leaving the water first.
6. Rotate the hand so that the little finger leads as the arm re-enters the water.

Breathing and Timing

- The arms move continuously in constant opposition to each other, one arm recovers while the other arm pulls.
- Use a regular breathing pattern during each stroke. Inhale when one arm recovers and exhale when the other arm recovers.
- The body rolls toward the recovery arm just before that hand enters the water.

Level 4 Back Crawl Stroke Performance Criteria

Body position	Trunk horizontal to 30 degrees from surface; ears may be out of water, chin on chest; hips may be bent; rudimentary body roll; slight side-to-side motion between shoulders and hips acceptable
Arms	Above-water arm recovery—elbows below surface acceptable; hands may enter at or above shoulder level; arm straight at elbow during power phase acceptable
Legs	Continuous kicking; occasional bicycling action acceptable; legs bent at knee acceptable; feet may break surface of water
Breathing and timing	Occasional breath-holding acceptable; arms in opposition—hesitation at finish acceptable

Improving Performance of the Back Crawl

Observations	Interventions
Extreme arch in back; head too far back	Tell participants to relax the back, tuck the chin in slightly and keep ears in water.
Hips bend excessively	Have participants practice flutter kick with arms extended behind the head. Have them focus on stretching body and keeping kick lower than body line.
Torso bends side-to-side	Check for proper body roll. Be sure head is aligned with spine and that hands enter water at 11:00 and 1:00 o'clock.
Legs too deep	Stress that toes should reach surface at end of each upward beat. The kick should churn the surface.
Knees bend too vigorously on downbeat	Stress starting the leg movement from the hips.
Hips too low in water	Emphasize body position, check head position.
Arm enters water with back of hand first	Have participants concentrate on arm rotation. Emphasize that the little finger enters first.
"Splash entry": bent arm recovery, elbow enters water first, forearm and hand are thrown into the water	Have participants practice arm strokes with legs supported. Have them do one-arm drills.
Arms overreach on water entry, and hands enter behind head or opposite shoulder	Have participants overcorrect point of entry outside of shoulders. Emphasize an earlier rotation so the body is rotated toward the arm entering the water sooner.

Swim on Side

TEACHING TIP

Refer to the Water Safety Instructor's CD-ROM *for activities and drills to help participants learn and improve the sidestroke.*

Sidestroke

In this level, participants should be able to swim the sidestroke at least 15 yards at the level of performance described in the stroke performance chart.

Body Position

Have participants–

- Move into a nearly, horizontal streamlined position on the side.
- Keep the head, back and legs in a straight line and with the legs together and fully extended.
- The lower ear resting in the water close to the shoulder, with the face just high enough to allow the mouth and nose to remain above the water.

Legs

Have participants–

1. Extend the bottom arm and put the head on the shoulder.
2. From the glide position, recover the legs by flexing the hips and knees and drawing the heels slowly toward the buttocks, keeping the knees close together.
3. At the end of the recovery, flex the top ankle and point the toes of the lower foot to prepare for the kick. Move the top leg toward the front of the body and the bottom leg toward the back. When extended, the top leg should be almost straight.
4. Without pausing, kick the top leg straight and press it backwards. At the same time, extend the bottom leg in a motion like kicking a ball until both legs are fully extended and together in the glide position.

Arms

With the leading arm, have participants–

1. From the glide position, rotate the arm slightly to position the palm down and angled slightly outward in the direction they are facing.
2. Bend the elbow and sweep the hand downward slightly and then back toward the feet, until the hand almost reaches the upper chest.
3. Without pausing, recover the arm by rotating the shoulder and dropping the elbow.
4. Pass the hand under the ear until the fingers point forward.
5. Thrust the arm forward, rotating it so the palm is down for the glide position.

With the trailing arm, have participants–

1. From the glide position, draw the forearm along the body until the hand is nearly in front of the shoulder of the leading arm.
2. Keep the palm down and angled slightly forward.
3. Sweep the hand downward slightly and then back toward the body and into the glide position.

Breathing and Timing

- Breathe with each stroke. Inhale while the trailing arm recovers and exhale as the trailing arm pushes back toward the feet.

- From the glide position, start the stroke with the sweep of the leading arm. Recover the trailing arm and the legs.
- Then kick and stroke with the trailing arm as the leading arm recovers. By the completion of the kick and the stroke of the trailing arm, the arms and legs should be fully extended.
- Glide until the speed slows.

Level 4 Sidestroke Stroke Performance Criteria	
Body position	Trunk horizontal to 30 degrees from surface; hips may roll away from midline; bottom ear may be out of water with head raised
Arms	Leading arm: hand may break surface of the water; elbow may be straight during catch; hand may continue past upper chest Trailing arm: hand may break surface of the water; elbow may remain close to body; hand may pass by thigh and recover past shoulder of leading arm; arm may be partially bent at elbow
Legs	Elements of breaststroke or flutter kick acceptable; legs may separate slightly as knees bend in recovery; any type of foot and ankle position acceptable; legs may bend at the knees and be held loosely together during glide
Breathing and timing	Any type of breathing pattern with minimal breath-holding; arms and legs may move simultaneously; arm action may be continuous; some glide occurs at end of power phase

Water Safety

The concept of water safety should be central to every part of an aquatics program. The following water safety topics are required for Learn-to-Swim Level 4:

- Reach or Throw, Don't Go
- Recreational water illnesses
- Think So You Don't Sink
- Look Before You Leap

As in earlier levels, some of the water safety topics are repeated for reinforcement. In this level, participants are introduced to entering the water in a headfirst position. Rules for headfirst entries should be repeated and built upon to ensure that participants clearly understand where and when it is appropriate to enter the water in a headfirst position. Vary your presentation approach to keep it interesting and to test the participants' level of understanding. Add topics as necessary so that you integrate water safety into each lesson. When selecting additional topics, think about current events in or special needs of your local area or region. Refer to **Chapter 4** for details on these topics and for additional topics. Wrap up each class session by emphasizing the safety component of the skills they learned.

Exit Skills Assessment

When participants complete Learn-to-Swim Level 4, they are starting to demonstrate effective and efficient strokes in the front crawl and elementary backstroke. They are starting to show stroke proficiency in the breaststroke, back crawl, butterfly and sidestroke. They can enter the water headfirst from both compact and stride positions. There are two parts to the exit skills assessment:

1. Perform a feetfirst entry into deep water, swim front crawl for 25 yards, change direction and position as necessary and swim elementary backstroke for 25 yards.
2. Swim breaststroke for 15 yards, change direction and position as necessary and swim back crawl for 15 yards.

Learn-to-Swim Level 5—Stroke Refinement

The objectives of this level are coordination and refinement of strokes. Participants refine their performance of all the strokes (front crawl, back crawl, butterfly, breaststroke, elementary backstroke and sidestroke) and increase their distances. Flip turns on the front and back are also introduced.

Learn-to-Swim Level 5—Stroke Refinement Outline

Equipment

- U.S. Coast Guard-approved life jackets (correct sizes for the participants)
- Flotation devices, such as kickboards and pull buoys

Skills	Completion Requirements	References
Water Entry and Exit		
Shallow-angle dive from the side*	Demonstrate, in water at least 9-feet deep	WSIM, page 232 SWS, page 127
Shallow-angle dive, glide two body lengths and begin any front stroke*	Demonstrate, in water at least 9-feet deep	WSIM, page 222
Breath Control and Submerging		
Tuck surface dive	Demonstrate, submerging completely	WSIM, page 222 SWS, page 90
Pike surface dive	Demonstrate, submerging completely	WSIM, page 223 SWS, page 90
Changing Direction and Position		
Front flip turn while swimming	Demonstrate	WSIM, page 222 SWS, page 135
Backstroke flip turn while swimming	Demonstrate	WSIM, page 223 SWS, page 137
Treading		
Tread water	Demonstrate, at least 5 minutes	WSIM, page 224 SWS, page 85
Swim on Front		
Front crawl	Demonstrate, at least 50 yards	WSIM, page 224 SWS, page 94
Breaststroke	Demonstrate, at least 25 yards	WSIM, page 224 SWS, page 103
Butterfly	Demonstrate, at least 25 yards	WSIM, page 225 SWS, page 107

** If water depth is not at least 9 feet, instructors SHOULD NOT teach headfirst entries.*

Skills	Completion Requirements	References
Swim on Back		
Elementary backstroke	Demonstrate, at least 50 yards	WSIM, page 225 SWS, page 112
Back crawl	Demonstrate, at least 25 yards	WSIM, page 225 SWS, page 100
Sculling ■ Standard scull	Demonstrate, at least 30 seconds	WSIM, page 226 SWS, page 83
Swim on Side		
Sidestroke	Demonstrate, at least 25 yards	SWS, page 115 WSIM, page 227
Water Safety		
How to call for help and the importance of knowing first aid and CPR	Discuss/demonstrate	WSIM, page 64 SWS, page 45
Recreational water illnesses	Discuss	WSIM, page 67 SWS, page 15 LWT
Reach or Throw, Don't Go	Discuss/demonstrate	WSIM, page 70 SWS, page 55 LWT
Look Before You Leap	Discuss/demonstrate	WSIM, page 75 SWS, pages 28 & 140 LWT
Think So You Don't Sink	Discuss	WSIM, page 76 SWS, pages 47 & 80 LWT
Think Twice Before Going Near Cold Water or Ice	Discuss/demonstrate	WSIM, page 78 SWS, pages 38 & 52 LWT
Wave, Tide or Ride, Follow the Guide	Discuss	WSIM, page 71 SWS, page 24 LWT

Exit Skills Assessment

1. Perform a shallow-angle dive into deep water, swim front crawl for 50 yards, change direction and position of travel as necessary and swim elementary backstroke for 50 yards.
2. Swim breaststroke for 25 yards, change direction and position of travel as necessary and swim back crawl for 25 yards.

* *If water depth is not at least 9 feet, instructors SHOULD NOT teach headfirst entries.*

Learn-to-Swim Level 5 Skills

Water Entry and Exit

Shallow-Angle Dive from the Side

Have participants–

1. Start on the edge of the pool with the feet about shoulder-width apart and the toes gripping the edge of the pool.
2. Flex the hips and knees and bend forward until the upper back is nearly parallel to the pool deck.
3. Focus on a target. To gain momentum for the dive, swing the arms backward and upward, letting the heels rise and the body start to move forward.
4. When the arms reach the farthest point backward, immediately swing the arms forward. Extend the hips, knees, ankles and toes one after another forcibly to drive forward in a line of flight over and nearly parallel to the surface of the water.
5. Keep the body stretched and the hands interlocked and out in front.
6. During the flight, drop the head slightly between the outstretched arms, which should be angled downward slightly.
7. Make the entry at roughly a 45-degree angle to the surface of the water. Once under water, steer upward toward the surface with the hands and head.
8. Keep the body fully extended and streamlined while gliding under water. Before losing too much speed, start the leg kick to rise to the surface and start swimming.

SAFETY NOTE

All headfirst entries must be taught in water at least 9-feet deep. If water depth is not at least 9 feet, instructors SHOULD NOT teach headfirst entries.

Shallow-Angle Dive, Glide 2 Body Lengths and Begin Any Front Stroke

Have participants follow steps 1–8 for the shallow-angle dive then glide 2 body lengths and begin any front stroke.

Breath Control and Submerging

Tuck Surface Dive

Have participants–

1. Use a swimming stroke and glide with the arms forward to gain forward momentum.
2. Take a breath, sweep the arms backward to the thighs then turn the palms downward.
3. Tuck the chin to the chest, bend the body at a right angle at the hips and draw the legs into a tuck position.
4. Roll forward until almost upside down.
5. Extend the legs upward quickly while pressing the arms and hands forward with the palms facing the bottom.
6. Use a breaststroke arm pull for greater depth after the initial descent slows down.
7. If depth of the water is unknown or if it is less than 8 feet, keep at least one arm extended over the head toward the bottom.

Pike Surface Dive

Have participants–

1. Use a swimming stroke and glide with the arms forward to gain forward momentum.
2. Take a breath, sweep the arms backward to the thighs and turn the palms downward.
3. Tuck the chin to the chest and flex at the hip sharply while the arms reach forward and downward toward the bottom.
4. Lift the legs upward, straight and together, putting the body into a fully extended, streamlined and nearly vertical position.
5. Allow the weight of the legs and forward momentum to cause descent.
6. If depth of the water is unknown or if it is less than 8 feet, keep at least one arm extended over the head toward the bottom.

Changing Direction and Position

TEACHING TIP

Refer to the Water Safety Instructor's CD-ROM *for tips on progressions for teaching front and backstroke flip turns.*

Front Flip Turn While Swimming

Have participants–

1. When one stroke length (3½ to 4 feet) away from the wall, keep the trailing arm at the side while taking the last stroke with the lead arm. Both hands will end up at the thighs with the palms facing up.
2. Perform a half-somersault by tucking the chin to the chest and bending at the waist while simultaneously using a single dolphin kick to push the hips forward and upward. Turn the palms down and push the hands toward the head in order to help the legs flip over the water.
3. During the somersault, bend the legs to prepare to hit the wall. The hands will have reached the ears, which helps complete the forward flip.
4. Plant the feet on the wall with the toes pointed up or slightly to the side and the knees bent.
5. Extend the arms into a streamlined position above the head. Push off while facing up or facing diagonally to the side; then rotate to a face-down position during the glide.
6. Before losing speed, start a steady kick and resume the arm stroke.

Backstroke Flip Turn While Swimming

Have participants–

1. Start the flip one stroke from the wall by turning the head and looking toward the pulling arm as it does the catch.
2. While pulling, rotate onto the stomach, drive the head downward and stop the pulling hand at the hips. At the same time, the other arm recovers across the body, enters the water in the same position as in the front crawl and pulls to the hips.
3. Drive the head down and start somersaulting while tucking the knees tightly to the chest. During the somersault, turn both palms down and push the hands toward the head to complete the flip. Keep the legs tucked until the feet contact the wall, toes pointed upward.
4. While still on the back, push straight off forcefully and go into a streamlined position while leaving the wall.
5. Before losing speed, start kicking to rise to the surface and resume the arm stroke.

Treading

Tread Water

Refer to Learn-to-Swim Level 3, page 198. In this level, participants should be able to tread water for 5 minutes.

Swim on Front

TEACHING TIP

Refer to the Water Safety Instructor's CD-ROM *for activities and drills to help participants learn and improve the front crawl, breaststroke and butterfly.*

Front Crawl

In this level, participants should be able to swim the front crawl at least 50 yards at the level of performance described in the stroke performance chart.

Level 5 Front Crawl Stroke Performance Criteria	
Body position	Body is nearly horizontal to the surface in a streamlined position; body roll is a fluid motion—head, trunk and legs are aligned
Arms	Above-water recovery with arm bent at elbow; arm relaxed as hand moves toward the head; arm extends fully in coordination with body roll; elbow and hand move just outside the shoulders as the arm travels straight backward; palm presses toward feet until arm reaches full extension during finish
Legs	Continuous kicking that starts from the hips and propels swimmer forward using a 2- to 6-beat kick; heels just break the surface
Breathing and timing	Exhale under water before the next breath during the power phase; head remains in line with the body—minimal head movement; alternate side breathing preferred

Breaststroke

In this level, participants should be able to swim the breaststroke at least 25 yards at the level of performance described in the stroke performance chart.

Level 5 Breastroke Stroke Performance Criteria	
Body position	Trunk horizontal to 15 degrees from surface during glide; body incline should become more level following kick
Arms	Palms begin moving outward at or narrower than shoulder width—arms slightly bent; in the mid-pull, sweep the hands downward and inward; bend at elbow increases as hands move toward chest—hands deeper than elbows by end of pull; hands should not sweep beyond the upper chest area; sweep hands back together so that hands travel along the midline underneath the body to a streamlined position
Legs	Legs bend at the knees bringing heels toward buttocks—legs bending slightly at hips; knees and hips should be aligned—knees do not separate beyond hip width; ankles bend and rotate outward with toes wider than the heel of foot; knees and ankles extend at the end of the power phase—legs partially bent at the knees and ankles acceptable
Breathing and timing	Pull, breathe, kick, glide sequence; rhythmic breathing with each cycle; glide after recovery with arms extended; slight hesitation before recovery acceptable

Butterfly

In this level, participants should be able to swim the butterfly at least 25 yards at the level of performance described in the stroke performance chart.

Level 5 Butterfly Stroke Performance Criteria	
Body position	Trunk horizontal to 15 degrees from the surface; head, trunk and legs are aligned with minimal movement to the left or right of the midline
Arms	Above-water arm recovery—straight elbow, occasional arm contact with the water acceptable; hands should enter at shoulder width, with fingertips facing down; arms partially bent at elbows; arms start wide then move to inside the width of body at waist; hands press back toward the feet past the hips
Legs	Legs may separate slightly at knees during kick with minimal flutter action; single kick action acceptable; hips flex and knees extended; knees slightly bent; hips raise as legs extend
Breathing and timing	Face-forward head lift begins at start of catch; head re-enters the water after taking breath and hands pull toward waist; one leg kick paired with each arm cycle at a minimum; arms should recover directly from the finish—minimal delay before recovery acceptable

Swim on Back

TEACHING TIP

Refer to the Water Safety Instructor's CD-ROM *for activities and drills to help participants learn and improve the elementary backstroke and back crawl.*

Elementary Backstroke

In this level, participants should be able to swim the elementary backstroke at least 50 yards at the level of performance described in the stroke performance chart.

Level 5 Elementary Backstroke Stroke Performance Criteria	
Body position	Body is nearly horizontal to the surface with arms at side during glide; chin up, ears in the water
Arms	Arms extend at or slightly above shoulder level with hands no further than top of head; fingers lead arm extension; palms face toward feet; elbows extend as palms push backward and inward, stopping at the hips
Legs	Heels drop by bending knees; ankles bend to 90 degrees and rotate outward with toes wider than heels of the feet; knees and ankles fully extending at the end of the power phase
Breathing and timing	Rhythmic breathing pattern—inhale during recovery and exhale during power phase; arm recovery begins slightly before leg recovery; arm and leg power phase begins simultaneously; extended glide after power phase

Back Crawl

In this level, participants should be able to swim the back crawl at least 25 yards at the level of performance described in the stroke performance chart.

Level 5 Back Crawl Stroke Performance Criteria

Body position	Body horizontal to 15 degrees from surface; head back with ears submerged; rudimentary body roll; trunk and legs should be aligned
Arms	Above-water recovery—arm may be partially bent at elbow; hands exit thumb-side or little finger first; hands enter little finger first about shoulder-width apart; arm partially bent at elbow during power phase; hand and forearm finish beyond hip
Legs	Continuous kicking that starts from the hips; legs slightly bent at the knee during upward kick and straight at knee with toes pointed during the downward kick; feet remain below the surface—moderate splashing acceptable
Breathing and timing	Relaxed rhythmic breathing pattern; arms in opposition—slight hesitation at finish acceptable

Sculling

Have participants–

1. Hold the hands just below the surface while standing in waist-deep water.
2. Keep the palms flat, facing downward, and rapidly move them side to side to create whirlpools. While holding the elbows about a tennis ball's distance from the ribs, move the forearms out and then back in. Keep your upper arms still while the lower arms and hands maintain consistent water pressure.

Standard Scull

To practice the sculling motion, have participants–

1. Move into a back float, lean the head back and place the arms at the side. Keep the hands flat and the fingers and wrists firm.
2. Press the shoulders down and back so that the hips are at the surface. Bend the arms at the elbows so that the hands are beside the hips, keeping the point of the elbow away from the body.
3. Keep the palms flat, while moving the forearms away from the body keeping the elbows wide.
4. Bend the elbows and move the arms back to the body so the hands are about 2 inches next to and slightly below the hips.
5. Continuously repeat Steps 3 and 4 to maintain the standard scull for at least 30 seconds.

Swim on Side

TEACHING TIP

Refer to the Water Safety Instructor's CD-ROM *for activities and drills to help participants learn and improve the sidestroke.*

Sidestroke

In this level, participants should be able to swim the sidestroke at least 25 yards at the level of performance described in the stroke performance chart.

Level 5 Sidestroke Stroke Performance Criteria

Body position	Trunk horizontal to 30 degrees from surface; hips may roll away from vertical; bottom ear in the water
Arms	Leading arm: hand may break surface of the water; elbow may be straight during catch; hand may continue past upper chest Trailing arm: hand may break surface of the water; elbow may remain close to body; hand may pass by thigh and recover past shoulder of leading arm; arm may be partially bent at elbow
Legs	Scissors kick; legs may separate slightly as knees bend in recovery; any type of foot and ankle position acceptable; legs may bend at the knees and be held loosely together during glide
Breathing and timing	Rhythmic breathing pattern; arms and legs may move simultaneously; some glide occurs at end of power phase

Improving Performance of the Sidestroke

Observations	Interventions
Body bent at hips or back severely arched; body almost turned onto stomach or back	Tell participants to stretch the body from the head to the toes during the glide and relax the neck and back muscles.
Head held too high, legs too low	Have participants relax neck muscles and lay the head on the shoulder.
Top and/or bottom knee drawn too far forward toward chest	Have participants keep the back straight. Emphasize relaxation and an easy recovery movement.
Top ankle not flexed during leg extension	Tell participants to flex top ankle while extending the leg so big toe points toward head.
Ineffective glide	Check whether power phase of kick and trailing arm are simultaneous. Have participants glide until momentum is almost lost.
Kick begins before trailing arm starts the power phase	Be sure trailing palm faces the feet before kicking.
Legs drop too deep	Have participants lower their heads into the water and start the next stroke sooner.
Legs open vertically on recovery	Have participants practice kick lying on deck to simulate scissors action.
Breaststroke kick	Have participants practice kick to simulate scissors action—extending top leg forward and bottom leg back—in bracket drill or with kickboard.

Water Safety

The concept of water safety should be central to every part of an aquatics program. The following water safety topics are required for Learn-to-Swim Level 5:

- How to call for help and the importance of knowing first aid and CPR
- Recreational water illnesses
- Reach or Throw, Don't Go
- Look Before You Leap
- Think So You Don't Sink
- Think Twice Before Going Near Cold Water or Ice
- Wave, Tide or Ride, Follow the Guide

As in earlier levels, some of the water safety topics are repeated for reinforcement. Vary your presentation approach to keep it interesting and to test the participants' level of understanding. Add topics as necessary so that you integrate water safety into each lesson. When selecting additional topics, think about current events in or special needs of your local area or region. Refer to **Chapter 4** for details on these topics and for additional topics. Wrap up each class session by emphasizing the safety component of the skills they learned.

Exit Skills Assessment

When participants complete Learn-to-Swim Level 5, they are starting to demonstrate effectiveness and efficiency in all strokes. They are starting to work on endurance through longer swims that require using open and flip turns. They can enter the water using the shallow-angle dive and can then continue swimming. There are two parts to the exit skills assessment:

1. Perform a shallow-angle dive into deep water, swim front crawl for 50 yards, change direction and position of travel as necessary and swim elementary backstroke for 50 yards.
2. Swim breaststroke for 25 yards, change direction and position of travel as necessary and swim back crawl for 25 yards.

Learn-to-Swim Level 6—Swimming and Skill Proficiency

The objectives of this level are to refine strokes so participants swim them with more ease, efficiency, power and smoothness and over greater distances. Level 6 also introduces other aquatic activities and offers three options–Personal Water Safety, Fundamentals of Diving and Fitness Swimmer. These options focus on preparing participants for more advanced courses, such as the Water Safety Instructor course, or other aquatic activities, such as competitive swimming or diving.

You should customize this level to meet the objectives of the participants. For instance, you can promote the course for participants who want to enter competition or who want to achieve a higher level of fitness. Because of the variety this level offers, participants can repeat it to focus on different goals each time.

Learn-to-Swim Level 6—Personal Water Safety Outline

Equipment

- Flotation devices, such as kickboards and pull buoys
- Diving brick or other object that sinks
- Clothing for in-water skill practice
- *Swimming and Water Safety* or *Water Safety Handbook* (one for each participant; recommended)

Skills	Completion Requirements	References
Swim on Front, Back and Side		
Front crawl	Demonstrate, at least 100 yards	WSIM, page 231 SWS, page 94
Elementary backstroke	Demonstrate, at least 100 yards	WSIM, page 231 SWS, page 112
Back crawl	Demonstrate, at least 50 yards	WSIM, page 231 SWS, page 100
Breaststroke	Demonstrate, at least 50 yards	WSIM, page 231 SWS, page 103
Sidestroke	Demonstrate, at least 50 yards	WSIM, page 232 SWS, page 115
Butterfly	Demonstrate, at least 50 yards	WSIM, page 232 SWS, page 107
Turns		
Front crawl open turn	Demonstrate while swimming	WSIM, page 233 SWS, page 132
Backstroke open turn	Demonstrate while swimming	WSIM, page 233 SWS, page 133
Front flip turn	Demonstrate while swimming	WSIM, page 233 SWS, page 135
Backstroke flip turn	Demonstrate while swimming	WSIM, page 233 SWS, page 137
Sidestroke turn	Demonstrate while swimming	WSIM, page 233 SWS, page 133

Skills	Completion Requirements	References
Turns *(continued)*		
Butterfly turn	Demonstrate while swimming	WSIM, page 233 SWS, page 137
Breaststroke turn	Demonstrate while swimming	WSIM, page 234 SWS, page 136
Review Skills and Information		
HELP position	Demonstrate, at least 2 minutes, in deep water	WSIM, page 234 SWS, page 53
Huddle position	Demonstrate, at least 2 minutes, in deep water	WSIM, page 234 SWS, page 53
Feetfirst surface dive	Demonstrate, in water at least 7-feet deep	WSIM, page 234 SWS, page 89
Tuck surface dive	Demonstrate, in water at least 7-feet deep	WSIM, page 234 SWS, page 90
Pike surface dive	Demonstrate, in water at least 7-feet deep	WSIM, page 234 SWS, page 91
Back float	Demonstrate, at least 5 minutes, in deep water	WSIM, page 234 SWS, page 80
Survival float	Demonstrate, at least 5 minutes, in deep water	WSIM, page 234 SWS, page 50
Survival swimming	Demonstrate, at least 10 minutes	WSIM, page 234 SWS, page 50
New Skills and Information		
Treading water, kicking only	Demonstrate, 2 minutes, in deep water	WSIM, page 234
Surface dive and retrieve an object from the bottom	Demonstrate, in water at least 7–10-feet deep	WSIM, page 235
Water Safety		
Think So You Don't Sink	Discuss/demonstrate	WSIM, page 76 SWS, pages 47 & 80 LWT
Swim with a Buddy in a Supervised Area	Discuss	WSIM, page 73 SWS, page 25 LWT
Learn About Boating Before You Go Floating	Discuss	WSIM, page 79 SWS, page 39 LWT

Exit Skills Assessment

1. Swim 500 yards continuously using any 3 strokes of your choice, swimming at least 50 yards of each stroke.
2. Jump into deep water, perform a survival float for 5 minutes, roll onto back and perform a back float for 5 minutes.
3. Perform a feetfirst surface dive, retrieve an object from the bottom of the pool at a depth of 7–10 feet, return to surface and return to starting point.

Learn-to-Swim Level 6—Personal Water Safety Skills

Swim on Front, Back and Side

TEACHING TIP

Refer to the CD-ROM for activities and drills to help participants learn and improve strokes.

Front Crawl

Refer to Learn-to-Swim Level 5, page 224. In this level, participants should swim at least 100 yards at the level of performance described in the Level 5 Front Crawl Stroke Performance Chart.

Elementary Backstroke

Refer to Learn-to-Swim Level 5, page 225. In this level, participants should swim at least 100 yards described in the Level 5 Elementary Backstroke Stroke Performance Chart.

Back Crawl

In this level, participants should swim at least 50 yards of back crawl at the level of performance described in the stroke performance chart.

Level 6 Back Crawl Stroke Performance Criteria

Body position	Body is nearly horizontal to surface in a streamlined position; head is still and aligned with body, no side-to-side movement; body roll is a fluid motion—head, trunk and legs are aligned
Arms	Above-water recovery—arm straight at elbow; hand enters just outside shoulder in coordination with body roll; hand enters little finger first reaching downward with elbow bent; fingertips pointing away from the body to the side; hand follows a straight path toward the feet; arm fully extended at elbow for the finish
Legs	Continuous kicking that starts from the hips and propels swimmer forward using a 2- to 6-beat kick; feet remain below the surface
Breathing and timing	Rhythmic breathing pattern—inhale as one arm recovers and exhale as the other arm recovers; arms in continuous opposition—no hesitation at finish

Breaststroke

In this level, participants should swim at least 50 yards of breaststroke at the level of performance described in the stroke performance chart.

Level 6 Breaststroke Stroke Performance Criteria

Body position	Body is nearly horizontal to the surface and streamlined during the glide position
Arms	Arms sweep outward from the glide position (arms extended narrower than shoulder width); bend at elbows increase as hands move toward chest; elbows remain high throughout the pull; hands come together at the midline under the chin; arms extend forward to a glide position
Legs	Heels drawn toward buttocks; heels remain under water; ankles rotate outward with toes wider than heels; knees and ankles fully extend at end of power phase
Breathing and timing	No delay from finish into recovery; face and head submerge during arm recovery, kick and glide; exhale under water

Sidestroke

In this level, participants should swim at least 50 yards of sidestroke at the level of performance described in the stroke performance chart.

Level 6 Sidestroke Stroke Performance Criteria

Body position	Body is nearly horizontal to the surface and streamlined during the glide position; hips and shoulders aligned; bottom ear and lower face in water
Arms	Leading arm: hand remains below the surface; palms angled down and slightly outward; elbow bends and hand sweeps slightly downward and slightly backward toward the feet; pull ends at upper chest; shoulder rotates and elbow drops; fingers lead arm extension as the hand passes the ear and the arm rotates so palm faces down; arm is parallel to and below the surface, inline with head, trunk and legs Trailing arm: hand remains below the surface of the water; palm presses downward and slightly backward at the beginning of the catch and continues backward throughout the pull; forearm travels along the midline close to the body during the recovery
Legs	Scissors kick on both sides; knees and hips bend, pulling heels toward buttocks; legs remain close together as knees bend; ankle of top leg begins the power phase in a bent position and extends as the leg returns to the glide position; ankle of the bottom leg remains extended with the toes pointed throughout the power phase
Breathing and timing	Regular rhythmic breathing pattern—inhale during leg recovery and exhale during power phase of the kick; arms alternate; recovery phase of kick occurs during leading arm pull and trailing arm recovery; extended glide after power phase

Butterfly

In this level, participants should swim at least 50 yards of butterfly at the level of performance described in the stroke performance chart.

Level 6 Butterfly Stroke Performance Criteria

Body position	Body is nearly horizontal to the surface in a streamlined position
Arms	Above-water arm recovery little or no bend in the elbows; hands enter thumb side first in front of or slightly outside the shoulders; arms extend and hands accelerate and press back past hips
Legs	Legs can separate slightly at knees during kick—no flutter kick motion; legs extend during downbeat; legs straighten with ankles relaxed during upbeat; heels just break the surface
Breathing and timing	Forward rhythmic breathing pattern on stroke each cycle; inhalation during face lift and arm recovery and exhalation during underwater arm pull; pivoting, up-and-down body action paired with arm action and two dolphin kicks; face exits water before the arms and re-enters the water before the arms

Turns

TEACHING TIP

Refer to the Water Safety Instructor's CD-ROM *for activities and drills to help participants learn and improve turns.*

Front Crawl Open Turn

Refer to Learn-to-Swim Level 4, page 210. In this level, participants should demonstrate the turn during a continuous swim.

Backstroke Open Turn

Refer to Learn-to-Swim Level 4, page 210. In this level, participants should demonstrate the turn during a continuous swim.

Front Flip Turn

Refer to Learn-to-Swim Level 5, page 223. In this level, participants should demonstrate the turn during a continuous swim.

Backstroke Flip Turn

Refer to Learn-to-Swim Level 5, page 223. In this level, participants should demonstrate the turn during a continuous swim.

TEACHING TIP

Refer to the Water Safety Instructor's CD-ROM *for tips on progressions for teaching the sidestroke, butterfly and breaststroke turns.*

Sidestroke Turn

Have participants–

1. Approach with the arm extended and touch the wall with the leading arm.
2. Bend the elbow, drop the opposite shoulder and rotate the back toward the wall.
3. Tuck the body, and swing the legs underneath the body to place them on the wall. Feet should be planted sideways with the foot on the lead arm side of the body placed above the foot on the trailing arm side of the body.
4. Take a breath and extend the trailing arm while pushing off the wall. During this step, the trailing arm now becomes the new leading arm. The leading arm used during the approach stays by the side and becomes the new trailing arm.
5. Once in the glide position, stay on the side and resume the stroke.

Butterfly Turn

Have participants–

1. Time the last stroke to allow the body to be fully stretched upon reaching the wall.
2. Place both hands on the wall at the same time then dip the shoulder in the direction of the turn. Tuck the hips and legs in tight as they continue to move toward the wall.
3. As the hands touch the wall, turn the head toward the left shoulder. Bend the left elbow and move the left arm backward as close as possible to the body.
4. When the legs pass under the body, move the right arm over the head, keeping it close to the head. Plant both feet on the wall with toes pointing toward the side and the knees bent.
5. Take a deep breath before the head submerges. Extend the arms into a streamlined position while pushing off with the body somewhat on its side.
6. Rotate into a face-down position while gliding about 1 foot below the surface.
7. After the turn, glide a short distance, then dolphin kick to the surface and start stroking.

Breaststroke Turn

Have participants–

1. Time the last stroke to allow the body to be fully stretched upon reaching the wall.
2. Place both hands on the wall at the same time then dip the shoulder on the side of the body that the turn will occur. Tuck the hips and legs in tight so that they are directly underneath the body as they continue to move toward the wall.
3. As the hands touch the wall, turn the head to the left shoulder. Bend the left elbow and move the left arm backward, keeping it as close as possible to the body.
4. When the legs pass under the body, move the right arm over the head, keeping it close to the head. Plant both feet on the wall with toes pointing toward the side and the knees bent.
5. Take a deep breath before the head submerges. Extend the arms into a streamlined position while pushing off with the body somewhat on its side.
6. Rotate into a face-down position while gliding below the surface.
7. Before losing speed, take a complete underwater breaststroke pull to the thighs, glide again and then kick upward as the hands recover close to the body. Return to the surface to resume stroking.

Review Skills and Information

HELP Position

Refer to Chapter 4, page 78.

Huddle Position

Refer to Chapter 4, page 79.

Feetfirst Surface Dive

Refer to Learn-to-Swim Level 4, page 209.

Tuck Surface Dive

Refer to Learn-to-Swim Level 5, page 222.

Pike Surface Dive

Refer to Learn-to-Swim Level 5, page 223.

Back Float

Refer to Learn-to-Swim Level 3, page 197. In this level, participants should back float for 5 minutes.

Survival Float

Refer to Learn-to-Swim Level 3, page 197. In this level, participants should demonstrate survival float for 5 minutes.

Survival Swimming

Refer to Learn-to-Swim Level 4, page 209. In this level, participants should survival swim for 10 minutes.

New Skills and Information

Treading Water, Kicking Only

In this level, participants should be able to tread water in deep water, kicking only, for at least 2 minutes. Participants determine which kick is the most efficient for them.

Surface Dive and Retrieve an Object from the Bottom

In this level, participants should be able to surface dive to retrieve objects from the bottom of a deep pool (7–10 feet). Participants may perform a feetfirst, tuck or pike surface dive, whichever is most efficient for them.

Water Safety

The concept of water safety should be central to every part of an aquatics program. The following water safety topics are required for Learn-to-Swim Level 6–Personal Water Safety:

- Think So You Don't Sink
- Swim with a Buddy in a Supervised Area
- Learn About Boating Before You Go Floating

Since the focus of this level is personal water safety, many of the skills are water safety skills. In addition to the required skills and topics from the outline, consider other topics that are relevent to participants, based on their interests and the types of aquatic enivronments in the area. By Level 6, participants should have a good understanding of how to be safe in, on and around the water so it is important to build on this knowledge, not simply repeat it. Refer to **Chapter 4** for details on the topics listed and for additional topics. Also, offer *Swimming and Water Safety* and the *Water Safety Handbook* as great resources to participants.

Exit Skills Assessment

When participants complete Learn-to-Swim Level 6–Personal Water Safety, they demonstrate effectiveness and efficiency in all strokes. They are able to swim continuously while using the appropriate turns for the stroke. They also have a solid understanding about how to be safe in, on and around the water. There are three parts to the exit skills assessment:

1. Swim 500 yards continuously using any 3 strokes of your choice, swimming at least 50 yards of each stroke.
2. Jump into deep water, perform a survival float for 5 minutes, roll onto back and perform a back float for 5 minutes.
3. Swim 20 yards, perform a feetfirst surface dive, retrieve an object from the bottom of the pool at a depth of 7–10 feet, return to the surface and swim 20 yards back to the starting point.

Learn-to-Swim Level 6—Fundamentals of Diving

Beginning with diving skills and information, you must follow the order that skills are presented in this outline.

Learn-to-Swim Level 6—Fundamentals of Diving Outline

Equipment

- Flotation devices, such as kickboards and pull buoys
- *Swimming and Diving Skills* DVD (recommended)
- *Swimming and Water Safety* (one for each participant; recommended)

Skills	Completion Requirements	References
Swim on Front, Back and Side		
Front crawl	Demonstrate, at least 100 yards	WSIM, page 239 SWS, page 94
Elementary backstroke	Demonstrate, at least 100 yards	WSIM, page 239 SWS, page 112
Back crawl	Demonstrate, at least 50 yards	WSIM, page 239 SWS, page 100
Breaststroke	Demonstrate, at least 50 yards	WSIM, page 239 SWS, page 103
Sidestroke	Demonstrate, at least 50 yards	WSIM, page 239 SWS, page 115
Butterfly	Demonstrate, at least 50 yards	WSIM, page 239 SWS, page 107
Turns		
Front crawl open turn	Demonstrate while swimming	WSIM, page 239 SWS, page 132
Backstroke open turn	Demonstrate while swimming	WSIM, page 239 SWS, page 133
Front flip turn	Demonstrate while swimming	WSIM, page 239 SWS, page 135
Backstroke flip turn	Demonstrate while swimming	WSIM, page 240 SWS, page 137
Sidestroke turn	Demonstrate while swimming	WSIM, page 240 SWS, page 133
Butterfly turn	Demonstrate while swimming	WSIM, page 240 SWS, page 133
Breaststroke turn	Demonstrate while swimming	WSIM, page 240 SWS, page 136

** If water depth is not at least 9 feet, instructors SHOULD NOT teach headfirst entries from poolside; if water depth is not at least 11½ feet (or deeper if state or local regulations require), instructors SHOULD NOT teach diving from a diving board.*

Skills	Completion Requirements	References
Diving Skills and Information*		
Basic stretching exercises	Discuss	WSIM, page 240
Body alignment and control	Demonstrate	WSIM, page 240 SWS, page 145
Surface dive	Demonstrate	WSIM, page 240 SWS, page 147
Diving from poolside		
■ Kneeling position	Demonstrate	WSIM, page 241 SWS, page 147
■ Forward dive fall-in	Demonstrate	WSIM, page 242 SWS, page 147
■ Standing dive	Demonstrate	WSIM, page 243 SWS, page 149
Diving from the Diving Board		
■ Kneeling position	Demonstrate	WSIM, page 244 SWS, page 151
■ Forward dive fall-in	Demonstrate	WSIM, page 244 SWS, page 152
■ Standing dive	Demonstrate	WSIM, page 245 SWS, page 153
Takeoff from the Deck		
■ One-part takeoff	Demonstrate	WSIM, page 246 SWS, page 153
■ Two-part takeoff	Demonstrate	WSIM, page 246 SWS, page 153
Takeoff from Poolside		
■ One-part takeoff	Demonstrate	WSIM, page 246 SWS, page 155
Takeoff from the Diving Board		
■ One-part takeoff	Demonstrate	WSIM, page 246 SWS, page 155
■ Two-part takeoff	Demonstrate	WSIM, page 247 SWS, page 156
Tuck Position	Demonstrate	WSIM, page 247 SWS, page 156
Forward Jump, Tuck Position		
■ With one-part takeoff from poolside	Demonstrate	WSIM, page 247 SWS, page 157

** If water depth is not at least 9 feet, instructors SHOULD NOT teach headfirst entries from poolside; if water depth is not at least 11½ feet (or deeper if state or local regulations require), instructors SHOULD NOT teach diving from a diving board.*

Skills	Completion Requirements	References
Forward Jump, Tuck Position *(continued)*		
■ With one-part takeoff from the diving board	Demonstrate	WSIM, page 247 SWS, page 157
■ With two-part takeoff from the diving board	Demonstrate	WSIM, page 247 SWS, page 158
Forward Dive, Tuck Position		
■ With one-part takeoff from poolside	Demonstrate	WSIM, page 248 SWS, page 158
■ With one-part takeoff from the diving board	Demonstrate	WSIM, page 248 SWS, page 159
■ With two-part takeoff from the diving board	Demonstrate	WSIM, page 248 SWS, page 159
Pike Position	Demonstrate	WSIM, page 248 SWS, page 160
Forward Jump, Pike Position		
■ With one-part takeoff from the diving board	Demonstrate	WSIM, page 248 SWS, page 160
■ With two-part takeoff from the diving board	Demonstrate	WSIM, page 248 SWS, page 160
Forward Dive, Pike Position		
■ With one-part takeoff from the diving board	Demonstrate	WSIM, page 249 SWS, page 160
■ With two-part takeoff from the diving board	Demonstrate	WSIM, page 249 SWS, page 160
Water Safety		
Look Before You Leap		WSIM, page 75 SWS, pages 12 & 140 LWT
Exit Skills Assessment		
1. Swim 500 yards continuously using any 3 strokes of your choice, swimming at least 50 yards of each stroke.		
2. Perform a two-part takeoff with a feetfirst entry from a 1-meter diving board.		
3. Perform a two-part takeoff with a headfirst entry from a 1-meter diving board.		

** If water depth is not at least 9 feet, instructors SHOULD NOT teach headfirst entries from poolside; if water depth is not at least 11½ feet (or deeper if state or local regulations require), instructors SHOULD NOT teach diving from a diving board.*

Learn-to-Swim Level 6—Fundamentals of Diving Skills

Swim on Front, Back and Side

TEACHING TIP

Refer to the CD-ROM for activities and drills to help participants learn and improve strokes.

Front Crawl

Refer to Learn-to-Swim Level 5, page 224. In this level, participants should swim at least 100 yards at the level of performance described in the Level 5 Front Crawl Stroke Performance Chart.

Elementary Backstroke

Refer to Learn-to-Swim Level 5, page 225. In this level, participants should swim at least 100 yards described in the Level 5 Elementary Backstroke Stroke Performance Chart.

Back Crawl

Refer to Learn-to-Swim Level 6–Personal Water Safety, page 231. In this level, participants should swim at least 50 yards at the level of performance described in the Level 6 Back Crawl Stroke Performance Chart.

Breaststroke

Refer to Learn-to-Swim Level 6–Personal Water Safety, page 231. In this level, participants should swim at least 50 yards at the level of performance described in the Level 6 Breaststroke Stroke Performance Chart.

Sidestroke

Refer to Learn-to-Swim Level 6–Personal Water Safety, page 232. In this level, participants should swim at least 50 yards at the level of performance described in the Level 6 Sidestroke Stroke Performance Chart.

Butterfly

Refer to Learn-to-Swim Level 6–Personal Water Safety, page 232. In this level, participants should swim at least 50 yards at the level of performance described in the Level 6 Butterfly Stroke Performance Chart.

Turns

Front Crawl Open Turn

Refer to Learn-to-Swim Level 4, page 210. In this level, participants should demonstrate the turn during a continuous swim.

Backstroke Open Turn

Refer to Learn-to-Swim Level 4, page 210. In this level, participants should demonstrate the turn during a continuous swim.

Front Flip Turn

Refer to Learn-to-Swim Level 5, page 223. In this level, participants should demonstrate the turn during a continuous swim.

Backstroke Flip Turn

Refer to Learn-to-Swim Level 5, page 223. In this level, participants should demonstrate the turn during a continuous swim.

Sidestroke Turn

Refer to Learn-to-Swim Level 6, page 233. In this level, participants should demonstrate the turn during a continuous swim.

Butterfly Turn

Refer to Learn-to-Swim Level 6, page 233. In this level, participants should demonstrate the turn during a continuous swim.

Breaststroke Turn

Refer to Learn-to-Swim Level 6, page 234. In this level, participants should demonstrate the turn during a continuous swim.

Diving Skills and Information

SAFETY NOTE

Beginning with this section, you must follow the order that skills are presented. Do not allow participants to wear goggles while practicing any of the diving skills.

Basic Stretching Exercises

Tell participants:

- **Stretching has been shown to be beneficial for strength, power and range of motion. Some examples of stretching exercises for divers include–**
  - **Jogging or fast walking.**
  - **Shoulder circles.**
  - **Leg swings–forward, backwards and sideways.**
  - **Pike stretch.**
  - **Special exercises (if needed).**
  - **Arm swings.**

Body Alignment and Control

Have participants practice proper body alignment on deck in the following way:

- Hand position: Place the palm of one hand on top of the back of the other and grip the bottom hand with the fingers of the top hand. Interlock the thumbs. Hyperextend both wrists so the palm of the bottom hand hits flat on the surface.
- Arm position: Raise the arms overhead with hands in line with the shoulders and hips. Lock the elbows. Press the upper arms tightly against the ears and head.

- Head position: Keep the head erect and tilted back very slightly to maintain alignment between the arms and with the torso.
- Upper body position: Lift the ribs up and align the back in a straight line.
- Hip position: Tilt the top of the pelvis (hips) backward to help reduce excess curvature or sway in the lower back.
- Leg and foot positions: Keep the legs straight at the hips and knees and the toes pointed.

Surface Dive

Have participants–

1. Push off the wall into a glide to gain forward momentum.
2. Take a breath then tuck the chin while sweeping the arms back toward the thighs and flex at the hip sharply. Once the hands reach the thighs, slide the arms above the head and reach forward and downward toward the bottom, stretching the arms over the head.
3. Lift the legs upward, keeping the knees straight and together so that the weight of the legs helps the downward descent.

Diving from Poolside

Kneeling Position

Have participants–

1. Kneel on one knee on the pool edge. The leg in front should be bent with the toes of the forward foot gripping the pool edge. The other leg should be bent at the knee and the foot bent at the ankle in a position for the toes to help push from the deck.
2. Extend the arms over head with the upper arms pressing together against the ears.
3. Focus on a target on the surface of the water about 2 feet from poolside.
4. Lean forward, keeping the chin tucked against the chest, try to touch the water with the hands and, when starting to lose balance, push with the legs. Dive downward, not outward.
5. On entering the water, straighten the body at the hips and extend both legs.

Instructor Assistance from Poolside

1. Stand on the side of the trail leg (**Fig. 9-1, A**).
2. Assist the participant by holding the trail leg above and below the knee. Lift the trail leg to keep the participant from doing a belly flop (**Fig. 9-1, B**).

Fig. 9-1, A

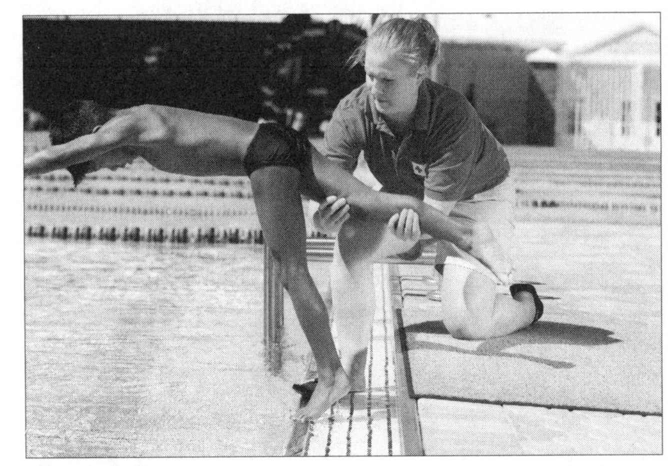

Fig. 9-1, B

Instructor Assistance from the Water

1. Position yourself in the water on the same side as the participant's kneeling leg. Do not get directly in front of the participant.
2. Hold your hand out, and have the participant place the palms of his or her hands on the upward facing palm of your hand (**Fig. 9-2, A**). Your hands should be in the location of the entry target.
3. Direct the participant to keep the head down as he or she begins leaning forward, pressing against your hands.
4. The participant pushes toward the water, staying in contact with your hand.
5. Lower your hand down as the participant begins to dive (**Fig. 9-2, B**).
6. When the participant's head reaches the surface, quickly move your hand away so the participant can enter the water cleanly and smoothly.

Forward Dive Fall-In

Have participants–

1. Stand with feet together or up to shoulder-width apart with the toes of both feet on the edge of the deck.
2. Bend at the waist so the upper body is at about a 45- to 90-degree angle to the legs and focus on a target on the surface of the water about 2 feet from poolside.
3. Tuck the chin to the chest and extend the arms overhead with the upper arms pressing together against the ears.
4. Rise up onto the balls of the feet and fall forward toward the water, keeping the knees straight.
5. Fall forward, lift the hips and extend the legs upward so they are in line with the torso.

Fig. 9-2, A

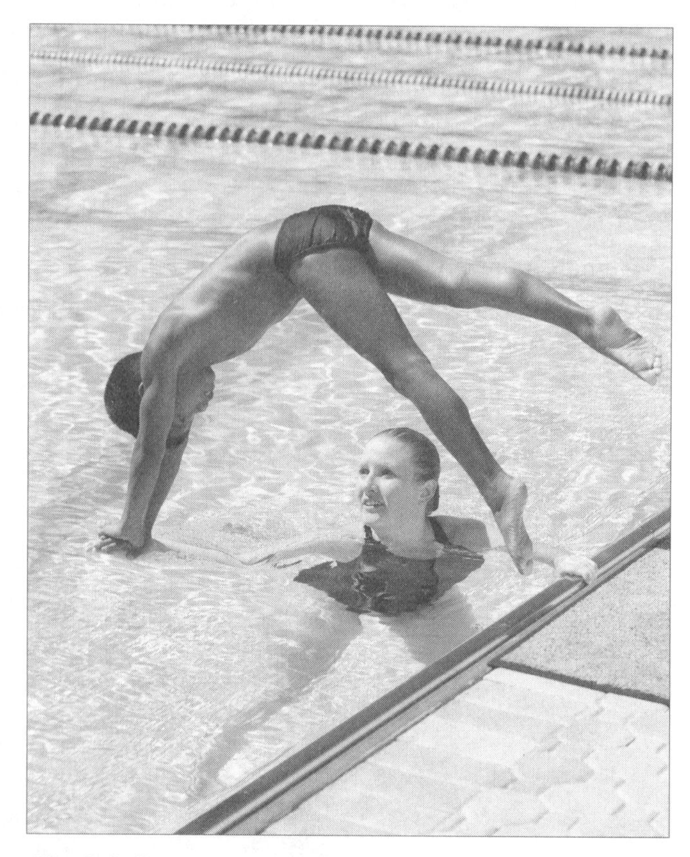

Fig. 9-2, B

Instructor Assistance from the Water

1. Position yourself in the water to the side of the participant, who is standing on the deck. Do not get directly in front of the participant.
2. Hold your hand out, and have the participant place the palms of his or her hands on the upward facing palm of your hand. Direct the participant to keep the head down.
3. Participant pushes toward the water, staying in contact with your hand (**Fig. 9-3**).
4. Lower your hand down as the participant pushes toward the water.
5. When the participant's head reaches the surface, quickly move your hand away.

Standing Dive

Have participants–

1. Stand with feet together or up to shoulder-width apart with toes gripping the edge of the deck.
2. Extend the arms over head with the upper arms pressing together against the ears.
3. Focus on a target on the surface of the water about 3 feet from poolside.
4. Bend at the knees and begin to angle the hands down toward the target.
5. Push off the deck, then lift the hips and extend the legs so they are in line with the torso, angle the hands down toward the target and keep the chin tucked toward the chest.

Instructor Assistance from Poolside

Use this technique only for a participant having difficulty lifting the legs during the dive.

1. Sit at the pool edge to one side of the participant. Place one arm in front of the participant midway between the feet and knees about 12 inches away from the legs (**Fig. 9-4**).
2. The participant dives over your arm, while angling down toward the water.
3. Move your arm away as the participant leaves the deck.

Fig. 9-3

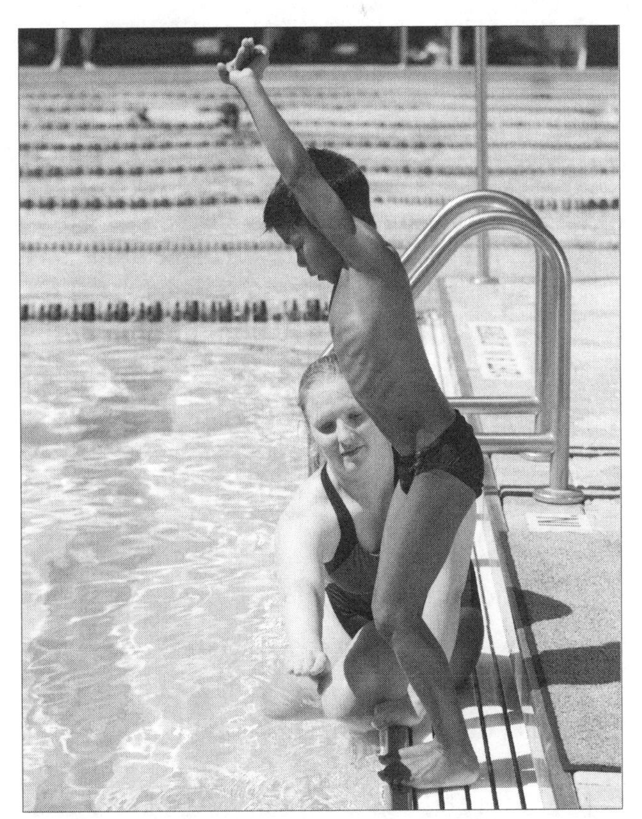

Fig. 9-4

Improving Performance of the Standing Dive	
Observations	**Interventions**
Diving too far out causing flat landing	Tell participant to aim at a closer target or dive just slightly closer than the target.
Lifting the head or arms up causing flat landing	Emphasize keeping the arms over the ears and squeezing the head between the arms. Emphasize proper body alignment, especially during the setup.
Pushing too late, causing legs to flip over head with arched back or roll into water	Tell participant to push off the deck earlier. Emphasize proper body alignment, especially as he or she enters the water.

Diving from the Diving Board

SAFETY NOTES

- *Do not use manual assistance for diving from the diving board. Make sure participants are proficient in diving from poolside before moving to the diving board.*
- *Move the fulcrum as far forward as possible to adjust the board to minimize bounce.*
- *Place a wet towel or chamois on the end of the board for dives from the kneeling position to help prevent knee abrasions.*
- *Ensure that participants keep the head and arms aligned during all steps. Participants should be practicing proper body alignment during dives from poolside.*
- *Ensure that participants choose a target that is appropriate for the skill. Choosing a target too far away may cause participants to dive too flat; a target that is too close may cause the legs to pass beyond vertical or the back to arch.*
- *Ensure that participants dive in a vertical, streamlined position.*

Kneeling Position

Have participants–

1. Kneel on one knee on the diving board. The leg in front should be bent with the forward foot flat on the board. The other leg should be bent at the knee with the foot bent at the ankle in a position for the toes to help push from the board.
2. Extend the arms over head with the upper arms pressing together against the ears.
3. Focus on a target on the surface of the water about 3 feet from the tip of the diving board.
4. Roll forward by dropping the hands and head, try to touch the water and, when starting to lose balance, push with the feet and legs.
5. Straighten the body, extend both legs and point the toes immediately upon leaving the board.

Forward Dive Fall-In

Have participants–

1. Stand with the toes at the tip of the diving board.
2. Grab the hands over head with the upper arms pressing together against the ears.
3. Bend at the waist so the upper body is at a 90-degree angle to the legs and focus on a target on the surface of the water about 3 feet from the tip of the diving board.
4. Rise up slightly onto the balls of the feet and fall forward toward the water, keeping focused on the target.

5. Squeeze the upper arms against the ears while falling toward the water. The head should remain aligned between the arms.
6. Extend the body to a streamlined position for the entry.

Improving Performance from the Diving Board

Observations	Interventions
Lifting the head from between the arms or ducking the head at entry	Emphasize keeping the arms over the ears and squeezing the head between the arms and keeping the head still.
Letting the hands and arms split apart before and when hitting the water	Emphasize gripping the hands, keeping the arms over the ears and squeezing the head between the arms.
Not extending the legs before entry causing the body to roll forward under water	Have participant practice the surface dive. Emphasize a streamlined body position during the dive.
Back overarches or knees flex on entry	Practice proper body alignment on the deck. Choose a target slightly farther away. Emphasize stretching the body through an imaginary hole in the water.

Standing Dive

Have participants–

1. Stand with feet together with the toes of both feet on the tip of the diving board.
2. Extend the arms over head with the upper arms pressing together against the ears.
3. Focus on a target on the surface of the water about 3 feet from the tip of the diving board.
4. Bend the knees slightly and begin to angle the hands down toward the target.
5. Push off the board, lift the hips and extend the legs so they are in line with the torso. Enter the water in a streamlined position.

Improving Performance of the Forward Dive, Tuck and Pike Positions

Observations	Interventions
Too much forward momentum	Emphasize body control maintaining a streamlined position, keeping the hips over the balls of the feet on the initial up motion to delay forward lean until the board begins to recoil.
Over rotating and passing vertical	Check to see if the participant is lowering the head too much or too quickly in flight. If so, tell the participant to continue watching the target during takeoff until they line up for the entry. If not, move the target slightly farther away from the board.
Swinging the arms directly forward in the "come out" (may cause the rotation past vertical)	Have the participant move the arms laterally and over the ears to prepare for the entry.
Incomplete pike position	The participant may need to improve lower back and hamstring flexibility or abdominal strength to assume a tighter pike position.
Under rotating and entering less than vertical	The participant may be keeping the head too far back or leaning back during the takeoff.

Takeoff from the Deck

SAFETY NOTE

Do these exercises only on a dry deck that is not slippery. When possible, have participants dry off to help keep the practice areas dry.

One-Part Takeoff

Have participants–

1. Slowly raise the heels up as the arms lift overhead into a "Y" position.
2. Circle the arms slowly back and down as the knees begin to bend.
3. With the feet flat on the ground, continue to bend the knees into a squat and swing the arms from behind the hips forward and upward, extending into a straight jump.

Two-Part Takeoff

Have participants–

1. Slowly raise the heels up as the arms lift overhead to a "Y" position.
2. Circle the arms slowly back and down as the knees begin to bend.
3. With the feet flat on the ground, continue to bend the knees into a squat and swing the arms from behind the hips forward and upward, extending into a straight jump that travels forward about 2-foot lengths.
4. Jump again immediately after touching down, circling the arms back and down while jumping high and traveling forward.

Takeoff from Poolside

One-Part Takeoff

Have participants–

1. Slowly raise the heels up as the arms lift overhead to a "Y" position.
2. Circle the arms slowly back and down as the knees begin to bend.
3. With the feet flat on the ground, continue to bend the knees into a squat and swing the arms from behind the hips forward and upward, extending into a straight jump that lands in the water.

SAFETY NOTE

Do not attempt a two-part takeoff from poolside for safety reasons.

Takeoff from the Diving Board

One-Part Takeoff

Have participants–

1. Stand upright at the tip of the diving board with the toes at the edge.
2. Slowly raise the heels up as the arms lift overhead to a "Y" position.
3. Circle the arms slowly back and down as the knees begin to bend.

4. With the feet flat on the board, continue to bend the knees into a squat and swing the arms from behind the hips forward and upward, extending into a straight jump that lands feetfirst in the water.

INSTRUCTOR'S NOTE

Having participants focus on a point in the middle of the pool helps keep the head in the proper position.

Two-Part Takeoff

Have participants–

1. Measure 2-foot lengths back from the tip of the board.
2. Slowly raise the heels up as the arms lift overhead to a "Y" position.
3. Circle the arms slowly back and down as the knees begin to bend.
4. With the feet flat on the board, continue to bend the knees into a squat and swing the arms from behind the hips forward and upward, extending into a straight jump that travels forward about 2-foot lengths.
5. Jump again immediately after touching down, circling the arms back and down while jumping high and traveling forward into a straight jump that lands feetfirst in the water.

Tuck Position

Have participants–

1. Sit or lie on the deck and pull the knees up to the chest.
2. Grab both legs at the shins midway between the ankles and knees, pulling the knees tight to the chest to form a tight ball shape.

Forward Jump, Tuck Position

With One-Part Takeoff from Poolside

Have participants–

1. Stand with feet together on the edge of the deck.
2. Perform a one-part takeoff, jumping as high as possible and moving through a straight jump position.
3. While in flight, pull the knees up to the chest and grab them briefly.
4. Kick the legs and straighten them toward the water. Enter feetfirst in a streamlined position.

With One-Part Takeoff from the Diving Board

- Combine the one-part takeoff with a tuck jump and kick out into deep water.
- Participants should perform the tuck on the way up and be stretched into a straight line on the way down.
- Participants should enter feetfirst in a streamlined position.

With Two-Part Takeoff from the Diving Board

- Combine the two-part takeoff with a tuck jump and kick out into deep water.

Forward Dive, Tuck Position

With One-Part Takeoff from Poolside

Have participants–

1. Focus on a target at a 45-degree angle across the pool.
2. Start by using the one-part takeoff. Just before the legs push against the deck to begin the dive, throw the arms overhead to propel the upper body, arms and head into a tuck position. The motion of the arms is similar to one used to throw a ball overhead using two hands.
3. Grab the middle of the shins for the tuck position with the thighs on the chest and the heels on the buttocks as the body rotates forward.
4. Attempt to kick the legs out on the way up.
5. While coming out of the tuck, bend the elbows and move the hands up the midline and grab the hands overhead to prepare for entry.
6. Align the body in a streamlined position and reach for the entry with the hands.

SAFETY NOTE

Watch that participants rotate properly. Remind them to press the arms to the side (laterally) and overhead in the "come out."

With One-Part Takeoff from the Diving Board

With toes on the tip of the board, repeat the forward dive tuck on the diving board using a one-part takeoff.

With Two-Part Takeoff from the Diving Board

1. Start 2-foot lengths back from the tip of the diving board.
2. Perform the two-part takeoff and combine it with a forward dive tuck.

Pike Position

Have participants–

1. Sit or lie on the deck and pull the legs up to the chest.
2. Reach for the toes with the fingertips and keep both legs straight.

Forward Jump, Pike Position

With One-Part Takeoff from the Diving Board

- Combine the one-part takeoff with a pike jump and kick out into deep water.
- Participants should perform the pike on the way up and be stretched into a straight line on the way down.
- Participants should enter the water feetfirst in a streamlined position.

With Two-Part Takeoff from the Diving Board

Combine the two-part takeoff with a pike jump and kick out into deep water.

Forward Dive, Pike Position

With One-Part Takeoff from the Diving Board

Have participants–

1. Focus on a target at a 45-degree angle across the pool.
2. Start by using the one-part takeoff. Just before the legs push against the board to begin the dive, throw the arms overhead to propel the upper body, arms and head into a pike position. The motion of the arms is similar to one used to throw a ball overhead using two hands.
3. Reach for the toes with the fingertips and keep both legs straight with the thighs on the chest as the body rotates forward.
4. Extend the legs into a streamlined position on the way up.
5. Bend the elbows and move the hands up the midline and grab the hands overhead to prepare for entry.
6. Align the body in a streamlined position and reach for the entry with the hands.

With Two-Part Takeoff from the Diving Board

1. Start 2-foot lengths back from the tip of the diving board.
2. Perform the two-part jump and combine it with a forward dive pike.

Water Safety

The concept of water safety should be central to every part of an aquatics program. The only required water safety topic for Learn-to-Swim Level 6–Fundamentals of Diving is diving safety in Look Before You Leap. Water safety should be integrated into the lesson every day, so consider other topics that are relevant to participants, based on their interests and the types of aquatic environments in the area. By Level 6, participants should have a good understanding of how to be safe in, on and around the water so it is important to build on this knowledge, not simply repeat it. Refer to **Chapter 4** for details on the topics listed and for additional topics. Also, offer *Swimming and Water Safety* and the *Water Safety Handbook* as great resources to participants.

Exit Skills Assessment

When participants complete Learn-to-Swim Level 6–Fundamentals of Diving, they demonstrate effectiveness and efficiency in all strokes. They are able to swim continuously while using the appropriate turns for the stroke. They also have a solid understanding about how to be safe in, on and around the water. Additionally, participants are able to perform headfirst dives from a diving board with confidence. There are three parts to the exit skills assessment:

1. Swim 500 yards continuously using any 3 strokes of your choice, swimming at least 50 yards of each stroke.
2. Perform a two-part takeoff with a feetfirst entry from a 1-meter diving board.
3. Perform a two-part takeoff with a headfirst entry from a 1-meter diving board.

Learn-to-Swim Level 6—Fitness Swimmer

Learn-to-Swim Level 6—Fitness Swimmer Outline*

Equipment

- Flotation devices, such as kickboards and pull buoys
- Swim paddles and fins
- Timing device, such as stopwatch or pace clock
- *Swimming and Water Safety* (one for each participant; recommended)

Skills	Completion Requirements	References
Swim on Front, Back and Side		
Front crawl	Demonstrate, at least 100 yards	WSIM, page 252 SWS, page 94
Elementary backstroke	Demonstrate, at least 100 yards	WSIM, page 252 SWS, page 112
Back crawl	Demonstrate, at least 50 yards	WSIM, page 252 SWS, page 100
Breaststroke	Demonstrate, at least 50 yards	WSIM, page 252 SWS, page 103
Sidestroke	Demonstrate, at least 50 yards	WSIM, page 252 SWS, page 113
Butterfly	Demonstrate, at least 50 yards	WSIM, page 252 SWS, page 107
Turns		
Front crawl open turn	Demonstrate while swimming	WSIM, page 253 SWS, page 132
Backstroke open turn	Demonstrate while swimming	WSIM, page 253 SWS, page 133
Front flip turn	Demonstrate while swimming	WSIM, page 253 SWS, page 135
Backstroke flip turn	Demonstrate while swimming	WSIM, page 253 SWS, page 137
Sidestroke turn	Demonstrate while swimming	WSIM, page 253 SWS, page 133
Butterfly turn	Demonstrate while swimming	WSIM, page 253 SWS, page 133
Breaststroke turn	Demonstrate while swimming	WSIM, page 253 SWS, page 136

**This option requires a preassessment and a postassessment of a swimmer. Perform the Cooper 12-minute swim test (Chapter 10 in Swimming and Water Safety) on the first day and last day of lessons, and compare the results.*

Skills	Completion Requirements	References
Fitness Skills		
Circle swimming	Demonstrate	WSIM, page 253 SWS, page 197
Using a pace clock	Demonstrate	WSIM, page 253 SWS, page 204
Swimming using equipment ■ Pull buoys ■ Fins ■ Paddles	Demonstrate, at least 25 yards	WSIM, page 254 SWS, page 200
Setting up an exercise program	Discuss/demonstrate	WSIM, page 254 WSIM CD-ROM SWS, page 187
Various training techniques	Demonstrate	WSIM, page 255 SWS, page 204
Calculating target heart rate	Demonstrate	WSIM, page 255 WSIM CD-ROM SWS, page 187
Aquatic exercise	Demonstrate	WSIM, page 255 SWS, page 200
Exit Skills Assessment 1. Swim 500 yards continuously using any 3 strokes of your choice, swimming at least 50 yards of each stroke. 2. Perform the Cooper 12-minute swim test, and compare results with the preassessment results.		

**This option requires a preassessment and a postassessment of a swimmer. Perform the Cooper 12-minute swim test (Chapter 10 in Swimming and Water Safety) on the first day and last day of lessons, and compare the results.*

Learn-to-Swim Level 6—Fitness Swimmer Skills

Preassessment—Cooper 12-Minute Swimming Test

Have participants–

- Swim for 12 minutes to cover the greatest distance possible, using whatever stroke is preferred.
- Rest as necessary, but go as far as possible.

Chart the distance traveled by participants to compare results at the end of the session.

Swim on Front, Back and Side

TEACHING TIP

Refer to the Water Safety Instructor's CD-ROM *for activities and drills to help participants learn and improve strokes.*

Front Crawl

Refer to Learn-to-Swim Level 5, page 224. In this level, participants should swim at least 100 yards at the level of performance described in the Level 5 Front Crawl Stroke Performance Chart.

Elementary Backstroke

Refer to Learn-to-Swim Level 5, page 224. In this level, participants should swim at least 100 yards described in the Level 5 Elementary Backstroke Stroke Performance Chart.

Back Crawl

Refer to Learn-to-Swim Level 6–Personal Water Safety, page 231. In this level, participants should swim at least 50 yards at the level of performance described in the Level 6 Back Crawl Stroke Performance Chart.

Breaststroke

Refer to Learn-to-Swim Level 6–Personal Water Safety, page 231. In this level, participants should swim at least 50 yards at the level of performance described in the Level 6 Breaststroke Stroke Performance Chart.

Sidestroke

Refer to Learn-to-Swim Level 6–Personal Water Safety, page 232. In this level, participants should swim at least 50 yards at the level of performance described in the Level 6 Sidestroke Stroke Performance Chart.

Butterfly

Refer to Learn-to-Swim Level 6–Personal Water Safety, page 232. In this level, participants should swim at least 50 yards at the level of performance described in the Level 6 Butterfly Stroke Performance Chart.

Turns

Front Crawl Open Turn

Refer to Learn-to-Swim Level 4, page 210. In this level, participants should demonstrate the turn during a continuous swim.

Backstroke Open Turn

Refer to Learn-to-Swim Level 4, page 210. In this level, participants should demonstrate the turn during a continuous swim.

Front Flip Turn

Refer to Learn-to-Swim Level 5, page 223. In this level, participants should demonstrate the turn during a continuous swim.

Backstroke Flip Turn

Refer to Learn-to-Swim Level 5, page 233. In this level, participants should demonstrate the turn during a continuous swim.

Sidestroke Turn

Refer to Learn-to-Swim Level 6, page 233. In this level, participants should demonstrate the turn during a continuous swim.

Butterfly Turn

Refer to Learn-to-Swim Level 6, page 233. In this level, participants should demonstrate the turn during a continuous swim.

Breaststroke Turn

Refer to Learn-to-Swim Level 6, page 234. In this level, participants should demonstrate the turn during a continuous swim.

Fitness Skills

Circle Swimming

In this level, participants should circle swim whenever doing continuous swims. To circle swim, have participants–

- Organize themselves in lanes by swimming speed.
- Swim in a counterclockwise pattern around the center of the pool lane, staying to the right of center in the lane.
- Stagger starts so that, in each lane, the fastest swimmer starts first, followed by slower swimmers at about 5-second intervals.
- Signal to pass by tapping the lead swimmer's foot, if passing is necessary. The lead swimmer stops at the wall and moves to a far corner to let the faster swimmer pass, then waits a few seconds before following the new lead swimmer.

Using a Pace Clock

- Position pace clocks where they can be seen by participants at each end of the pool. Be sure to synchronize the pace clocks.
- Have participants learn the basics of using a pace clock by having them swim two different types of sets.
- Have participants first practice while swimming a fixed rest set. Explain that they will swim a series of four 50-yard swims with a rest of 20 seconds between each. Have participants–
    1. Be ready to push off at a certain time on the clock and swim. The first swimmers in each lane start when the second hand is at the "top" or on the "0" or "60" on the clock. The next swimmers push off when the second hand is at "5," the next swimmers push off when the second hand is at "10," etc.

2. Upon completion of the first 50 yards, rest for 20 seconds.
3. After 20 seconds has passed, push off and repeat the series of swimming 50 yards and resting 20 seconds until completing the set of four.

- Next, have participants practice while swimming a straight set. Explain that they will swim a series of four repetitions of 50 yards on the minute. This means that they will swim 50 yards and then rest until the clock reaches 1 minute. As the second hand reaches the 1-minute mark, participants push off and swim again. Have participants–

1. Be ready to push off at a certain time on the clock and swim. The first swimmers in each lane start when the second hand is at the "top" or on the "0" or "60" on the clock. The next swimmers push off when the second hand is at "5," the next swimmers push off when the second hand is at "10," etc.
2. Upon completion of the first 50 yards, rest until the clock reaches 1 minute.
3. After the clock reaches 1 minute, push off and repeat the series of swimming 50 yards and resting in periods of 1 minute until completing the set of four.

INSTRUCTOR'S NOTE

The fixed rest and straight sets provided are examples only. Be sure to have participants swim distances and rest appropriate to their level of skill and fitness.

Swimming Using Equipment

Refer to **Chapter 3**, page 200 for information on using equipment during training.

TEACHING TIP

Refer to the Water Safety Instructor's CD-ROM *for activities and drills that use equipment to help participants learn and improve strokes.*

Pull Buoys

Have participants swim at least 25 yards using pull buoys.

Fins

Have participants swim at least 25 yards using fins.

Paddles

Have participants swim at least 25 yards using paddles.

Setting Up an Exercise Program

- Have participants set up an exercise program using the "Setting Up an Exercise Program" worksheet on the *Water Safety Instructor's CD-ROM.*
- Review with participants the components of a workout. Have them check their own worksheets to see that they included all components for each exercise day.
  - Warm-up
  - Stretching

- Aerobic set
- Muscular development set
- Cool-down

■ Review with participants the elements of a sound fitness program. Have them check their own worksheets to see that they included all elements in their programs.
- Frequency–how often the exercise is done
- Intensity–how much the person works
- Duration–time spent during the exercise session
- Type–kind of exercise performed

INSTRUCTOR'S NOTE

Refer participants to Chapter 10 in Swimming and Water Safety *for more information on setting up workouts and an exercise program.*

Various Training Techniques

Refer to *Swimming and Water Safety*, page 204, for information on various training techniques. Develop short workouts to meet the specific fitness levels of participants. The distance and speed swum will depend on the amount of time set aside for this portion of each lesson and the fitness levels of participants. Consider introducing a different training technique each lesson.

Calculating Target Heart Rate

Have participants calculate their target heart rate range using the "Target Heart Rate" worksheet on the *Water Safety Instructor's CD-ROM.*

Aquatic Exercise

■ Tell participants that aquatic exercise workouts and programs vary in many ways, but these workouts and programs should have the same components as a swimming workout.

■ Have participants try each of the following moves commonly used in aquatic exercise workouts:
- Jog in place forward and backward.
- March, step sideways, skip, gallop, leap and hop.
- Step-ups–Begin with the legs in the stride position. Bend the back leg; bring forward into a knee lift; return to stride position; repeat. Reverse legs; repeat. Move opposite arm forward at the same time as the leg moves forward (right arm forward with left leg, left arm forward with right leg).
- Leg kicks–Begin with the legs together, knees slightly bent. Lift one leg at a time forward toward the surface, knee slightly bent. Do not kick the legs higher than the hips. Move arms in opposition to the legs–right arm forward with left leg, left arm forward with right leg.
- Alternate strides–Begin with the legs in the stride position. Position the arms in opposition to the legs. Reverse legs and arms. Keep arms under the water.
- Scissors–Begin with the legs together. Move legs into stride position, one forward, one back, moving opposite arms and legs forward and back at the same time. Repeat several times. Return to the starting position and switch the lead leg and arm.
- Heel lifts–Begin with the legs together. Keeping the knees directly under the hips, pull the heel of one foot toward the buttocks, then straighten and return to the starting position. Alternate legs.

Water Safety

The concept of water safety should be central to every part of an aquatics program. There are no required water safety topics for Learn-to-Swim Level 6–Fitness Swimmer. However, water safety should be integrated into the lesson every day, so consider other topics that are relevant to participants, based on their interests and the types of aquatic environments in the area. By Level 6, participants should have a good understanding of how to be safe in, on and around the water so it is important to build on this knowledge, not simply repeat it. Refer to **Chapter 4** for details on topics. Also, offer *Swimming and Water Safety* and the *Water Safety Handbook* as great resources to participants.

Exit Skills Assessment

When participants complete Learn-to-Swim Level 6–Fitness Swimmer, they demonstrate effectiveness and efficiency in all strokes. They are able to swim continuously while using the appropriate turns for the stroke. They also have a solid understanding about how to be safe in, on and around the water. Additionally, participants are working to improve their level of fitness. There are two parts to the exit skills assessment:

1. Swim 500 yards continuously using any 3 strokes of your choice, swimming at least 50 yards of each stroke.
2. Perform the Cooper 12-minute swim test and compare results with the preassessment results. (Swim for 12 minutes to cover the greatest distance possible, using whatever stroke is preferred. Rest as necessary, but go as far as possible.)

Part E

Teaching Water Safety

CHAPTER

10

Water Safety Courses and Presentations

Teaching people to be safe in, on and around the water is critical for someone who teaches others how to swim. Teaching water safety is integrated throughout the Parent and Child Aquatics, Preschool Aquatics and Learn-to-Swim levels. As a Water Safety instructor, you can expect that people will look to you to share your knowledge and to help people understand how to prevent, prepare for and respond to emergencies in and around the water. You must lead by example by always demonstrating examples of safe practices and behaviors and promoting a safety-first mindset and attitude.

The American Red Cross Swimming and Water Safety program offers a variety of ways for you to share water safety information. This chapter outlines the Water Safety courses and presentations you are authorized and encouraged to teach. By knowing the intended audience and what they hope to achieve, you can be sure to select and customize a course or presentation that meets their needs.

Basic Water Rescue

Basic Water Rescue is a 4-hour certification course that provides participants with the knowledge and skills necessary to prevent, recognize and respond to aquatic emergencies. It also prepares participants for aquatic emergencies by teaching them how to protect themselves while assisting others. Basic Water Rescue does not provide participants with all the knowledge and skills needed to be certified as a lifeguard.

Target Audience

Basic Water Rescue is targeted to public safety personnel, camp personnel and day trip leaders, daycare workers, school teachers, aquatic fitness instructors, aquatic therapists, anyone involved in aquatic activities and others who work around water.

Instructor's Materials

The Basic Water Rescue course outline, including the lesson plan, is on Instructor's Corner (*www.instructorscorner.org*). There are no videos or DVDs required for this course; however, the *Small Craft Safety* video is suggested.

Participants' Materials

It is recommended that all participants have a copy of the *Basic Water Rescue* reference guide or *Swimming and Water Safety*. Both books are designed to help participants learn the basic principles of emergency prevention, planning and assisting others using nonswimming rescues in an aquatic emergency.

Safety Training for Swim Coaches

Safety Training for Swim Coaches, developed in collaboration with USA Swimming, is designed to provide participants training in aquatic safety and focuses on basic knowledge and skills to prevent and respond appropriately to many of the emergencies that can occur in a competitive swimming environment.

All coach members of USA Swimming are required to fulfill safety training requirements as established by the USA Swimming Board of Directors. USA Swimming coach members must maintain current certifications in the following: Safety Training for Swim Coaches, CPR and First Aid. The American Red Cross Sport Safety Training course does not meet or replace the Safety Training for Swim Coaches course requirement. However, it does fulfill USA Swimming's first aid and CPR requirements for the Coaches Safety Curriculum. USA Swimming recommends coaches take Sport Safety Training because of its coaching-specific content and materials.

Target Audience

Safety Training for Swim Coaches is targeted to aquatic professionals, such as competitive swim coaches, officials, athletic trainers and other individuals involved in aquatic competition or exercise programs.

Instructor's Materials

Instructors use the *Safety Training for Swim Coaches Instructor's Manual* to teach the course, which is available in an electronic format from your local Red Cross chapter.

Participant's Materials

Participants should obtain and retain *Swimming and Water Safety* and the *Safety Training for Swim Coaches Supplement*. The supplement is available in electronic format from your local Red Cross chapter and on the Health and Safety Services section of the Red Cross Web site at *www.redcross.org*. These two books work together to provide participants information and skill techniques on preventing and responding to possible life-threatening or hazardous situations in and around the water.

Water Safety Today

This 2-hour presentation teaches participants how to recognize, prevent and respond to emergencies in, on and around the water.

Target Audience

Water Safety Today is intended for anyone with an interest in learning water safety knowledge and skills.

Leader's Materials

The presentation outlines and lesson plans for each presentation are included on Instructor's Corner (*www.instructorscorner.org*).

Participants' Materials

It is recommended that all participants have a copy of *Swimming and Water Safety* or the *Water Safety Handbook.*

Personal Water Safety

This 5-hour course teaches participants how to prevent personal injuries and emergencies in, on and around the water. Participants will also learn survival and self-rescue techniques. It provides basic information on ocean safety (rip currents), safety at waterparks and boating.

Target Audience

Personal Water Safety is intended for anyone who wants to learn about how to be safe in, on and around the water.

Leader's Materials

The course outline and lesson plan is included on Instructor's Corner (*www.instructorscorner.org*).

Participants' Materials

It is recommended that all participants have a copy of *Swimming and Water Safety* or the *Water Safety Handbook.*

General Water Safety

This 30-minute presentation provides individuals with an awareness of the importance of water safety training and key information on being safe in, on and around the water.

Target Audience

General Water Safety is intended for individuals who want to learn about the importance of water safety and how to be safe in, on and around the water.

Leader's Materials

The presentation outlines and lesson plans for each presentation are included on Instructor's Corner (*www.instructorscorner.org*).

Participants' Materials

It is recommended that all participants have a copy of *Swimming and Water Safety* or the *Water Safety Handbook.*

Home Pool Safety

This 30-minute presentation provides information for home pool owners and apartment pool users on how to keep their family and guests safe in an aquatic environment.

Target Audience

Home Pool Safety is intended for home pool owners and apartment pool users.

Leader's Materials

The presentation outlines and lesson plans for each presentation are included on Instructor's Corner (*www.instructorscorner.org*).

Participants' Materials

It is recommended that all participants have a copy of *Swimming and Water Safety* or the *Water Safety Handbook.*

Parent Orientation to Swim Lessons

This 30-minute presentation provides an orientation for parents to American Red Cross swim lessons offered at local aquatic facilities.

Target Audience

Parent Orientation to Swim Lessons is intended for parents of young children enrolled in Red Cross swim lessons for the first time.

Leader's Materials

The presentation outlines and lesson plans for each presentation are included on Instructor's Corner (*www.instructorscorner.org*).

Participants' Materials

It is recommended that all participants have a copy of the *Water Safety Handbook.*

Sun Safety

This 30-minute presentation teaches participants the dangers of too much exposure to direct sunlight. Participants learn how to protect themselves and others when enjoying activities in the sun.

Target Audience

Sun Safety is intended for any general audience who enjoys outdoor activities.

Leader's Materials

The presentation outlines and lesson plans for each presentation are included on Instructor's Corner (*www.instructorscorner.org*).

Participants' Materials

It is recommended that all participants have a copy of *Swimming and Water Safety* or the *Water Safety Handbook*.

Rip Current Safety

This 30-minute presentation provides individuals with an awareness of the dangers of rip currents. Participants learn how to recognize rip currents, how to avoid them and what to if caught in one.

Target Audience

Rip current safety is intended for families and individuals interested in learning about or who spend time at surf beaches.

Leader's Materials

The presentation outlines and lesson plans for each presentation are included on Instructor's Corner (*www.instructorscorner.org*).

Participants' Materials

It is recommended that all participants have a copy of *Swimming and Water Safety* or the *Water Safety Handbook*.

Longfellow's WHALE Tales

Longfellow's WHALE Tales is a dry land water safety program that includes information on the following topics:

- Be Cool, Follow the Rule
- Don't Just Pack It, Wear Your Jacket
- Swim with a Buddy in a Supervised Area
- Look Before You Leap
- Think So You Don't Sink
- Reach or Throw, Don't Go
- Think Twice Before Going Near Cold Water or Ice
- Know About Boating Before You Go Floating
- Too Much Sun Is No Fun
- In Your House and In Your Yard, Watch for Water, Be on Guard
- Wave, Tide or Ride, Follow the Guide

Target Audience

Longfellow's WHALE Tales is targeted at children ages 5 to 12.

Leader's Materials

Longfellow's WHALE Tales K–6 Educational Packet consists of a CD-ROM containing lesson plans, handouts and participant activities as well as printed posters to reinforce water safety topics. The optional *Longfellow's WHALE Tales* DVD supports nine of the 11 safety topics. The DVD features experiences elementary school-aged children may encounter related to water safety. Think Twice Before Going Near Cold Water or Ice and Know About Boating Before You Go Floating are two topics that do not have DVD segments that support the lesson plans.

Participants' Materials

Supporting materials, such as activity and fact sheets, are available for download on the CD-ROM that is included in the *Longfellow's WHALE Tales K–6 Educational Packet.*

Sources

Adams, J. A. "A Closed-Loop Theory of Motor Learning." *Journal of Motor Behavior* 3 (1971): 111–150.

American Academy of Pediatrics. Committee on Sports Medicine and Fitness and Committee on Injury and Poison Prevention. "Swimming programs for infants and toddlers." *Pediatrics*, Vol. 105, No. 4, April 2000, 868–870. Reaffirmed October 1, 2004. Available at http://aappolicy.aappublications.org/cgi/content/full/pediatrics;105/4/868. Accessed August 2008.

American Academy of Pediatrics. The Injury Prevention Program (TIPP). Available at http://www.aap.org/FAMILY/tippmain.htm. Accessed August 2008.

American National Red Cross. *Adapted Aquatics: Swimming for Persons with Physical or Mental Impairments.* Garden City, New York: Doubleday, 1977.

American National Red Cross. *Fundamentals of Instructor Training.* Washington, D.C.: American National Red Cross, 2000.

_____. *Guide for Training Instructors: Adapted Aquatics Programs.* Washington, D.C.: American National Red Cross, 1980.

_____. *Lifeguard Management.* Yardley, Pennsylvania: StayWell, 2007.

_____. *Lifeguarding.* Yardley, Pennsylvania: StayWell, 2007.

_____. *Methods in Adapted Aquatics: A Manual for the Instructor.* Washington, D.C.: American National Red Cross, 1980.

_____. *Water Safety Instructor's Manual.* Yardley, Pennsylvania: StayWell, 1992, revised 2004.

Anshel, M. H. "Cognitive Strategies to Teach Motor Skills to Elderly Learners in Nursing Homes." Paper presented to American Alliance for Health, Physical Education, Recreation and Dance, Atlanta, April 17–21, 1985.

Arthur, M., and Ackroyd-Stoland, S. A. *A Resource Manual on Canoeing for Disabled People.* Toronto: Canadian Recreational Canoeing Association, (n.d.).

Bain, L. L. "Physical Education Teacher Education." In *Handbook of Research on Teacher Education,* edited by W. R. Houston. New York: Macmillan, 1990.

Berliner, D. C., and Rosenshine, B. V., editors. *Talks to Teachers.* New York: Random House, 1987.

Brancazio, P.J. *Sport Science: Physical Laws and Optimum Performance.* New York: Simon & Schuster, 1984.

Brems, M. *Swimming–Going for Strength and Stamina.* Chicago, Illinois: Contemporary Books, 1988.

British Sports Association for the Disabled. *Water Sports for the Disabled.* Woking, England: Adlard Coles Nautical, 1983.

Brophy, J. E., and Good, T. L. "Teacher Behavior and Student Achievement." In *Handbook of Research on Teaching,* edited by M. C. Wittrock. 3rd ed. New York: Macmillan, 1986.

Bruya, L. D., and Langendorfer, S. J. "Decrease Liability Risks with Proper Documentation." *Aquatics* 1 (1989): 21–24.

Canadian Red Cross. *Assistant Water Safety Instructor Manual.* Guelph, Ontario, Canada: Canadian Red Cross Society, 2005.

_____. *Manual on Teaching Swimming for the Disabled.* Toronto: Canadian Red Cross Society, (n.d.).

Centers for Disease Control and Prevention, Division of Parasitic Diseases. *Healthy Swimming.* Available at http://www.cdc.gov/healthyswimming. Accessed August 2008.

Collins, M. *A DAM Good Year, Davis Aquatic Masters.* Pittsburgh, Pennsylvania: Sports Support Syndicate, Inc., 1992.

Colwin, C.M. *Swimming into the 21st Century.* Champaign, Illinois: Human Kinetics, 1992.

Councilman, J. E. *The Science of Swimming.* Englewood Cliffs, New Jersey: Prentice-Hall, 1968.

Fitts, P. M. "Factors in Complex Skill Training." In *Training Research and Education,* edited by R. Glasser. New York: John Wiley, 1965.

_____. "Perceptual-Motor Skill Learning." In *Categories of Human Learning,* edited by A. W. Melton. New York: Academic Press, 1964.

Fitts, P. M., and Posner, M. I. *Human Performance.* Belmont, California: Brooks/Cole Publishing, 1967.

Gabrielsen, M. A. In *Diving Injuries: A Critical Insight and Recommendation,* edited by R. D. Clayton. Indianapolis: Council for National Cooperation in Aquatics, 1984.

Gage, N. L. *Hard Gains in the Soft Sciences: The Case of Pedagogy.* Bloomington, Indiana: Phi Delta Kappa, 1985.

_____. *The Scientific Basis of the Art of Teaching.* New York: Teachers College Press, 1978.

Gentile, A. M. "A Working Model of Skill Acquisition with Application to Teaching." *Quest* 17 (1972): 3–23.

_____. "The Structure of Motor Tasks." In *Mouvement. Actes du 7e Symposium en Apprentissage Psycho-moteur et Psychologie du Sport.* Quebec City, Canada, 1975.

Grosse, S. J. "It's a Wet and Wonderful World." *Palaestra* 2 (1985): 14f.

_____. "Use and Misuse of Flotation Devices in Adapted Aquatics." *Palaestra* 4 (1987): 31f.

Harrod, D. L., and Langendorfer, S. J. "A Scalogram Analysis of the American Red Cross Beginner Skill Order." *National Aquatic Journal* 6 (1990): 12–16.

Hay, J. G., and Reid, J. G. *The Anatomical and Biomechanical Basis for Human Motion.* Englewood Cliffs, New Jersey: Prentice Hall, 1982.

Haywood, K. M. and Getchell N. *Life Span Motor Development,* 4th ed. Champaign, Illinois: Human Kinetics, 2005.

Heckathorn, J. *Strokes and Strokes: An Instructor's Manual for Developing Swimming Programs for Stroke Victims.* Reston, Virginia: American Alliance for Health, Physical Education, Recreation and Dance, 1981.

Hedley, E. *Boating for the Handicapped.* Albertson, New York: National Center for Disability Service, 1979.

Hellison, D. R., and Templin, T. J. *A Reflective Approach to Teaching Physical Education.* Champaign, Illinois: Human Kinetics, 1991.

Jackson, E. "Cultural Diversity: "Attracting Minority Staff, Participants, Requires Understanding and Perseverance." *Aquatics International* (November/December 1991):14–18.

Johnson, B. L., and Nelson, J. K. *Practical Measurements for Evaluation in Physical Education.* 4th ed. New York: Macmillan, 1986.

Kids Health for Parents. *Learning Disabilities: Understanding Dyslexia.* Available at http://www.kidshealth.org. Accessed August 2008.

Langendorfer, S. J. "Aquatic Movement Patterns: Developmental and Environmental Perspectives." *Children and Water, Special Issue of Children's Environments Quarterly,* 1987.

_____. "Aquatics for the Young Child: Facts and Myths." *Journal of Physical Education, Recreation, and Dance* 57 (1986): 63–69.

_____. "Aquatics for Young Children with Handicapping Conditions." *Palaestra* (Spring 1989): 17–19, 37–40.

_____. "Early Childhood Aquatics: Risks and Benefits." *Pediatric Exercise Science* 1 (1989): 30–43.

_____. "Separating Fact From Fiction in Preschool Aquatics." *National Aquatics Journal* 3 (1987): 1f.

Langendorfer, S. J., and Bruya, L. D. *Aquatic Readiness: Developing Water Competence in Young Children.* Champaign, Illinois: Human Kinetics, 1995.

Langendorfer, S. J., and Bruya, L. D. "Developmental Aquatics: Water Experiences for Preschool Children." *Future Focus* (Winter 1989): 6–9.

Langendorfer, S. J., Bruya, L. D., and Reid, A. "Facilitating Aquatic Motor Development: A Review of Developmental and Environmental Variables." In *Advances in Motor Development Research,* Vol. 2, edited by J. H. Humphrey and J. E. Clark. Brooklyn, New York: AMS Press, 1987.

Langendorfer, S. J., German, E. W., and Kral, D. "Aquatics Games and Gimmicks for Young Children." *National Aquatics Journal* 4 (1988): 14–16.

Langendorfer, S. J., Gray, D. P., and Bruya, L. D. "Children's Aquatics: Managing the Risks." *Parks and Recreation* (February 1989): 20–24.

Langendorfer, S. J., Harrod, D. L., and Bruya, L. D. "Perspective Aquatic Instruction." *National Aquatics Journal* 5 (1989): 10, 12.

Langendorfer, S. J., Roberts, M., and Ropka, C. R. "Aquatic Readiness: A Developmental Test." *National Aquatics Journal* 3 (1987): 9–12.

Learning Disabilities Association of America. *Dyslexia, Attention Deficit Disorder/Attention Deficit Hyperactivity Disorder.* Available at http://www.ldanatl.org. Accessed August 2008.

Magill, R. A. *Motor Learning: Concepts and Applications.* Dubuque, Iowa: W. C. Brown, 1989.

Maglischo, E. *Swimming Faster.* Palo Alto, California: Mayfield, 1984.

Mosston, M., and Ashworth, S. *Teaching Physical Education,* 3rd ed. Columbus, Ohio: Merrill, 1986.

National Dissemination Center for Children with Disabilities. *Emotional Disturbance Fact Sheet 2004.* Available at http://www.nichcy.org. Accessed August 2008.

Newman, J. *Swimming for Children with Physical and Sensory Impairments: Methods and Techniques for Therapy Recreation.* Springfield, Illinois: Charles Thomas, 1976.

Porter, E. R. *All Visitors Welcome, Accessibility in State Park Interpretive Programs and Facilities.* Edited by M.A. Helmich, M. A. and D.C. Pozzi. California State Parks, Interpretation and Education Division. 2008. Available at http://www.parks.ca.gov/pages/735/files/allvisitorswelcome2008.pdf. Accessed August 2008.

Priest, L. "Diving for the Disabled." *National Aquatics Journal* 1 (1985): 14f.

_____. "Lifeguarding the Disabled." *National Aquatics Journal* 5 (1989): 17f.

Rink, J. E. *Teaching Physical Education for Learning.* St. Louis: Mosby, 1985.

Roberton, M. A., and Halverson, L. E. *Developing Children–Their Changing Movement.* Philadelphia: Lea and Febiger, 1984.

Robinson, J., and Fox, A. D. *Diving With Disabilities.* Champaign, Illinois: Leisure Press, 1986.

Rosenshine, B., and Stevens, S. "Teaching Functions." *In Handbook of Research on Teaching,* edited by M.C. Wittrock. 3rd ed. New York: Macmillan, 1986.

Safrit, M. J. *Introduction to Measurement in Physical Education and Exercise Science.* St. Louis: Mosby-Year Book, 1990.

Sage, G. H. *Motor Learning and Control: A Neuropsychological Approach.* Dubuque, Iowa: W. C. Brown, 1984.

Schmidt, R. A. "A Schema Theory of Discrete Motor Skill Learning." *Psychological Review* 82 (1975): 225–260.

_____. *Motor Control and Learning.* Champaign, Illinois: Human Kinetics, 1982.

Siedentop, D. *Developing Teaching Skills in Physical Education.* 3rd ed. Palo Alto, California: Mayfield, 1989.

Silverman, S. "Research on Teaching Physical Education." *Research Quarterly for Exercise and Sport* 62 (1991): 352–364.

Smith, D. W., Bierman, E. L., and Robinson, N. M. *The Biological Ages of Man From Conception Through Old Age.* Philadephia: W. B. Saunders Co., 1978.

Smith, E. L., and Serfass, R. C. "Exercise and Aging." Papers presented at the ACSM annual meeting, Las Vegas, May 28–30, 1991.

Smith, Y. R. "Issues and Strategies for Working with Multicultural Athletes." *Journal of Physical Education, Recreation, and Dance* (March 1991): 39–44.

Stankov, L., Seizova-Cajic, T. and Roberts, R. "Tactile and Kinesthetic Perceptual Processes within the Taxonomy of Human Cognitive Abilities." *Intelligence* January-February 2001 (29)1. Elsevier Science. Available at http://www.sciencedirect.com. Accessed August 2008.

USA Diving. *USA Diving Coach Development Reference Manual.* Indianapolis, Indiana: USA Diving Publications, 2007.

U.S. Department of Health and Human Services. Leading Health Indicators. *Healthy People 2010.* Available at http://www.healthypeople.gov. Accessed August 2008.

Whitbourne, S. K. *The Aging Body: Physiological Changes and Psychological Consequences.* New York: Springer-Verlag New York Inc., 1985.

YMCA of the USA. *Principles of YMCA Competitive Swimming and Diving,* 2nd ed. Champaign, Illinois: Human Kinetics Publishers, 2000.

_____. *The Parent/Child and Preschool Aquatic Program Manual.* Champaign, Illinois: Human Kinetics Publishers, 1999.

_____. *The Youth and Adult Aquatic Program Manual.* Champaign, Illinois: Human Kinetics Publishers, 1999.